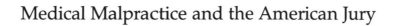

Medical Malpractice and the American Jury

Medical Malpractice and the American Jury

Confronting the Myths about Jury Incompetence, Deep Pockets, and Outrageous Damage Awards

Neil Vidmar

Ann Arbor

THE UNIVERSITY OF MICHIGAN PRESS

Published in the United States of America by
The University of Michigan Press
Manufactured in the United States of America
♾ Printed on acid-free paper

1998   1997   1996   4   3   2

A CIP catalog record for this book is available from the British Library.

Library of Congress Cataloging-in-Publication Data

Vidmar, Neil.
    Medical malpractice and the American jury : confronting the myths
about jury incompetence, deep pockets, and outrageous damage awards
/ Neil Vidmar.
        p.   cm.
    Includes bibliographical references and index.
    ISBN 0-472-10639-2 (hardcover : acid-free paper)
    1. Medical personnel—Malpractice—United States. 2. Jury—United
States. 3. Verdicts—United States. 4. Damages—United States.
I. Title.
KF2905.3.V53 1995
346.7303'32—dc20
[347.306332]   95-21343
                                                              CIP

For my mom and dad
Joseph Vidmar—January 26, 1910 to February 8, 1994
Leola McKinney Vidmar—March 16, 1915

Contents

4. Damages

5. Conclusion

Preface

In this book I examine the civil jury as it carries out its duties with respect to one particular class of lawsuit—that involving medical negligence or, a term I will use synonymously, *medical malpractice*. Why medical negligence? There are three reasons. First, medical negligence is one of the most controversial areas in which civil juries decide cases. It seems that no critic of the present tort system can write more than a paragraph without citing jury behavior in medical negligence cases as a prime example of the evils and ills that are alleged to characterize that system. Claims of jury malfeasance are made, for example, by the American Medical Association (AMA), by serious scholars and other authors writing about the tort system, and by judges and politicians urging reforms in the civil justice process. Second, as will be abundantly clear in the first several chapters of this book, the claims about juries are founded, in some instances, solely on thin-air conjecture; in others on misrepresentation of data; in still others on misunderstanding of data. This does not mean that the claims are untrue, only that the claims have no foundation that can be considered methodologically and scientifically legitimate. Third, in the course of a larger project involving the study of medical malpractice litigation in North Carolina I have accumulated a substantial amount of data bearing on jury performance that provides answers to many of the controversial issues that surround the contemporary malpractice jury. These core data, moreover, are strongly supported by recent studies undertaken by researchers in other locations around the United States.

This book is about medical malpractice juries, not about the whole tort litigation system for medical malpractice. Nevertheless, in part 2 I show that jury outcomes cannot be understood independently of the dynamics of the litigation process and of the mass of cases from which jury trials arise. At the same time, any conclusions about how juries perform unavoidably have important implications for the debate on the merits of the tort system. I deal with this issue in the final chapter of this book.

The principal subject of my investigation is how juries decide medical negligence cases not other types of cases, such as products liability, antitrust claims, or automobile injuries. Part of my argument is that malpractice cases are different from these other categories of litigation. Yet I must use information bearing on these other types of juries throughout the book partly because the malpractice jury debate is often framed in comparison to these other cases and, equally, because data from studies of these other areas richly inform our understanding of malpractice juries. On the output side, the understandings and insights that are generated from this study help us to better understand jury behavior in these other cases. I would not want it to be otherwise.

Although I examine the subject matter primarily from a social science perspective I intend the book to reach a broader audience of lawyers, doctors, politicians, and policy makers in addition to social scientists. As a result, I have tried, successfully I hope, to eliminate unnecessary technical jargon from the social sciences and statistics as well as from law and medicine.

Finally, because the subject of medical malpractice is a controversial issue and because I will charge that many commentators and critics of malpractice juries have made unfounded or misleading claims, I need to acknowledge my previous writings on the subject of juries. In these writings, and in my teaching about the jury system, I have frequently argued that although juries do make errors and sometimes perform poorly, the bulk of empirical studies show that, on average, both civil and criminal juries perform much better than their critics assert. I began the present project with this bias but tried strongly to keep in mind the fact that malpractice trials involve technical and other complexities not present in other types of cases and that, therefore, malpractice juries might be an exception to the rule. As the reader will discover, my ultimate conclusion about medical negligence juries is consonant with my prior conclusions, namely, that juries perform their functions reasonably well. Readers can judge for themselves whether my conceptual analyses, the case studies, and the statistical data that I and other authors have collected justify the conclusion. At the very least I expect the detailed treatment of the issue to force closer attention on the complexity of the issues involved in the debate about medical malpractice juries and the civil jury system in general.

Acknowledgments

Like all authors, I have my debts.

Financial support for my research was provided by the following: the Robert Wood Johnson Foundation (a grant with Thomas B. Metzloff as co-investigator); the State Justice Institute (a grant with Thomas B. Metzloff as co-investigator); a Perry Nichols Fellowship Grant from the National College of Advocacy; a Duke University Research Council Grant; and Eugene T. Bost Professorship funded by the Charles A. Cannon Charitable Trust. Several of the students who worked on the project were supported, in part, by the Fuller-Perdue Trust Fund of Duke Law School. A great deal of financial support was also provided by Duke Law School, initially under the leadership of Dean Paul D. Carrington and then by his successor, Dean Pamela B. Gann.

The list of colleagues, lawyers, judges, court administrators, insurance company executives, and students who, in one way or another, helped in the gathering of the data would be so long that I hesitated to create it for fear that some participants would be left out. Despite my fears, I made the list anyway and apologize in advance to anyone whose name I have inadvertently omitted. Professor David Warren provided intellectual insight and political skills, particularly in the early stages of the research. Dr. Laura Donnelly's skills at data analysis were invaluable as were the general skills of Julia Burchett. Judges Anthony M. Brannon, W. Douglas Albright, and Robert L. Farmer of the North Carolina Superior Court gave me permission to recruit jurors for experiments. Some of the lawyers from both the plaintiff and defense bars who rendered extraordinary time and help are as follows: Grover McCain, Edward Bryson, Donald Beskind, and Elizabeth Kunniholm. Kathy Shuart and Daniel Becker of the North Carolina Administrative Office of the courts spent many valuable hours assisting us. Several medical liability insurer executives gave us advice and access to data, but Wayne Parker of the Medical Mutual Insurance Company of North

Carolina was exceptional in his help and cooperation, even when he agreed to disagree with some of my conclusions. Jeffrey Rice, who was finishing a joint J.D./M.D. degree at Duke, coauthored two articles with me and explained many medical issues. Susan Smith, Anne Stewart, Elaina Cohen, Jessica Lee, Martha Wach, Laura Ann Hellstern, and David Landau were student collaborators on various research projects reported in the book. Other students who helped collect data from court and insurer records are as follows: Alyse Bass, William Broun, Bruce Burchett, John Kongable, Heather Mackenzie, Debra Marcus, Andy Martin, Brad Mindlin, Tricia Romano, Steve Sagretto, Jackie Shogan, Paul Sun, Maurice Taylor, Ann Uglietta, Greg Weiss, Tricia Wilson, Matt Woods, Bar Flynn, Karen Johnson, Adam Kingsley, and Marilyn Sandbeck (I apologize for any omissions from this list). René Stemple Ellis and Carmon Stuart of the Private Adjudication Center also helped in many ways.

In thanking those colleagues who offered criticism and insight on the book manuscript, I want to begin with David Landau, my law student research assistant and editor for two years. For his editorial duties I instructed David to pull no punches; he didn't; and many parts of the final draft reflect his suggestions. Martha Wach, Jessica Buranosky Lee, and Elaina Cohen also served ably as student editors for some chapters. My colleagues—Shari Diamond, Valerie Hans, Herbert Kritzer, and Stephen Landsman—and my wife—Joanne Ernteman—offered valuable commentary on the manuscript as it neared completion. My colleagues George Christie, Terence Dunworth, Samuel Gross, Richard Lempert, James Levine, Michael Saks, Joseph Sanders, and Clive Seligman offered important criticism of manuscripts that were published as independent articles before being incorporated in this book. I also want to thank Steve Cohen for permission to reprint his article from NEW YORK as a chapter. Finally, my secretary, Donna Mooney, deserves mention for her patience with a professor who still composes in longhand and revises "finished" drafts too many times.

In acknowledging financial and intellectual debts, authors are obliged to state that the opinions and conclusions expressed in their books are their own and do not necessarily reflect the views of the funding sources or colleagues. That is as it should be, and I accept personal responsibility for opinions, conclusions, and any errors in this book.

1. The Debate and
the Evidence

1

Are Medical Malpractice Juries Engaged in Malpractice?

For more than two decades the jury has played a central role in an ongoing debate about the viability and fairness of the American tort system.[1] Critics of that system, and there are many, argue that the jury is the primary flaw in the legal procedures through which disputes over liability and compensation for injuries alleged to be caused by the negligence of another are resolved. For them, juries are the apotheosis of irrationality, incompetence, and injustice. The critics allege not only that jury verdicts are often unfair in individual cases but, equally important, that the consequences of the verdicts redound throughout the whole legal system and beyond. Although only about 10 percent of lawsuits reach the stage of jury trial and about 40 percent are dropped without payment to the plaintiff, settlements in the remaining cases are argued in the shadow of what the jury will do if the case goes to trial. High damage awards in jury trials, the logic goes, increase the amount of settlements in other cases by setting the standards for compensation. Moreover, it is argued, overgenerous awards rendered at trial encourage even more litigation by plaintiffs and their attorneys as they seek a windfall in the "jury lottery." The costs of the awards and settlements are passed on to all of us through higher costs for products, the discouragement of innovation that could produce new and better products if not for the risk of lawsuits, the driving of service providers out of business, and increased insurance liability premiums.[2]

While the criticisms of civil juries are also extended to products liability cases and to non-tort cases such as antitrust and business contract disputes, to take a few examples, it seems that no discussion is complete without particular reference to medical malpractice. Indeed, malpractice verdicts are identified in many quarters as the

3

central villain in the illnesses of the American system of health care. Unjustified awards to plaintiffs, it is asserted, occur in such numbers that doctors are fleeing from high-risk specialties like obstetrics. Unfair jury verdicts produce fears of lawsuits that create mistrust that, in turn, destroy doctors' relations with their patients. To avoid lawsuits based on claims that they did not do everything possible, doctors order unnecessary and expensive medical tests. Finally, the unjustified awards increase the rates of professional liability insurance that, in turn, raise the overall costs of medical treatment that are passed on to the patients.[3] But I will let some of these critics speak in their own words about jury performance.

In a submission to a federal government study, the North Carolina Plastic Surgery Society said:

> The jury system seems to show a desire for punitive [action] and retribution above and beyond the degree of injury—"let's get the rich doctor."[4]

The North Carolina Hospital Association claimed:

> Often awards have little relationship to the seriousness of injury. This is no way to predict how a jury will rule on a particular set of facts. . . . Often awards bear no relationship to economic losses. . . . today juries often make awards regardless of the "fault" of anyone—out of sympathy for an injured person. More and more the public attitude is that insurance will compensate the injured party and the defendant will not sustain any loss . . . ; [t]oo often juries appear to award on [the] bases of emotion as opposed to facts and/or realistic evaluation of case circumstances.[5]

In 1988 a task force of the AMA declared:

> In the medical liability context, a source of at least some of the problem for physicians and other health care providers . . . appears to many to be the jury. . . . [Problems with the jury] include decisions that are not based on a thorough understanding of the medical facts and awards that increase at an alarming rate

and in a fashion that seems uniquely to disadvantage physicians as compared with other individuals who have acted negligently.[6]

Physicians do not stand alone. For instance, James Griffith, a lawyer specializing in the defense of medical malpractice cases, asserted, "There's no limit on what jurors can award for pain and suffering, so too often they act like Santa Claus, handing out millions of dollars in cases involving comparatively minor injuries."[7] In the mid-1980s the insurance brokerage firm Johnson and Higgins took out advertisements in the WALL STREET JOURNAL declaring that there was a litigation crisis in which juries "tripled their awards in just one decade" and that the average medical malpractice award in 1984 was $950,000.[8] In 1986 a report on tort policy produced by the U.S. Department of Justice asserted that between 1975 and 1985 the average medical malpractice jury award had increased from $220,108 to $1,017,716.[9]

Popular writer Peter Huber's book on the tort system, LIABILITY: THE LEGAL REVOLUTION AND ITS CONSEQUENCES, is sprinkled with anecdotes about malpractice cases.[10] He asserts that, "[i]nflation-adjusted awards in medical malpractice cases have doubled about every seven years" and concurs with the doctors and liability insurers when he says of trial outcomes in the 1970s and 1980s,

> But judges and juries were, for the most part, committed to running a generous sort of charity. If the new tort system cannot find a careless defendant after an accident, it will often settle for a merely wealthy one.[11]

Huber then offers an explanation:

> The only human reaction to the individual tragedy viewed close up, is unbounded generosity, which any large corporation or insurer can surely afford to underwrite.[12]

Similar sentiments are expressed by Huber's colleague, Walter Olson, in THE LITIGATION EXPLOSION.[13] TIME, NEWSWEEK, THE WALL STREET JOURNAL, and READER'S DIGEST, among other widely read publications, have repeated and popularized these claims.[14]

In 1988 President Bush's administration proposed placing a cap on pain and suffering awards in malpractice cases, presumably on the assumption that this component of damages is one of the causes of "runaway" verdicts.[15] Senator Pete Dominici and C. Everett Koop, the former U.S. Surgeon General, cowrote an article in the NEW YORK TIMES that made similar charges.[16]

Serious scholars voice these views as well. In his widely read and influential book MEDICAL MALPRACTICE ON TRIAL, Professor Paul Weiler writes about "spiraling jury verdicts" and explains that

> juries have become accustomed to huge award requests and they are more willing to reach into the deep pocket of malpractice insurers to compensate the victims generously—more willing than when they encounter the victims of automobile accidents, for in these cases the insurance premiums at risk are paid directly by the jurors themselves.[17]

Elsewhere in the book he comments that "the most troublesome feature of large tort verdicts is the amount of damages awarded for pain and suffering, not for direct medical costs."[18] He also questions the ability of juries composed of laypersons to competently judge the highly technical issues bearing on causation and liability in medical negligence.[19]

Complaints about malpractice juries are not new. Medical malpractice lawsuits were known in England, for example, where Sir William Blackstone mentioned them in his famous COMMENTARIES on the law of England, published in 1803.[20] Professor Kenneth Allen DeVille's book MEDICAL MALPRACTICE IN NINETEENTH-CENTURY AMERICA documents accusations of malpractice in colonial times, a substantial number of cases in the early 1800s, and many more after midcentury.[21] DeVille's scholarship also reveals complaints about the jury system that are very similar to those made today. An 1847 editorial in a medical journal, for example, referred to the "glorious uncertainty of legal justice and of medical testimony," and "bewildered" juries.[22] In 1854 an outraged New York doctor complained that "[a] single dissenting voice among the surgeons on the stand is enough to turn the scale in favor of the plaintiff, toward whom the sympathies of the jury invariably run."[23] A medical editorial in 1865 stated that the "sympathy of a jury of citizens is not generally with the doctor, but rather on the side of the poor, ill-advised, unfortunate victim of incurable injury."[24]

A Summary of Charges against Juries

If the claims of such a variety of critics have validity then we should be forced to conclude that medical malpractice juries themselves are rather consistently engaged in malpractice. The critics offer a list of overlapping indictments that, placed in summary form, are as follows.

- Over recent decades juries have increasingly favored plaintiffs over physician and hospital defendants.
- Jury damage awards are increasing at an alarming rate and in amounts that cannot be justified.
- Juries are biased against doctors and hospitals.
- Juries often give awards to plaintiffs out of sympathy for their plight, even if there is no evidence of negligence.
- There is a "deep pockets" effect whereby, as contrasted to negligent automobile drivers, jurors give larger awards against doctors because they assume that doctors can more afford to pay.
- Jury largess mainly revolves around the "pain and suffering" component of damage awards.
- Punitive damages are also a problem because they are given frequently and without warrant.
- Juries are not competent to decide the complex technical issues in medical negligence cases.
- Juries are often confused by the testimony of experts, particularly "hired gun" experts, and they evaluate the expert evidence on legally irrelevant dimensions.
- Juries are unreliable and capricious in their decisions about both liability and damages.
- Doctors can make "better" decisions than juries on the issue of negligence.
- Legal professionals can make "better" decisions than juries on the issue of damages.

These charges raise serious questions not only about how malpractice cases are resolved but about the whole institution of the civil jury. We should not expect such misbehavior to be confined exclusively to the domain of medical negligence. Even though the right to jury trial in many civil matters is guaranteed by the Seventh Amendment to the U.S. Constitution and to a great extent in the constitutions of the 50 states, perhaps it is time to consider serious curbs on juries or even replacing the jury with some alternative method of deciding law-suits—but only if these extreme claims are true.

Let us not rush to such hasty conclusions. We need to examine the evidence supporting these claims and any contrary evidence. The jury has served a central role in the civil justice system for more than 200 years—it was in use in colonial America long before the framing of the Constitution.[25] Contemporary studies of public opinion show high support for it.[26] Although some members of the legal profession have been critical of it—Judge Jerome Frank described civil juries as applying law they don't understand to facts they can't get straight—recent surveys of judges show that the vast majority consider juries to be competent and conscientious.[27]

Thus, before we even consider abandoning the jury system for medical malpractice disputes we need to evaluate how it performs. We also need to consider whether any weaknesses it has might be corrected by modifying the way it is asked to perform. This book's organizing theme is the extent to which malpractice juries deviate from legal norms and, if so, for what reasons. To undertake this analysis I will examine jury performance at an absolute level and in relation to standards of how doctors and judges might perform in its place. The analyses separate the issues of deciding liability and decid-ing damage awards. While my focus is on malpractice juries this study has broader implications for understanding juries in other con-texts and about the role of the jury in our system of civil justice. These latter themes will be addressed in the final chapter.

Data Sources

The research underlying this book is empirically based—by which I mean that it places heavy emphasis on systematically collected data rather than on anecdotes. Nevertheless, case studies are used in abun-dance to develop conceptual points and give flesh to the hard statis-tics. For my analyses I draw upon an eclectic set of sources that include the following:

- A database of court records consisting of approximately 95 percent of the malpractice cases filed in North Carolina state and federal

courts between the beginning of July 1984 and the end of June 1987:
a sample of 895 cases
- A second database of court records for state malpractice cases filed
  in 14 North Carolina counties beginning July 1987 and terminating
  at the end of December 1989: a sample of 326 cases
- A sample of 154 "closed claim" files obtained from three medical
  malpractice liability insurers in North Carolina covering roughly the
  same period as the court file data
- Case studies of malpractice trials in North Carolina, involving observations of the trials and interviews with jurors who rendered the
  verdicts in those trials
- Experimental studies involving persons awaiting jury duty and senior lawyers, including former judges, in various jurisdictions in
  North Carolina
- Personal interviews and questionnaire responses from plaintiff and
  defense attorneys involved in malpractice litigation. There are also
  interviews and conversations with insurance company personnel
  bearing on their roles in the litigation process and on specific cases
  that formed part of our sample.
- Studies by other researchers of malpractice juries in other jurisdictions in the United States

An Overview

In the remainder of this first part of the book I review the sources of
evidence upon which the assertions about jury misbehavior are apparently based and offer a detailed critique of some of this evidence
(chap. 2). I then profile medical malpractice jury verdicts in North
Carolina (chap. 3) and compare North Carolina statistics with statistics from other states and federal courts (chap. 4).

Part 2 develops my thesis that some unknown, but probably substantial, portion of malpractice jury outcomes can be ascribed to the
types of cases selected for trial and that the understanding of jury
behavior is incomplete without understanding of this aspect of the
litigation process. Chapter 5 presents a profile of the cases that went
to trial, and chapter 6 uses a number of case studies to demonstrate
the dynamics that propel cases to trial. Chapter 7 puts the case studies
into context, and chapter 8 develops the theme that trial cases are
often weak on the issue of defendant liability.

Part 3 is devoted to the exploration of how juries decide liability. Chapter 9 is a reprinted article by Steve Cohen, an alternate juror in a New York malpractice trial. Cohen's article gives a unique insight into the minds of the jurors that decided one very contentious malpractice case. It is followed by a brief chapter that discusses the trial judge's review of the reasonableness of the New York jury's decisions. Chapter 11 describes what malpractice juries are asked to do and reviews the claims about jury incompetence and bias with regard to liability. Chapter 12 presents studies of cases that, I argue, contradict the claim that all malpractice trials are technically complex. Chapter 13 presents case studies in which the issues were indeed complex. Chapter 14 extends these case studies describing studies that help us compare jury performance against the decisions of doctors and legal professionals. Chapter 15 closes this part of the book with a summary perspective on liability decisions.

Part 4 turns to the issue of damage awards. Chapter 16 provides an overview of the jury's task. Chapter 17 describes and analyzes the claim that juries favor plaintiffs who sue "deep pockets" defendants, such as doctors. It is frequently said that when jurors perceive that a defendant is rich (hence has "deep pockets") and can afford the loss they are inclined to give big awards regardless of negligence. Chapter 18 presents two experiments with jurors that put the deep pockets hypothesis to empirical test. Chapter 19 examines the claim that judges rather than juries are more competent to decide the amount of awards for pain and suffering and describes experiments bearing on this hypothesis. Chapter 20 presents some case studies that give more insight into how jurors deliberate and arrive at damage awards. Chapter 21 reports additional data bearing on punitive damages and on the correspondence of damage awards with actual economic losses. Chapter 22 presents a summary perspective on damages.

Part 5 brings the book to a conclusion. It first addresses the question of why the widespread beliefs about jury incompetence and misbehavior are so discrepant from the empirical portrait painted in this book. It then attempts to assess the meaning of the findings in the context of the broader debate about tort reform.

2

Proplaintiff Bias, Rising Win Rates, and Deep Pockets: Some Major Problems with the Critics' Evidence

In this chapter I want to consider the grounds on which claims about jury behavior in medical negligence cases are made. I will set forth a methodological critique of these claims. My conclusion from the critique is that they offer no scientifically adequate evidence bearing on the question of whether juries perform their duties improperly.

Anecdotal Evidence

Anecdotes have played an important role in assertions about irresponsible jury behavior. But scholars who have studied these anecdotes have concluded that some are fabricated while others involve distorted reports of actual cases.[1] For instance, one story about the psychic and her CAT scan was reported in a widely quoted 1985 speech by a leading business executive.[2] According to the story, a Philadelphia jury awarded a woman almost $1 million after she claimed that the CAT scan performed at Temple University Hospital made her lose her psychic abilities. This story clearly suggests an irresponsible jury at work, but the actual facts of the case on which the story was based, *Haimes v. Hart* in the Philadelphia Court of Common Pleas, are different.[3] Indeed, the woman did make a claim for economic loss asserting that she was unable to continue her business as a psychic. However, she also sustained permanent brain damage due to an allergic reaction to a contrast dye that she claimed was negligently administered prior to the CAT scan. The judge instructed the jury to disregard the claim about the loss of psychic abilities and consider only the evidence on brain damage. Despite the fact that the true story about the psychic's lawsuit was publicized in 1986 and 1987, the inaccurate version continues to be repeated.[4] It appeared, for example, in the 1991 report of former Vice President Quayle's Council on Competitiveness, in books published in 1991 by tort reform advocates Peter Huber and Walter Olson and by economist Kip Viscusi, and in a 1993 article in NEWSWEEK.[5]

Similar anecdotes are pervasive in the overall debate about the behaviors of civil juries. Another widely reported case involved a "burglar" who sued a school system after he fell through a skylight, winning damages of $206,000 plus $1,500 per month for life. The actual facts of the case are that the "burglar" was a teenager who climbed on the roof of a high school to get a floodlight and was rendered a quadriplegic by the fall; the school officials had contracted to have the skylights covered in order to "solve a . . . safety problem"; and a similar incident in a neighboring school eight months earlier had killed a student. Finally, the "award" was *not* the result of a jury trial but rather resulted from a settlement with the school board.[6]

While these selected examples of fabrication or distortions in reporting are striking, it must be observed that many case anecdotes about jury verdicts may indeed be true. No one can reasonably claim that juries always make correct decisions. However, the problem, as Professor Michael Saks has observed, is that anecdotes can mislead us into thinking that they are representative of a class of cases, that they are typical cases, when in fact they may be aberrations.[7]

In MEDICAL MALPRACTICE ON TRIAL, for example, Professor Weiler relates the case of *Baez v. Dombroff*, involving a plaintiff who was left with disfigured breasts from a breast-reduction operation and received a $2.625 million award that was eventually reduced to $750,000 by an appeals court.[8] The reader is left with the impression that this is typical of what occurs when juries decide these cases. Perhaps the *Baez* verdict (and some might even say the final award by the court of appeal) was out of line, but is it representative of most or even many jury verdicts? Or is it the exception? Without information about other cases, including those in which juries rule against plaintiffs, we cannot say.

The appeal of anecdotes, accurate or inaccurate, however, is often compelling, particularly if the anecdotes support strongly held beliefs. Professor Robert Hayden has speculated that anecdotes about egregious legal cases have strong appeal because they portray a threat to important American cultural values related to equality, individual responsibility, and economic redistribution.[9] Consequently, when the story is told of a woman who sought $10 million because her physician failed to replace her nipples after breast reconstruction and the author claims that she didn't notice that they *were missing until six months after the surgery*, it may be believed and told to others. This anecdote was actually put into print by a defense lawyer in a scholarly publication called MEDICAL ECONOMICS.[10] Stereotypes of greedy people and lawyers with shark fins protruding out of their Saville Row suits will cause many persons to fail to question the face plausibility of the story. The facts of the case are quite different. According to testimony of operating room personnel, a plastic surgeon made pre-surgery markings while the patient was prone rather than erect, a violation of standard surgical procedures in such cases. As a consequence, the surgery virtually removed the woman's breasts and left her scarred, deformed, and with nipples too high and uneven on her breasts. Eventually the case was settled for a figure reported to be in the range of $2.5 million.[11]

The long and the short of it, then, is that anecdotal horror stories, though widely reported and used in condemnation of the jury system, tell us little about the system. While plaintiff lawyers have recently taken to reporting anecdotes suggesting that deserving plaintiffs have been deprived of just and fair compensation, the same principle holds: anecdotes, even ones that are absolutely accurate in reporting details, can tell us little about the overall jury system—at least absent solid corroborative evidence that indicates the anecdotes are representative of specified percentages of legal cases.[12]

Unrepresentative Verdict Data

Every year the NATIONAL LAW JOURNAL, a newspaper for the legal profession, and Jury Verdicts, Inc., an organization that provides various services for lawyers, produce reports of the previous year's largest jury awards and statistics on average awards. The statistics contained in the reports are cited in speeches and writings by critics of the jury system and in testimony before Congress.[13] Thus, in 1984 the Subcommittee on Health of the Committee on Ways and Means heard one statement saying that the average malpractice award was $962,258, a figure derived from statistics published by Jury Verdict Research.[14]

Articles in the WALL STREET JOURNAL, TIME, and BUSINESS WEEK, to take other examples, have carried charts from Jury Verdict Research in major articles about the "tort crisis."[15] In the mid-1980s the insurance brokerage firm Johnson and Higgins took out advertisements in the WALL STREET JOURNAL declaring that there was a litigation crisis in which juries "tripled their awards in just one decade" and that the average medical malpractice award in 1984 was $950,000.[16] In 1986 a report on tort policy produced by the U.S. Department of Justice asserted that between 1975 and 1985 the average medical malpractice jury award had increased from $220,108 to $1,017,716.[17]

As striking as these statistics are, and as readily accepted as they are in many quarters, they can be completely misleading. Russell Localio, Director of Research at the Risk Management Foundation in Cambridge, Massachusetts, investigated the way that the Jury Verdict Research data are collected and analyzed.[18] He discovered that there is no systematic sampling scheme to ensure that the cases are representative. Jury Verdict Research relies on court clerks, newspaper clipping services, local verdict reporting services, and attorneys who report on verdicts from trials in which they have been involved or know about. You do not have to hold a Ph.D. in one of the social sciences to recognize the problems with these data. Newspapers are quick to report megaverdicts but tend to ignore cases in which plaintiffs lose or receive only a modest award. The latter are not newsworthy. Similarly, a plaintiff's lawyer who loses a big case will not be as likely to rush to the nearest pay phone to report the outcome as when a big award is involved—and probably she will forget to call after she gets back to the office. An additional problem is that, not infrequently, settlements and verdicts rendered by a judge have been included in figures attributed to jury awards.[19]

Another major problem is that frequently the reported increases in awards have not been adjusted for inflation. As Stephen Daniels has pointed out, an award of $360,000 in 1970 would be equivalent to $1 million in 1985.[20] In fact, the inflation problem is even more serious since medical costs, which constitute a large portion of most malpractice claims, have increased more rapidly than the general rate of inflation.[21] Thus, comparing award changes over time without inflation adjustments can mislead us into believing juries have become more generous when in fact they have not. Still another problem involves the reporting of statistical averages, which may be

inflated by a relatively small number of large awards.[22] To take a
very simple example, suppose nine of ten juries rendered awards of
$10,000, but the remaining jury rendered a verdict for $1 million.
Setting aside the question of whether the first nine awards were too
low or the last was too high, we can calculate that the average award
in this example is $109,000. This average, of course, may be telling
us something important about the overall effect of the "jury system"
defined by those 10 cases, but it is highly misleading regarding what
the typical jury does. We shall return to this issue of averages elsewhere in the book.

The crux of the above discussion, then, is that, like anecdotes,
unrepresentative data on verdicts may give a totally misleading view
of jury decisions.

Representative Verdict Data

The final source of evidence against the jury comes from more systematic studies based on verdict reports and to a lesser extent on statistics
from the records of malpractice insurance companies. In a number of
jurisdictions around the country, records of all, or almost all, jury
trials are compiled and sold to lawyers in the form of publications
called verdict reporters.[23] Most of these publications provide not only
the jury verdict but also summary information on other aspects of the
case, such as the alleged seriousness of the plaintiff's injuries.

Researchers at the Rand Corporation's Institute for Civil Justice
used verdict reporters as a source of data to study trends in jury
verdicts over time and across various types of cases. The findings
from their initial studies have been cited many times by jury critics.
One study examined 9,000 state and federal civil jury trials that took
place in Cook County (Chicago) Illinois between 1960 and 1979.[24] The
data showed that medical malpractice plaintiffs won their cases only
about one-third of the time, but they obtained large awards when
they did win. Moreover, the awards were larger when doctors and
hospitals were charged with malpractice than when they were defendants in other types of cases, such as slip and fall or automobile
accidents. Finally, the size of average awards against doctors grew
larger over the period covered by the research.

In a subsequent study, data on jury verdicts in Cook County and
San Francisco were compared over a 25-year period spanning 1960

through 1984.[25] The data showed that in both jurisdictions the plaintiff win rates in malpractice cases almost doubled: from one win in four trials to one in two.[26] And the size of awards for winning plaintiffs increased even more rapidly, even when the awards were adjusted for inflation. The mean and median figures for San Francisco, for example, were as follows.[27]

	Mean	Median
1960–64	$ 125,000	$ 64,000
1965–69	306,000	157,000
1970–74	449,000	124,000
1975–79	644,000	99,000
1980–84	1,162,000	156,000

Figures for Cook County were similar. The fact that the median awards were so much lower than the mean awards suggests that there were a number of relatively large awards and many more smaller awards, but the increasing figures certainly cause anyone to pause. The study also concluded that awards for work injuries were less than half those given in medical malpractice and products liability cases.[28] Taken at face value, the study suggests increasing jury profligacy, but as I will argue in a moment, taking these statistics at face value can be very misleading. Even seasoned researchers, including those at the Rand Corporation, were initially led into drawing conclusions that should not have been made.

Professor Patricia Danzon conducted a study similar to the verdict reporter studies just discussed, except that her source of data was approximately 6,000 claims from private insurance company files in California for the years 1974 and 1976.[29] The most important difference between her study and the ones just described is that it contained information not only on jury verdicts but also on claims that were settled. About 7 percent of the cases in her study were resolved by a jury, and, of these, plaintiffs prevailed about one time in four. When they did win the average award was $102,000. This figure can be contrasted with settled claims, which averaged $26,000.[30] Danzon, however, concluded that the cases that went to trial involved more serious injuries and larger potential awards than those that were settled. In her words, the cases that are actually litigated to verdict constitute a small, atypical subset, self-selected to that stage of disposition precisely because the outcome was unpredictable to the litigants, the potential award was larger, and the evidence for the plaintiff was weak. Thus we get a very biased impression of the operation of the malpractice system from observing the minority of more visible cases that are litigated to verdict rather than the great majority of cases that are settled out of court.[31]

Danzon's insight was directed toward her own data, but it strongly hints at the difficulties in drawing facile conclusions from any jury verdict research. Of particular importance here is the fact that the Rand studies just described contained no information to let us know how and why they were selected for trial and if the selection patterns changed over time.

The Tip-of-the-Iceberg Problem

Jury verdicts represent only the tip of the iceberg of the total number of claims that are actually filed in court and become legal cases. Research indicates that across all types of cases roughly 10 percent of legal claims go before a jury, with the remainder being settled or dropped by the plaintiff without any compensation.[32] However, the studies also show that settlement rates may vary between types of cases and that the mix of cases going to the jury or being settled may vary over time.[33] These facts make it very difficult to rule out alternative hypotheses when the rates of plaintiff wins or the amounts of those wins change over time or when there are differences between malpractice verdicts and verdicts in, say, automobile injury cases. The thrust of this insight is that rather than deciding cases differently juries may be deciding very different cases.

Since this fact seems to have escaped even some experienced researchers, let me provide an elementary example:[34] Take any state or jurisdiction. Assume for the moment that the only cases that go before juries are ones in which defendants are found liable and that the only task of the jury is to decide damages. Assume further that at year 1, two types of cases are selected for jury trial: type A cases are worth $10,000, and type B cases are worth $100,000. During year 1, 10 type A cases and 10 type B cases are tried and the juries are consistent so that, on average, plaintiffs in type A cases each receive $10,000 and plaintiffs in type B cases receive $100,000. If we calculate the average jury award for year 1, we get: (10 trials × 10,000) + (10 trials × $100,000) ÷ 20 trials = $55,000. Assume now that between year 1 and year 5 the state introduces an alternative dispute resolution program for cases involving $10,000 or less. It is so successful that all type A cases are settled by the process, leaving only type B cases, of which there are still 10 per year, that go to jury trial. These latter cases still each receive a $100,000 award. What is the average award at year 5? It is: (10 × $100,000) ÷ 10 = $100,000. Thus, the average jury award has increased $45,000, or approximately 82 percent, from year 1 to year 5. Can we conclude that juries have become more magnanimous over the five-year period? Of course not. The change in the average award is caused by the change in the types of cases going to trial. The lesson is that juries are deciding different cases, not deciding cases differently.

My hypothetical example has one less obvious implication. It is very easy to construct scenarios to show absolutely no differences in average awards between year 1 and year 5 but in which juries actually do decide cases differently. In the most extreme scenario, suppose at year 5 juries perversely give 10 type A cases $100,000 and 10 type B cases only $10,000. The average would be the same as year 1— $55,000—and the enormous change in jury behavior would not be reflected as even a ripple in the averaged awards for that year.[35]

We can vary the above example with any number of permutations and combinations, such as, say, only half of the type A cases are shunted into alternative dispute resolution. We can vary the example from damages to verdicts on liability, proposing, for example, that from year 1 to year 5 plaintiffs (and their lawyers) stop litigating cases in which there is a low chance of prevailing at trial. This basic problem of changes in samples between year 1 and year 5 affecting our ability to rule out plausible alternative hypotheses to the claim of change in verdicts is a very common one in the social sciences.[36] In an elegant and insightful article Professor Michael Saks has demonstrated this problem's relevance to understanding many key aspects of the whole tort litigation system.[37]

The example's application to the present problem leads directly to the conclusion that, absent knowledge about changes in how cases are selected for trial, changes in average plaintiff win ratios or amounts of awards tell us almost nothing about what juries may be doing relative to what they were doing in the past. The verdict reporter data tell us nothing about these unseen cases that form the base of the iceberg.

We do know, however, that settlement patterns frequently do vary over time. The adoption of alternative dispute resolution procedures may encourage settlements; delays in court processing encourage parties to settle; outcomes of high-profile cases encourage or discourage trials; changes in substantive or procedural law or a host of other local "legal culture" factors may individually and collectively affect the process. Strikingly, the data in the second Rand study, described above, strongly suggest that such factors may have been operating. For example, in San Francisco the number of malpractice jury trials *decreased* by almost half between the 1960–64 period and 1980–84 period, from 95 trials to 55.[38] Unless we assume that the number of malpractice suits in San Francisco also declined by half between 1960 and 1984—a most unlikely hypothesis—we must infer that cases were being settled differently.

In contrast the Rand data show that the number of malpractice trials in Cook County almost tripled over the same period, from 56 in 1960–64 to 162 in 1980–84.[39] This difference between Cook and San Francisco counties points to another problem with focusing only on jury trials and ignoring the base of the iceberg: because of different local legal cultures, different jurisdictions may have quite distinct processes for selecting cases for trial. The Rand report in fact took cognizance of some of the differences between Cook and San Francisco counties with respect to overall patterns of litigation. Noting the large number of automobile accident trials in Cook County it commented,

At the least, [the finding] suggests that there is a substantial number of lawyers in Chicago who were willing to try cases that involved small stakes. The pattern might also reflect less aggressive use of methods of alternative dispute resolution in Cook County than in other jurisdictions. Cook County courts made less use of mechanisms similar to California's court-annexed arbitration program which seemed to have contributed to the sharp reduction of automobile accident trials in San Francisco after 1980.[40]

If patterns are so distinct between two jurisdictions on automobile injuries who is to say that other processes do not affect malpractice case patterns? Stephen Daniels studied malpractice jury verdicts in 43 different counties in 10 different states; his data showed enormous variations from jurisdiction to jurisdiction, hinting strongly at different selection processes.[41]

Finally, the tip-of-the-iceberg problem with respect to verdict reports also creates difficulty in making comparisons across case types. Take the comparison between malpractice verdicts and automobile injury verdicts. Evidence indicates that while between 7 and 10 percent of malpractice cases go to trial, only between 1 and 2 percent of automobile cases go to trial.[42] And while the plaintiff win rate in malpractice cases hovers around 30 percent, the rate for auto injuries is between 60 and 70 percent.[43] We do not have to be able to specify precisely how and why trial selection differs between case types to have strong suspicions that they are different.

In the Rand research, attempts were made to statistically control for the most obvious factors—ones that could be gleaned from the verdict reporters—such as the alleged seriousness of the injury and party characteristics.[44] However, these variables account for only a minute fraction of the potential factors that could possibly differentiate cases.

To sum up, because jury verdict data by themselves do not provide information about the proportion of cases selected for trial or the various dimensions along which cases may differ as a result of changing or different trial selection processes, it is not possible to conclude one way or another what changes may be occurring in jury behavior or what differences in jury behaviors may exist between malpractice and other types of cases or between different jurisdictions.

Imputed Motives

Finally, consider the following statements made about motives of juries.

Professor Weiler complains, "jurors have become accustomed to huge award requests, and they are more willing to reach into the deep pockets of malpractice insurers to compensate the victims generously—more willingly than when they encounter the victims of automobile accidents, for in these cases the insurance premium at risk are paid by the jurors themselves."[45]

In a videotape produced by the Manhattan Institute for Policy Research, former U.S. Surgeon General C. Everett Koop poses a hypothetical example of a child born with cerebral palsy; the doctor has no control over this unfortunate event, but, nevertheless, the family sues the doctor. Dr. Koop then says, "[Patients who sue their family physician are] very likely to find a sympathetic jury that will award something to that family, not necessarily because they think their doctor is guilty of negligence or malpractice but because their sympathy with the family dictates it."[46]

These claims are, purely and simply, unsupported assertions about what goes on in the minds of jurors. Other than anecdotes of questionable reliability, there appears to be not a shred of evidence behind them. Juror motives, attitudes, and perceptions cannot be derived from court records, closed claim files, or verdict reports because interviews with the jurors are not contained anywhere in these reports. The assertions appear, instead, to be based solely on inferences and stereotyped assumptions of what jurors might be doing. Even if it turns out that juries are giving larger awards today or larger awards in malpractice than in automobile injuries, such assertions about the minds and motives of jurors from trial outcomes alone are, quite simply, unwarranted.

Other Methodological Issues

There are more methodological issues beyond the problems of anecdotes, unrepresentative data, tip-of-the-iceberg statistics, and missing data on juror motives. I will address them in subsequent chapters. However, my critique to this point should be sufficient to raise doubts about the validity of the foundation on which claims against malpractice juries are based. The critique does not allow the conclusion that the claims are wrong or that juries are, to the contrary, doing a good job; it merely raises serious doubts about the grounds on which the claims about jury misbehavior are made and indicates the need for other types of data and a careful interpretation of the meaning of statistical data.

Summary and Concluding Comments

The widespread criticism of juries in medical negligence cases appears to be based on anecdotes and on findings from several studies of jury verdicts. The data from the studies do not allow the conclusions that have been drawn from them because very plausible alternative hypotheses that could explain the results cannot be ruled out.

The methodological critique I have offered does not allow the inference that juries are doing a good job; it only says that the evidence does not allow us to say one way or the other. Indeed, if some of the plausible alternative hypotheses were to turn out to be true, we might still draw the conclusion that juries are acting improperly.

This chapter has not addressed all of the problems alleged to plague juries: for example, a propensity to weigh expert evidence on the basis of irrelevant factors; a tendency to award excessive amounts for pain and suffering; or a tendency to assess punitive damages without warrant. These will be raised at appropriate times in subsequent chapters, but now it is time to present a profile of outcomes in jury trials involving medical negligence.

3

A Profile of Jury Verdicts in North Carolina

This chapter presents a basic profile of the malpractice litigation "iceberg" and jury verdicts in North Carolina. The profile of verdicts seems at considerable variance with the claims about jury license, caprice, and bias since defendants prevail in most trials. But there are some additional surprises when we look just a little bit behind these statistics: sometimes "winning" plaintiffs are losers and sometimes "losing" plaintiffs are winners.

The Sources of the Statistics

For the profile I draw upon two data sets covering two consecutive time periods. As part of the Duke Law School and Private Adjudication Center's Medical Malpractice Project an attempt was made to identify every medical malpractice case filed in the state and federal courts in North Carolina between July 1, 1984, and June 30, 1987.[1] Rigorous screening procedures captured an estimated 95 percent of the cases filed during that period: a total of 895 lawsuits. Using these court files I and a research team systematically identified essential substantive and procedural information about each case on a 19-page structured questionnaire.[2] Each of these cases was followed until it was closed. At the termination of data collection efforts, all but nine cases were closed.

A second sample involved cases filed in 14 of the state's 100 counties between July 1, 1987, and December 31, 1990: a sample of 326 cases. These 14 counties include the most populous counties in the state, and, based on the previous sample, we estimate that they constitute approximately 52 percent of the malpractice cases filed in North Carolina's superior courts during that period. At the close of data collection in July 1992, three cases were still pending. A data collection instrument and procedures similar to the first study were used to follow these cases through closure. For both sets of data, attorneys were surveyed to obtain additional information when it was missing from court files.

In addition to the main data sets, three malpractice liability insurers provided samples of closed claim files that were accessible in their offices at the time that we requested them. These constituted a total of 154 cases. While I do not claim that these data are a representative sample, they appear typical. Moreover, they provide additional information on important aspects of the malpractice cases, particularly on amounts of settlements that were not contained in court records.[3]

Jury Verdicts and Settlements in North Carolina

Percentage of Jury Trials

Of the 895 cases in the 1984–87 study, approximately 50 percent were "settled," meaning that the plaintiff received money from the defendant.[4] Slightly over 40 percent were dropped, either because the plaintiff withdrew the claim, allowed it to lapse beyond procedural or statutory deadlines, or received a judicial ruling that terminated the case in favor of the defendant through summary judgment on the merits of the evidence or law. Out of the 895 cases, only 118 reached the stage of trial. However, three cases were tried by a judge, and 31 were either settled after the trial had begun, disposed of by a directed verdict from the judge, or withdrawn by the plaintiff, leaving a final tally of 84 jury trial cases. Thus, 9.4 percent of all medical malpractice cases eventually were placed in the hands of a jury.

In the second study, covering the 1987–90 period, approximately 51 percent of the 326 cases resulted in a settlement, 40 percent were dropped or terminated without payment to the plaintiff, and 9 percent went to trial. Of the 32 trial cases, three were still pending at the end of data collection, two were settled during trial, one resulted in the judge directing the jury to return a verdict for the defendants, and one was decided by a judge. Not including the three cases still pending, 25 cases, or 7.7 percent of all malpractice suits, went before a jury for a decision.

This slight drop in the number of jury trials between the first and second study, from 9.4 percent to 7.7 percent, is not statistically significant. It may or may not portend a slight change in settlement practices.[5] Our safest course is to say that between 7 and 10 percent of malpractice cases were decided by juries.

Who Wins at Trial and How Much?

Of the 84 cases tried by juries in the 1984–87 study, plaintiffs prevailed on the issue of liability in 17 instances, or 20 percent of the time. In the 1987–90 study, plaintiffs prevailed in only four of the 25 trials, a win rate of 16 percent.

Table 3.1 summarizes the allegations of malpractice and the injuries suffered by the plaintiffs plus the amounts of the awards for all of the 21 cases in the combined samples in which plaintiffs prevailed. The table shows that there were three awards of at least $1 million: $1.28 million, $1 million, and $3.5 million. There was also an award for $750,000 and two for $300,000. The remainder of the trials, however, resulted in much more modest sums, with the lowest being $4,000. The mean award for the 21 cases in which plaintiffs prevailed was $367,737, but, reflecting the large number of low awards, the median was just $36,500.

Another way to think about the jury awards is to ask about the plaintiff's expected value of going to trial. The expected value is equal to the average award when plaintiffs prevail multiplied by the probability of obtaining a verdict.[6] To calculate this figure we simply divide the total of all awards in the sample ($7,722,488) by the total number of jury trials (109). This yields a figure of $70,849. Put in other words: every plaintiff who went to trial could expect, on average, to win $70,849. However, as already described, most either came away with nothing or received only modest awards. Only 9 of the 109 plaintiffs whose cases were decided by juries received more than the expected value of their claims.

The most striking impression from these verdict statistics is that plaintiffs did not do well with juries. They won less than one case in five. When they did receive an award, the amount was usually low. The expected value at trial—$70,849—is not a very large sum when the costs of litigation are considered. There are discovery expenses, including travel costs, fees for expert witnesses, and trial costs. Under contingency fee arrangements the attorney will receive 30 to 40

TABLE 3.1. Summary of Alleged Malpractice, Injury, and Award in the
21 Trials in Which Plaintiffs Prevailed: 1984–90 (combined samples)

Case	Allegation/Injury	Award
106501	Podiatrist gave cortisone without authorization, causing disintegration of femur and requiring hip replacement.	$12,787
110511	After surgery on coccyx silver nitrate was placed on wound causing second-degree burns and scars.	$15,200
115402	Resection (removal) of enlarged prostate gland damaged nerves and urinary sphincter, resulting in incontinence and persistent pain.	$127,500
125516	Plaintiff admitted to hospital with fever, feeding tube inserted in lung rather than stomach, necessitating partial lung removal; patient relapsed and feeding tube inserted in other lung; patient now requires nursing home care.	$750,000
125522	Erroneous diagnosis of advanced prostate cancer; prostatectomy resulted in impotence and requirement of urinary sphincter prosthesis.	$20,000
128710	Plaintiff treated for cut; ensuing gangrene diagnosed but not treated; as a result surgery and hospitalization were required and a disfigurement resulted.	$33,000
133752	During knee surgery improper anesthetic intubation into esophagus; tube removed once and reinserted, again improperly. Patient suffocated and died. Punitive damages asked.	$1,280,000
13635	During testing for chest pain improper insertion of needle led to cellulitis and phlebitis.	$25,500
135742	Physician prescribed medicine for bursitis despite manufacturer's warning not to use it for bursitis. Patient dies from toxic reaction.	$4,000
155501	Surgeon performs unauthorized tubal ligation on a schizophrenic woman during an abortion.	Compensatory: $1.00 Punitive: $6,000

(continued)

TABLE 3.1.—*Continued*

Case	Allegation/Injury	Award
159407	During hysterectomy surgical tape left in body causing severe infection and complications.	$40,000 Loss of consortium: $1,000
159527	During molar extraction plaintiff complains about pain of anesthetizing needle but dentist refuses to stop and insults patient; charges of lack of consent, false imprisonment; battery.	$7,000 (Punitive)
159529	During cancer chemotherapy patient given 10 times required dosage resulting in nerve damage, paralysis, organ damage, and loss of sexual function.	$300,000
173614	Seventy-four-year-old patient dropped by attendants, fracturing her femur, which was not set for two weeks resulting in amputation nine months later.	$75,000
178602	Pregnant woman with hypertension; only a nurse and not the physician examined her. Fetus died at 34 weeks; complications to mother.	$195,000
197-708	Physician diagnosed thrombophlebitis in legs despite information about recurrent Hodgkin's disease. This diagnosis and treatment shortened life expectancy and patient died two years later.	$300,000
197725	Surgery on middle-age accident victim improperly performed causing drooping eyelid.	$5,000
3-00-810	Patient in detoxification facility given Dilantin despite his protests that he was allergic to it; became critically ill with a skin disorder.	$18,000
3-25-703	Pregnant woman with hypertension, anemia, and mononucleosis went into labor and went to hospital. High-risk pregnancy specialists did not appear. Delay caused severe retardation of baby.	$3,500,000
3-25-924	Permanent paralysis and brain damage following drug overdose subsequent to heart surgery.	$1,000,000
3-33-702	Surgery on wrong foot of minor with claim of permanent minor disability.	$7,500

percent of the award. Assuming, very conservatively, that expenses and fees averaged $10,000 and that the attorney's share was 35 percent, or roughly $25,000, the plaintiff who went to trial would expect to recover $35,849.[7] Indeed, when the hours and days spent in preparing the case and going to trial are considered, even the plaintiff attorneys did not do very well. Of course, in a few cases plaintiffs and their attorneys did much better than average. On the other hand, in the majority of cases they did much worse. It would seem from these surface statistics that after expenses and hours of effort, not to mention the emotional drain on plaintiffs, many plaintiffs actually lost money going to trial.

We should, however, approach any analysis of verdicts with caution. In addition to the tip-of-the-iceberg problem described in chapter 2 the statistics mask some important complexities that have been ignored in most empirical research as well as by commentators on jury behavior.

Some Case Studies

I want to begin my analysis with some selected case studies and the lessons that are learned from them. The cases were constructed from court files, interviews with attorneys, and the insurers' closed claim files. They provide examples of certain patterns that recur in medical malpractice litigation.

Five Cases

In case 1 a jury rendered a verdict for the defendants in a suit involving brain damage to an infant during childbirth. The mother was 34-weeks pregnant and involved in an automobile accident; she was rushed to a hospital and connected to a fetal monitor. On the second day of her hospitalization, doctors observed signs of fetal distress and ordered an immediate cesarean section, but the child was born with severe brain damage. Subsequently, a suit was brought against the hospital and three physicians. After an initial period of discovery, the process in which both parties exchange documents and seek expert advice, the lawsuit was amended to include the obstetrician, the neonatologists, and the physicians' clinic. Ultimately, a total of eight defendants were named in the suit. The plaintiff's allegations were that the defendants had failed to identify and treat the fetal distress in time despite clear warnings from the fetal monitor reading and an ultrasound reading. The plaintiff's initial claim was for $6 million, though subsequently an offer was made to settle the case for $3 million. During the pretrial phase of the litigation significant procedural maneuvers occurred, including defense motions to dismiss some of the defendants from the suit (which were denied) and a plaintiff motion to limit the number of defense experts on the grounds that it was unfair and subjected the plaintiff to excessive deposition costs. Behind the scenes the personal attorney for several of the defendants demanded that their insurer settle the case for the policy limits. The defendants' legal counsel also uncovered the fact that the plaintiff's main expert had been forced to resign from a university position under allegations of falsified research data. Ultimately, three of the defendants settled their portion of the suit for a sum exceeding $500,000. Twenty-four months after the suit was filed, a nine-day trial against the remaining defendants was held. The jury rendered a verdict in favor of the defendants.

In case 2 a 63-year-old female went to an emergency room with chest pains. She was examined solely by a student in a physician's assistant program (who consulted with the physician on call), but no tests were conducted. She was discharged within an hour with a prescription for Motrin. She died later that day from a heart attack. The lawyer for the woman's spouse attempted to settle the case against the hospital for around $100,000 and did manage to settle with the physician's insurer for $80,000. The hospital felt it had a valid defense as an independent contractor, but it raised its indemnity reserves from $50,000 to $75,000. (Indemnity reserves are the amounts that insurers set aside against their assets in the event that they lose the case and must pay the plaintiff.) At the end of discovery defense counsel for the hospital made a $40,000 settlement offer, but it was refused. Defense counsel believed that the refusal was due in part to the fact that plaintiff counsel was involved in a similar case involving hospital liability and wanted to use the trial as a "dry run." The husband died before the case went to trial, but the couple's children pursued the case on behalf of the estate. At the eight-day trial, the jury absolved the hospital of the claim of nursing negligence, but on another claim against it returned a verdict of $18,000. Defense counsel requested a "set off" from the judgment due to the $80,000 settlement and moved for one-half of defense costs since defense prevailed on the nursing issue.[8] The judge denied costs but set the recovery figure for the plaintiff at zero because of the prior settlement.

In case 3 a black female child was taken to a hospital's emergency room with a two-day history of nausea, vomiting, and fever. A diagnosis of upper respiratory tract infection was made, and the child was sent home. The next morning the child was found dead in her bed. An autopsy indicated that the death was caused by meningitis. After a suit was filed against the hospital and the doctor defense counsel received two expert opinions that there was no medical negligence, but the liability insurer's indemnity reserves were nevertheless set at $150,000. In the defense counsel's opinion the plaintiff's expert "performed well" during the deposition; defense counsel believed the expert "was damaging to our case" and estimated a 50-percent chance of winning on liability and $100,000 to $300,000 exposure on damages. At the end of a four-day trial the jury deliberated from 4:00 P.M. to 7:00 P.M., and as they left for the day, the court reporter overheard a juror say they were divided eight to three for the plaintiff with one person undecided. The reporter quietly (and inappropriately) told the defense counsel.[9] Fearing the prospect of an adverse verdict or a hung jury, defense counsel offered the plaintiff $50,000 to settle. While the jury was deliberating the following day the plaintiff accepted the offer, and the jury was dismissed. Interviews with jurors indicated they were 11 to 1 in favor of the plaintiff; no information about the probable amount of the damage award was obtained.

Case 4 involved a pregnant woman who requested a cesarean section because of a problem with her spine that was the result of childhood scoliosis. After getting an opinion from another doctor, the physicians decided a cesarean was unnecessary. During birth, the baby turned and had to be delivered with forceps. The child was born with hypoxia, was quadriplegic, and had no bowel control. The woman, on behalf of her child, sought $15,500,000 against the hospital, the physician, and the obstetrical clinic. The hospital report indicated that the baby suffered from a congenital condition, but defense expert consultants gave the opinion that the condition had resulted from an injury at birth. The child died at around two years of age and about 18 months after the suit was filed. An autopsy concluded that the injury occurred at or near the time of birth. The insurers offered a settlement exceeding $1 million, and it was accepted. About three-quarters of a million dollars of the award went to the county health department, which had assumed responsibility for costs of the child's medical care.

Case 5 involved a 57-year-old male who was partially disabled by a heart attack. Subsequently, he underwent unrelated surgery for a growth on his lungs, which turned out to be benign. In his complaint the plaintiff stated that although the anesthesia used in the operation paralyzed him, he could still feel the incision being made and hear and see the operating team. As a consequence, he suffered recurrent nightmares about the surgery. In his deposition, taken early in the case, the plaintiff was assessed by defense lawyers as "rambling and tedious" and as displaying inconsistencies about the facts. For example, he stated that his eyes were open and that he saw the surgeon when in fact his eyes had been taped shut. Initially, the plaintiff's attorney requested $800,000 to settle the case; this offer was rejected and the plaintiff subsequently demanded $1.5 million. Experts who reviewed the case for the defendants stated that "recall syndrome," whereby the patient has conscious memories of surgery, is not unusual. However, the experts also offered the opinion that the dose of anesthesia administered to the man was proper for 99 percent of patients and that the plaintiff's deposition was inconsistent with true "recall syndrome." The plaintiff again offered to settle—for $900,000—but the insurer for the physician assessed the likelihood of a jury finding liability as low and estimated that the award would be only about $50,000 if the plaintiff did win. The hospital defendant estimated the damage award would be between $35,000 and $50,000 if they lost. At the end of the six-day trial, the jury returned a verdict for the defendants.

No practitioner or academic familiar with medical malpractice litigation will find anything atypical about these case synopses. They capture some of the grist of day-to-day medical malpractice litigation. Practitioners may complain that I have failed to capture the complexities of developing the evidence and the many pretrial procedural maneuverings that affect the litigation process.[10] I will attend to some of these issues in the following chapters, but the case synopses, combined with other data, provide some crucial insights and hypotheses that bear upon the interpretation of surface statistics about jury verdicts.

Conceptual Insights from the Case Studies

The first insight that can be derived from the examples is that malpractice cases typically involve multiple defendants (cases 1, 3, 4, and 5). Sometimes an extra defendant is simply the physician's clinic or other professional association. However, most malpractice injuries that result in lawsuits involve incidents that occur in hospitals.[11] The modern practice of medicine involves a team approach with different health care providers bearing responsibility for the well-being of the patients. One doctor may diagnose, another may perform the surgery after the patient has been rendered unconscious by an anesthesiologist, a gastroenterologist may be responsible for the patient's nutritional needs while he or she is recovering, and the hospital may provide nursing care and other services. When something goes wrong it may not be clear which providers are legally responsible or to what degree. Sometimes the facts are unclear when the suit is filed. Everyone may be sued or only some providers. As the evidence develops, some defendants may be dropped or others may be added to the lawsuit. The liability of those remaining in the suit may differ; some may settle and others may contest the claims at trial.

The second insight is that jury verdicts do not tell the whole story about the outcomes of litigation. In my discussion of the plaintiff "wins" reported in table 3.1 I drew attention to the fact that some of the awards are so small that they may not have covered expert fees and other expenses, let alone expectations of plaintiffs and their attorneys. Cases 1 and 2, for example, demonstrate the opposite result, namely, that plaintiffs who lost at trial did not always come away empty-handed: settlements with some of the parties to the suit occurred prior to trial. (It is important to state here that ordinarily the jurors would not be informed of these prior settlements.)

A third insight is that some cases that were settled might have yielded some very large jury awards if they had gone to trial. Cases 3 and 4 are probable examples. I will examine some of the dynamics of settlement and failures of settlement in chapter 4.

Some Statistics Bearing on the Conceptual Insights

To what degree do the conceptual insights just discussed characterize malpractice cases? The following data bear on each of these insights.

The Number of Defendants

In the 1984–87 data set, only 32 percent of the cases filed had a single health care provider as a defendant. There were two defendants in 26 percent of the cases, three in 15 percent of the cases, four in 11 percent, and five or more in the remaining 16 percent. Overall, the average malpractice case initially had 3.2 defendants. Of the cases that actually went to trial, however, only 15 percent initially had a single defendant, while 59 percent of these cases initially had four or more defendants.

In the 1987–89 sample, 30 percent were filed against a single health care provider. There were two defendants in 30 percent of the cases, three in 17 percent, four in 8 percent, and five or more in the remaining 15 percent. Overall, the average malpractice case began with 3.1 defendants. Of the cases that went to trial 72 percent initially had multiple defendants. [12]

Settlements in Trial Cases

Documenting the number of pretrial settlements by one or more defendants in the cases that went to trial proved to be a difficult task because unambiguous evidence of a settlement was usually missing from court files. [13] I did obtain additional information from insurance company files and from attorneys. It is likely, however, that the final estimates understate the number of settlements because when there were doubts the cases were coded as not involving settlements.

In the 1984–87 data, we were able to document prior settlements by one or more defendants in 14 percent of trial cases. For the 1987–89 data set we sent questionnaires to both plaintiff and defense attorneys for all trial cases in an attempt to obtain more systematic settlement information. We received information on 25 of the 32 trial cases. These cases initially had an average of 2.5 defendants named in the suit. The number of trial defendants, however, averaged only 1.7. Some of the defendants had been voluntarily dropped from the suit, and others had been dismissed through judicial action. In 21 percent of the cases, however, one or more of the defendants settled with the plaintiff prior to trial, leaving the remaining defendants to argue their case before the jury.

Information on the amount of settlements in trial cases was difficult to obtain because of confidentiality agreements between the parties.

Nevertheless, we were able to obtain this information in 22 cases. Some settlements were in the range of $10,000 to $25,000, but others were more substantial. In one case, the prior settlement was $1,031,885, and in another it was $1,385,000. Two other cases exceeded $500,000, and two others exceeded $150,000. We ascertained prior settlements ranging between $50,000 and $122,000 in four other cases.

However incomplete and unsatisfactory the available statistics are on prior settlements in trial cases they do demonstrate that plaintiffs who lose at trial do not necessarily come away from the lawsuit with empty hands.

Settlement Amounts versus Jury Awards

Systematic information on settlements in cases that did not go to trial was also difficult to obtain, but searches of court records, surveys of lawyers, and closed claim files yielded information on 133 settlements in the combined data sets. These data yield a striking conclusion: a number of cases resulted in settlements that approached or exceeded the largest jury awards reported in table 3.1.

One case involved a claim of failure to timely diagnose and treat meningitis in a four-year-old girl. Ultimately, both her arms and legs had to be amputated. The parties reached an agreement on a structured settlement of approximately $9 million. Other settlements exceeding $1 million were as follows: $3.1 million, $2.9 million, $2.8 million, $2.51 million, $2.5 million, $2.4 million, $1.85 million, $1.75 million, $1.46 million, $1.35 million, $1.22 million, $1.20 million, and $1.03 million. There were nine settlements between $500,000 and $1 million, 10 settlements between $250,000 and $499,000, and 32 between $100,000 and $249,000. Recall that of the jury trials reported in table 3.1 only 6 of 109 cases involved verdicts that exceeded $250,000. In contrast, 32 of the 133 known settlements exceeded $250,000. Once again let me caution that since juries may be deciding different types of cases than those that are settled we cannot conclude anything about jury behavior relative to settlements.

Summary of the Profile

This chapter provides an initial profile of jury verdicts and settlements in North Carolina and demonstrates in a concrete way some of the inherent problems in looking only at jury verdict statistics. The fact that plaintiffs win only one case in five seems to contradict the extreme claim that juries are prone to side with plaintiffs regardless of the evidence on liability. The statistics on awards suggest that the claims of jury profligacy also may be overstated. I will reserve discussion of the appropriateness of awards—both large ones and small ones—for later chapters. Nevertheless, at this point it is reasonable to say that the findings do not support the conclusion that million-dollar or even quarter-million-dollar awards are typical. The findings also raise the question of whether some of the plaintiffs receiving the lower awards might better be considered losers than winners because their award may not have exceeded litigation costs. In contrast, the data on settlements in cases that go to trial suggest that a certain percentage of plaintiffs who lose at trial may actually be considered winners; they may receive substantial monies from defendants who settle prior to trial. The data on cases that are settled without trial indirectly raise questions about whether some of the large jury awards are necessarily unreasonable since many settlements exceed most jury awards; that is, perhaps juries are giving awards commensurate with the evidence on the economic and other costs of the injury. All of these factors raise the issue of how cases are selected for trial, a topic I will address in the chapters in part 2. However, we should first compare North Carolina to other jurisdictions around the United States.

4

How Typical Is North Carolina?
Data from Elsewhere in America

How typical are the cases and verdict patterns in the North Carolina data when compared to other states? This is a worthwhile question if we wish to generalize the results. It is also relevant to subsequent chapters where I will draw upon data from studies of juries in other states. Although I do not have the data to answer the question without qualification, it is likely that on balance North Carolina is probably not atypical.

The Absence of Baseline Data

The question of whether North Carolina is typical cannot be answered to my satisfaction because of the absence of data from other jurisdictions about the mass of cases from which jury trial cases arise: the iceberg problem arises again. The central lesson of chapter 2 was that different case selection patterns among states or jurisdictions may result in different cases being tried before juries. The verdict reporter data from these other jurisdictions tell us nothing about the cases that make it to trial. Likewise, closed claim studies of insurance files, such as those conducted by the General Accounting Office (GAO) and by Sloan and Hsieh, did not make clear distinctions between trial cases and settled cases.[1]

Data compiled by the National Association of Insurance Commissioners (NAIC) for the years 1981–85 suggested that the number and dollar value of malpractice claims in North Carolina were lower than most of the rest of the nation.[2] However, absent further comparative information from other states, we cannot tell what this means. Perhaps the lower rates are due to the fact that patients were injured less frequently, either because they underwent fewer risky procedures or because their doctors were more careful or less legally negligent. Perhaps, for whatever reasons, North Carolinians were less likely to make claims when they were injured, or perhaps North Carolina plaintiff attorneys were more reluctant to take cases than attorneys in other states. Perhaps when they file suits, plaintiffs ask for lower damages than they do elsewhere, or perhaps more claims can be settled amicably without the plaintiff filing a lawsuit.[3] Additionally, North Carolina retains the legal concept of contributory negligence whereas most other jurisdictions use a comparative negligence rule for determining liability.[4] Further complicating the picture is the fact that statistics are compiled differently in various states.[5] Thus, even these statistics about numbers and amounts tell us nothing about the typicality of North Carolina jury cases.

Any answer to the question of North Carolina's typicality must be consistent with what I said in chapter 2 about treating statistics cautiously. Accordingly, my data cannot definitely answer the question we want to investigate. It does not prevent us, however, from making educated guesses using indirect data and statistics.

Plaintiff Win Rates

Data on plaintiff win rates in a number of jurisdictions have been reported in various studies. Table 4.1 summarizes these data, giving the authors of the study in which the data were reported, the dates covered by the verdicts, the jurisdiction, the sample size, and the plaintiffs' win rates.[6] The table shows that plaintiff win rates varied from 13.5 percent to 53 percent, with a median win rate of around 29 percent.

The Daniels study involved 42 counties in 11 states. While it concluded that overall the plaintiff win rate was 32.4 percent, there was considerable variability between jurisdictions.[7] Of 32 counties having 10 or more malpractice cases, the plaintiffs' success at trial ranged from 8.3 percent in Fresno County, California, to 55.8 percent in Bronx County, New York. Considering only counties with 50 or more malpractice cases (there were eight such counties), the success rates varied from 10.3 percent in Harris County, Texas, to 48.2 percent in Queens County, New York. In a related study, Daniels and Andrews separated obstetrics-gynecology (OB-GYN) cases from the other malpractice cases and found plaintiff win rates in these cases averaged 36.8 percent.[8] Once again, the lessons of chapter 2 need to be repeated. Because the Daniels study tells us nothing about how the base rates of filed malpractice cases or settlement rates affected the cases that went to trial, we cannot say whether the different win rates are due to juries deciding cases differently or juries deciding different cases. Nevertheless, the conclusion from the Daniels study and from the data summarized in table 4.1 is that, for whatever reasons, the plaintiff win rates in North Carolina, while lower than those in some jurisdictions, do not appear to deviate substantially from those of other jurisdictions.

TABLE 4.1. Plaintiff Win Rates in Studies of Jury Verdicts

Source	Dates of Verdicts	State/Jurisdiction	Sample Size	Win Rate (%)
Vidmar	1984–87	North Carolina	84	20
Vidmar	1987–89	North Carolina	25	16
Danzon (1985a)	1974+1976	California	420[a]	28
Danzon (1985b)	1983	Florida	322	13.8
NAIC (1980)	1975–78	Nationwide study	2,539[b]	13.5
Peterson (1987)	1960–64	San Francisco	95	27
	1965–69	San Francisco	88	35
	1970–74	San Francisco	98	43
	1975–79	San Francisco	81	32
	1980–84	San Francisco	55	53
Peterson (1987)	1960–64	Cook Co., IL	56	25
	1965–69	Cook Co., IL	68	29
	1970–74	Cook Co., IL	100	29
	1975–79	Cook Co., IL	134	33
	1980–84	Cook Co., IL	162	49
Hubbard (1987)	1976–85	South Carolina	117	35
Daniels (1990)	1981–85	42 counties in 11 states	1,886	32.4
Gross & Syverud (1992)	1985–86	California	65	29.2
Bovbjerg et al. (1991)	1980–85	5 jurisdictions	426	33
Clermont & Eisenberg (1992)	1979–87	Federal courts/ nationwide	759	30
Taragin et al. (1992)	1977–92	New Jersey	988	24
Sloan et al. (1993)	1986–89	Florida	37	27

[a]Estimate: Database was approximately 6,000 claims of which 7 percent went to verdict = 420.
[b]These data include an unknown number of bench trials along with jury trials.

Settlement Rates, Settlement Dynamics, and Outcomes

There are a few studies by which we may take some rough comparative measure of North Carolina settlement patterns. Recall that, as
stated in chapter 3, approximately 50 percent of all malpractice cases
in North Carolina resulted in some payment to the plaintiff, 40 percent were dropped by the plaintiff or dismissed through judicial action, and the remaining 10 percent went to trial.

A nationwide study by the NAIC (1980) found that 46 percent of
malpractice insurance claims were settled with a payment.[9] Daniels
reported that the Texas Board of Medical Examiners found that only
20.5 percent of all malpractice insurance claims were settled with a
payment.[10] The GAO nationwide study of claims closed in 1984 concluded that 43 percent of claims were closed with an indemnity payment.[11] A companion study to the GAO report dealing with North
Carolina found that in 1984, 38 percent of claims against hospitals
were closed with an indemnity payment to the plaintiff; no comparable data were reported for claims against physicians.[12] These closed
claims studies do not distinguish between claims settled prior to or
after a formal lawsuit, but they suggest that North Carolina was not
very different from the rest of the nation.

Danzon's study of closed claims in California for the years 1974
and 1976 did distinguish trials from other dispositions.[13] Approximately 43 percent of claims were dropped without payment, 50 percent were settled with an indemnity to the plaintiff, and the remaining 7 percent went to trial for a verdict. Of trial cases, plaintiffs
prevailed 28 percent of the time. These figures roughly coincide with
those reported in chapter 3. The average award for settled cases was
$26,000, and the average trial award, when plaintiffs prevailed, was
$102,000. Danzon speculated that there was a difference between
settled and trial cases. The trial cases constituted "a small atypical
subset, 'self selected' to that stage of disposition precisely because
the outcome was unpredictable to the litigants, the potential award
was large, and the evidence for the plaintiff was weak."[14] It is difficult to use Danzon's data to make comparisons with our North Carolina data because they are about 20 years older. Indeed, they probably do not apply to California today because of the many changes in
California laws and settlement practices since 1976. Danzon's conclusions that in trial cases "the outcome was unpredictable" and the

"evidence for the plaintiff was weak" appear to have been based on speculation rather than on any evidence in her data set.[15] However, these problems do not necessarily render Danzon's conclusions invalid. Three other studies seem to support this conclusion.

First, Professors Henry Farber and Michelle White examined 252 cases filed against a large, self-insured hospital between 1977 and 1989.[16] Of these cases, 36.5 percent were dropped by the plaintiffs or dismissed by the judge, and 58.3 percent were settled out of court. Of the remaining 5.2 percent that were tried in court—a total of only 13 cases—all were decided in the hospital's favor. An important feature of the Farber and White study was that the hospital's experts had evaluated each case according to whether the standards of care had been met. Care was coded as good, bad, or ambiguous. When the experts classified the case as involving good quality care, two-thirds of the cases were dropped or dismissed. When they classified the case as bad, only 10 percent of cases were dropped or dismissed; patients received damage payments in 89 percent of bad care cases. Trial cases appeared to be indistinguishable from dropped or dismissed cases, causing Farber and White to conclude that cases go to trial because "some plaintiffs fail to drop cases even when it is relatively clear that negligence did not occur, rather than because bargaining over a settlement breaks down."[17] This last conclusion hints that there is a tendency for the evidence bearing on defendant liability in trial cases to be weak, a hypothesis that will be investigated more in part 2. Farber and White also concluded that their data support an interpretation that cases eventually dropped by plaintiffs are frequently not "nuisance" suits that disappear because the plaintiffs become discouraged by the litigation process. Rather, it is because plaintiffs file promising suits but drop them when they learn during discovery that negligence was unlikely.[18]

Professors Roger Rosenblatt and Andy Hurst conducted a somewhat similar study.[19] They reviewed 54 obstetric malpractice claims in the files of a physician-sponsored malpractice liability insurance company between 1982 and 1988. They attempted to assess each case for medical negligence and concluded that

> no payments were made in the 42 percent of cases in which there were no significant deviations from prevailing standards of care. For those cases in which payments were made, there was general

consensus among insurance company staff, medical experts, defense attorneys, and the physician defendants that some lapse in standard of care contributed to the observed outcome.[20]

A third study was conducted by Mark Taragin and his co-researchers. They examined malpractice cases in the state of New Jersey that were closed between 1977 and 1992, a total of 8,231 cases involving 12,829 physicians.[21] Insurance company experts systematically rated the quality of medical care. Physician care was rated defensible in 62 percent of the cases, indefensible in 25 percent of the cases, and unclear in the remaining 13 percent. A payment to the plaintiff was made in 21 percent of the cases in which medical care was rated defensible, in 91 percent of the cases that were rated indefensible, and in 59 percent of the unclear cases. Twelve percent of cases went to trial, and the plaintiff win rate at trial was approximately 25 percent.

Taragin et al.'s discussion of the reasons why payment occurred in cases classified as defensible deserves to be quoted at length.

> First, the determination of physician care was made very early after a claim was generated and may have been inaccurate as more information became available. Second, a physician-based review process may be biased toward assessing physician performance in the physician's favor. Third, the insurance company may err toward an initial determination of physician care as defensible to avoid unnecessary payments. The possibility that new information rendered the original assessment of defensibility incorrect was supported by the fact that 68% of defensible cases that resulted in payment were settled before trial, in half of these before discovery was complete.[22]

In short, Taragin et al. concluded that cases are fluid and subject to revision as each case progresses. The Taragin et al. data seem consistent with a view that insurance companies attempted to settle cases where physician liability was clear and that the majority of cases that proceeded to trial involved a judgment by the insurer that the case was defensible.

Professor Frank Sloan and his colleagues produced a study that yielded somewhat similar results.[23] These researchers obtained a sample of 187 malpractice cases involving both OB-GYN and emergency room injuries occurring in Florida between 1986 and 1989. They had panels of physicians review the medical records and code each case according to three categories of defendant liability: liable, not liable, and uncertain liability. Statistically significant relationships were found between the liability ratings and the type of resolution of the case. Here is their conclusion:

> Among the dropped cases, the physician panels found the defendants not liable almost three times as often as liable. Among cases settled before trial, the ratio was reversed; in about twice as many cases, one or more defendants were classified as "liable." Among cases settled at trial, the ratio of liable to not liable cases was four to one, but there were only ten such cases. Cases whose outcomes were decided at verdict or subsequently were assigned almost evenly to the three categories. Thus, the patterns are consistent with the view that cases with low defendant liability are comparatively likely to be dropped, those with high defendant liability are more likely to be settled, and a more mixed pattern is apparent for the cases decided at verdict and beyond.[24]

The Sloan et al. study involves a special subset of malpractice cases of which 19.7 percent went to trial and 24 percent of those were won by the plaintiffs. The actual sample of trial cases was only 37. The physician panels rated only 32 percent of the cases as those in which the defendant was liable with 17 percent categorized as not liable and 51 percent as uncertain.[25] These patterns of settlement and their relationship to assessments of liability seem generally consistent with the other studies.

These various findings lead me to infer that plaintiff win rates in North Carolina are within the normal range of win rates in other states. They also cause me to infer that insurers tend to settle cases where defendant liability is clear and to contest cases where they conclude that there is no liability.

Win Rates in Other Types of Personal Injury Cases

A question may have arisen in some readers' minds about how plaintiff win rates in malpractice trials compare to those in other personal injury cases. Such information will also be useful in the chapters that follow. I do not have good data for North Carolina, but some of the other studies reported in table 4.1 do have these figures.

Peterson reported data on plaintiff win rates for San Francisco and Cook counties.[26] Data for 1980–84 in San Francisco are as follows: medical malpractice, 53 percent; product liability, 52 percent; work injury, 66 percent; auto accident, 70 percent; injury on property, 61 percent; common carrier, 41 percent; and intentional torts, 53 percent. For Cook County for the same period the figures are: medical malpractice, 49 percent; product liability, 52 percent; work injury, 72 percent; auto accident, 64 percent; injury on property, 68 percent; common carrier, 60 percent; and intentional tort, 56 percent. Observe from table 4.1 that the plaintiff win ratios for malpractice were highest in the Peterson study.

Daniels and Andrews found a success rate for all malpractice cases to be 32.4 percent and for OB-GYN cases a rate of 36.8 percent.[27] In contrast, the success rate for all civil jury verdicts involving money damages, drawn from a database of 24,625 cases, was 57 percent.

Bovbjerg et al. found that while the success rate in malpractice trials was 33 percent, in automobile injury cases it was 64 percent. Cases involving government defendants and products liability defendants had success rates of 48 and 44 percent, respectively.[28]

Clermont and Eisenberg's study of win rates for plaintiffs in over 17,000 jury trials in federal courts found plaintiffs prevailing 28 percent of the time in malpractice cases and 29 percent of the time in products liability cases.[29] In comparison, the win rates for other types of personal injury cases were as follows: motor vehicle, 60 percent; fraud, 59 percent; negotiable instruments, 73 percent; contract, 66 percent; marine personal injury, 64 percent; assault, libel, or slander, 49 percent; and federal employer's liability, 72 percent.

These various studies make it very clear that malpractice cases yield among the lowest success rates of personal injury suits, often by a very substantial margin.

Wrapping Up: Chapters c and d

The data on jury verdicts from North Carolina indicate that plaintiffs won only about one case in five that went to trial. Median and expected values of awards when plaintiffs prevailed were modest in comparison to widely asserted claims about what juries do and in comparison to the monetary value of settlements in cases that did not go to trial. Further analysis suggests that in cases that did go to trial there was a tendency for plaintiff cases to be weak on the issue of defendant liability. Data from studies in other jurisdictions show similar plaintiff win ratios and settlement patterns, creating a prima facie argument that, while plaintiff win rates are a little below the average overall, North Carolina does not appear atypical from other states.

2. Case Selection and Its Importance in Understanding Jury Outcomes

The Cases That Went to Trial
(*with Laura Donnelly*)

The discussion and data in chapters 3 and 4 documented low plaintiff win rates, prior settlements in some of the cases that went to trial, and settlements in some nontrial cases that equaled or exceeded most jury awards. This raises important questions about the characteristics of cases that juries are asked to decide. Take, for example, the finding that plaintiffs prevailed on the issue of liability in only one case in five. Are we to conclude that, exactly contrary to what critics have claimed, juries are in fact strongly biased against plaintiffs rather than against health care defendants? Or should we entertain a competing hypothesis that states that in many cases that proceed to trial, the plaintiff's claim about liability is weak and perhaps litigated by plaintiff attorneys who cannot tell good cases from bad ones? This last hypothesis was suggested by the authors of several studies involving other jurisdictions that were discussed in chapter 4. Or are there other characteristics that differentiate trial cases from settled cases?

In this chapter, Laura Donnelly and I begin to explore these issues using data from our North Carolina studies. The analyses lend support to the general thesis that trial cases have some interesting characteristics that can be detected only by studying trial cases in comparison to the remaining 90 percent of cases that never progressed to trial.

Severity and Nature of Injury

Cases that are filed on behalf of plaintiffs vary by the alleged seriousness of the injury. Following a classification system used in other studies,[1] we categorized the severity of injury for all malpractice cases on a nine-point scale. However, because of the small numbers of cases in some of the categories, we subsequently collapsed the system into five categories:

1. Emotional or Minor Injury: e.g., fright; temporary pain and suffering; lacerations; contusions; minor scars; rashes; no delays in recovery
2. Temporary Disability: e.g., infection; miss set fracture; fall in hospital; burns; surgical material left in body; drug side effect; delayed recovery
3. Permanent Partial Disability: e.g., loss of fingers; damage to organs; deafness; loss of one limb, eye, kidney, or lung
4. Permanent Total Disability: e.g., paraplegia; blindness; loss of two limbs; brain damage; quadriplegia; lifelong care or fatal prognosis
5. Death

Variable 1a in table 5.1 reports the percentage of each type of injury for all malpractice cases in the 1984–87 data set discussed in chapter 3. It shows that minor or emotional injuries accounted for only 5 percent of claims, temporary disability accounted for 27 percent, permanent partial disability involved 39 percent, permanent total disability involved 8 percent, and 21 percent of the cases involved death. Variable 1b shows the percentage of cases that resulted in trial, in a settlement with the plaintiff, and in no payment to the plaintiff for each of the types of injury. We see that jury trials occurred less frequently when the injury involved only minor or emotional injury (9 percent) or temporary disability (7 percent) and that they occurred more frequently when the injury involved permanent total disability (13 percent) or death (13 percent); permanent partial disability cases fell in the middle, with trials occurring in 10 percent of cases. Equally as interesting are the settlement and nonpayment patterns. In minor or emotional and temporary disability cases, 52 and 47 percent of claims, respectively, resulted in no payment to the plaintiff. In contrast, only 19 percent of permanent total injuries and 31 percent of death injuries resulted in no payment. Put another way, settlements occurred with greater frequency in cases involving the most serious injuries, but proportionately more jury trials of serious injuries occurred as well. The pattern in the 1987–89 data set was similar.

Variable 2 in table 5.1 reports the case types by form of medical

TABLE 5.1. Injury Characteristics and Form of Disposition: 1984–87 Sample

Variable 1: Severity of Injury	Minor/ Emotional	Temporary Disability	Permanent Partial Disability	Permanent Total	Death	All
(a) Percentage by injury type	5	27	39	8	21	100
(b) Percentage by disposition						
Jury trial	9	7	10	13	13	10
Settled	39	46	47	67	56	50
No payment	52	47	43	19	31	40

Variable 2: Primary Allegation by Form of Medical Error	Diagnosis	Surgery	OB-GYN	Treatment	Anesthesia	Monitor	All
(a) Percentage by medical care type	22	31	9	21	10	7	100
(b) Percentage by disposition							
Jury trial	11	9	12	7	16	7	10
Settled	47	45	56	55	53	58	50
No payment	42	46	32	39	31	35	40

Variable 3: Age of Patient at Time of Injury	Birth to One Year	Over One Year	All
(a) Percentage by age	8	92	100
(b) Percentage by disposition			
Jury trial	18	9	10
Settled	64	48	50
No payment	18	42	40

Note: Because of rounding, percentages may not total 100 percent.

error divided into one of six categories: diagnosis, surgery, Ob-Gyn, treatment (including lack of informed consent), anesthesia, and monitoring. These must be treated as very rough categories on two grounds. First, we collapsed a number of possible subcategories of diagnoses in order to maintain reasonable numbers of cases within each category.[2] Second, many pleadings made multiple claims covering different categories, and, therefore, a judgment had to be made to determine the primary allegation for each case. Variable 2a reports the percentage of each category of medical care for all filed cases; and variable 2b gives the breakdown of trials, settlements, and no payment within each category. One interesting finding from these data is that allegations of negligence involving anesthesia constituted a relatively small (10 percent) proportion of cases overall but resulted in a higher proportion of trials (16 percent) than any of the other cases. Ob-Gyn error also constituted a relatively small proportion of cases (9 percent), but it had the second highest percentage of trials (12 percent). Both of these types of cases were more likely to result in very serious injury. Thus, the findings seem consistent with variable 1: that is, cases involving death or serious permanent injury were more likely to go to trial.

Variable 3 in table 5.1 helps us explore the data a little further. The court pleadings allowed us to categorize cases according to whether the plaintiff's injury occurred birth to under one year of age, or over one year of age. We see from variable 3a that injuries from birth to one year constituted 8 percent of all malpractice lawsuits. Their trial rate, however, was double that for patients over one year. Note, further, that the number of settlements for children under one year (including birth injuries) was substantially higher (64 percent) than for plaintiffs who were over one-year old (48 percent).

Table 5.1, then, provides us with some insight that cases involving the most serious injuries were more likely to go to trial. Additionally, it shows that a higher percentage of serious cases were also more likely to result in some sort of settlement with the plaintiff. I will discuss the possible meaning of this finding after we consider other data.

Number of Defendants

In chapter 3 I showed that cases frequently involve more than a single defendant. Variable a in table 5.2 reports these data again, showing that only 32 percent of cases involved a single defendant, and 26 percent involved two defendants while the remaining cases involved three (15 percent), four (11 percent), or five or more defendants (16 percent). Variable b in table 5.2 shows that cases initially involving four or five or more defendants were more likely to result in trial (18 and 14 percent, respectively) than cases involving fewer defendants (6 to 8 percent trial rates). Or more accurately stated in the light of the conceptual analysis reported in chapter 3, the cases with four or more initial defendants were more likely to go to trial against at least *some* of the defendants. Some of the defendants settled before trial (recall my estimate in chap. 3 that a minimum of 21 percent of trial cases fall into this category), and other defendants were dismissed from the suit prior to trial, either because the plaintiff's lawyer or a judge concluded that liability against them could not be proved.[3] Using the court statistics and a survey of lawyers involved in the trial cases in the 1987–90 data set, I determined that trial cases initially had an average of 2.75 defendants, but by the time of trial they had an average of 1.86 defendants.

Hospitals As Defendants

Hospitals were named as one of the defendants in 56 percent of the cases that were filed between 1987 and 1990. When named as defendants, however, hospitals went to trial only 3 percent of the time.[4] Although the data are incomplete, there is evidence that hospitals settled with a payment in one-third to one-half of the cases. Some of

TABLE 5.2.   Number of Defendants and Form of Disposition: 1984–87 Sample

Variable: Number of Defendants	Number of Defendants					
	One	Two	Three	Four	Five or More	All
(a) Percentage of cases	32	26	15	11	16	100
(b) Percentage by disposition						
Jury trial	8	6	8	18	14	10
Settled	50	48	53	46	45	50
No payment	41	46	39	36	41	40

Note: Because of rounding, percentages may not total 100 percent.

these settlements were for very small amounts, but in other instances hospitals participated in substantially larger settlements.

Plaintiff Attorney Experience

Plaintiff attorneys' experience with malpractice litigation varies. Some devote most or all of their practice to medical negligence cases. In contrast, some malpractice cases are filed by lawyers who do not specialize in the area. Given that plaintiffs won only one case in five, a plausible hypothesis is that nonspecialist lawyers were more likely to take cases to trial because they inaccurately assessed liability and thus brought weak cases to trial.

As a rough substitute for experience on specialization, lawyers in the 1984–87 data set were classified according to the number of malpractice cases that were filed with their name or the name of their firm as legal counsel for the plantiff.[5] These data are presented as variable a in table 5.3. Fully 34 percent of the lawyers filed only one malpractice suit in the period, 28 percent had two or three cases, 23 percent had four to seven cases, and 16 percent filed eight or more. Thus, there was considerable variation in plaintiff attorneys' experience with malpractice litigation. The data reported as variable b contradict the hypothesis that inexperienced lawyers are primarily the ones who take cases to trial. Lawyers with only one malpractice case took 6 percent of their cases to trial, but lawyers with four to seven cases went to trial 13 percent of the time, and those with eight or more cases took 12

TABLE 5.3.   Lawyer Experience with Malpractice Cases and Form of Disposition: 1984–87 Sample

Variable: Plaintiff Lawyers	Number of Times				
	One (%)	Two to Three (%)	Four to Seven (%)	Eight or More (%)	All (%)
(a) Percentage of all cases	34	28	23	16	100
(b) Percentage by disposition					
Jury trial	6	10	13	12	10
Settled	46	50	45	60	50
No payment	48	40	43	28	40

Note: Due to rounding, percentages may not total 100 percent.

percent to trial. The lawyers with eight or more cases were interesting in another respect: their rates of successfully settling their cases were much higher (60-percent settlement rates) than for those attorneys with fewer cases (who had 45- to 50-percent settlement rates).

We investigated these findings further by comparing lawyer experience with the variables of injury seriousness (variable 1 in table 5.1) and the number of defendants in the case (table 5.2), the two factors also positively associated with higher proportions of jury trials. These comparisons showed that lawyers with many cases were more likely to have cases involving serious injury and a greater number of defendants. That specialist lawyers got the bigger stake cases and were more successful in obtaining settlements should not be surprising: they probably were contacted by more clients and clients with bigger cases; in addition, they may have screened those cases more carefully, chosen bigger cases, and negotiated from a position of strength.

In a sample of birth and emergency room injuries in Florida, Professor Frank Sloan and his colleagues found that claimants who were represented by specialist attorneys were more likely to receive greater amounts than when they were represented by nonspecialists.[6] Sloan et al. hypothesized that their specialists may have been more skillful in selecting cases, needed to invest less time in cases because of their accumulated experience and that their threat of going to trial was more credible, resulting in increased bargaining power. Unlike our findings, however, Sloan et al. did not find that specialists were more likely to go to trial. These contradictory findings may be a result of differences, such as the fact that the Sloan et al. study involved only birth and emergency room injuries whereas our data set contained cases of all types. Or it could be any number of other factors that differentiate our studies; I cannot say. In any event, I have confidence in the relationships found in the North Carolina data and will proceed on the assumption that specialists got more settlements *and* tended to go to trial more often than nonspecialists.

We could not conduct similar analyses on defense attorneys because almost all of them were specialist lawyers who were repeat players with malpractice cases. Insurers tend to maintain a pool of lawyers who are repeat players and become specialists. Even in those rarer cases when a relatively less experienced defense attorney was retained for one or more defendants, this was usually offset by the fact that other defendants in the suit were represented by experienced counsel. Thus, malpractice litigation experience tended to be high among defense attorneys and did not vary enough to allow meaningful correlations.

Request for Punitive Damages

Punitive damages were requested against the health care defendants in only 13 percent of the cases. The court records, moreover, indicated that most of these claims were dropped by the plaintiff or disposed of by summary judgment before the case went to the jury. However, the presence of such a claim in the pleadings suggests that there was a judgment on the part of the plaintiff's lawyer that the defendants' behavior went beyond mere negligence. However, it is also possible that requests for punitive damages were sometimes made for strategic reasons. Punitive damage requests increase the financial stakes for the defendant; they are difficult to assess and perceived to be unpredictable. Furthermore, punitive damages cannot be covered by liability insurance and thus pose a direct threat to the defendant's finances.[7]

Defendants appear to have responded more vigorously in fighting cases when punitive damages were asked. Of the cases that went to trial, 27 percent had initially involved a claim for punitive damages. Thus, although punitive damage requests were made in the pleadings of only 13 percent of all cases, they were represented in 27 percent of trial cases. It is possible that a claim for punitive damages threatens both the purses and the reputation of doctors more than suits over ordinary negligence. In short, a request for punitive damages might increase the degree of conflict and work against settlement.

Summary

These empirical analyses of case characteristics are only suggestive, but they do provide some important insights about the cases that go before juries. Perhaps the most important finding is that specialist lawyers, who are by definition involved in multiple malpractice cases, are more likely to be involved in jury trial cases than inexperienced lawyers. These specialists are more likely to handle cases with severe injuries and multiple defendants. They are also more likely to settle cases than plaintiff lawyers who are only occasional players in medical malpractice litigation.

The findings also hint that cases that proceed to trial may not, on average, be strong cases for plaintiffs. The finding of a higher incidence of requests for punitive damages suggests that many trial cases begin on a contentious note. However, the data do not answer the question of whether punitive damages requests are justified or whether they set an adversarial tone for the litigation that hinders settlement.

The fact that hospitals were named as defendants in over half the cases but went to trial in only 3 percent of the cases in which they were named suggests that their liability may be weak in many cases because it is the physicians who are the principal defendants when medical accidents occur. However, some hospitals do make settlements in a significant number of cases in which they are named as defendants. The findings may reflect a tendency to attempt to settle cases and avoid trial.

None of the data presented in this chapter provide much insight on why plaintiffs go to trial against such stiff odds of winning before juries. I explore the reasons why cases may go to trial against the odds in the next chapter.

6

Case Studies of
Settlement Failure

Chapter 5 reported empirical analyses that did not provide much help in understanding why plaintiffs and their attorneys go to trial against such odds. In this and the next three chapters I will engage in a more qualitative analysis. My analysis is derived from the insurance companies' claim files and from interviews with plaintiff and defense attorneys who litigated those cases.

The Litigation Process: An Overview

A nutshell overview of the malpractice litigation process will help readers not familiar with these matters to understand the case studies.[1] After a plaintiff files a lawsuit and the defendant(s) formally denies(y) liability, lawyers for both sides seek information about the plaintiff and defendant(s) through the process called "discovery." During discovery both plaintiff and defendant can be legally compelled to provide medical and financial records, answer written questions, or "interrogatories," and be questioned under oath in depositions. As will be discussed further in chapter 11, one unique characteristic of malpractice litigation is the requirement that at trial the plaintiff must prove that the defendant(s) breached a "standard of medical care" or "practice" that a physician or other health care provider in his or her field should have followed. Ordinarily, to carry this burden the plaintiff must find a medical expert who is qualified and willing to testify that the standard of care was violated. Typically, defendants, too, must find their own experts to testify that the standard of care was not violated. In addition, either or both sides may call experts to testify on other matters such as the nature of the injuries suffered, the extent of any preexisting medical conditions, the rehabilitative or palliative care that the plaintiff requires, and estimates of the past and future financial losses expected to result from the injuries. All of the experts may be deposed, that is, examined under oath by both sides, before trial so that the other side will have prior knowledge of what they will testify about. Recall also that many malpractice cases involve more than one defendant. Because of possibly conflicting interests, each may have his or her own attorney.

Not surprisingly, the discovery process takes time. Expert witnesses willing to testify must be found, and they may reside in different parts of the country. Depositions have to be arranged to accommodate the professional and personal schedules of these witnesses and those of the attorneys. Often, after taking the deposition of an expert witness, the lawyer for the other side may decide to seek additional experts to counter that witness. During discovery the lawyers for the plaintiff and defendant(s) typically engage in negotiations to determine if the case can be settled without trial. Overall, the discovery process is expensive and time-consuming.

In the 1984–87 sample of North Carolina cases the average time elapsed from the filing of the lawsuit to trial was 26 months, but a few cases exceeded 60 months, that is, five years. In the 1987–89 sample the average time was 25.6 months. Cases that were settled or dropped usually took less time to terminate than trial cases. Cases involving very serious injuries took longer to resolve than those with less serious injuries. For example, 19 months after the suit was filed about 75 percent of cases involving temporary disability to the patient had been resolved; in contrast, during the same 19-month period, less than 50 percent of cases involving permanent total disability were closed.[2]

The litigation process is also expensive. Experts have to be found and hired, not infrequently at rates of $300 to $500 per hour. If the experts are in distant locations, sometimes even in another country, the lawyers may have to travel there to take a pretrial deposition and arrange to pay for a stenographer and transcripts of the deposition. There are numerous other costs for documents and materials bearing on the case. If the experts have to travel to testify at the trial, their travel costs, as well as their fees, must be added to the bills. Defense lawyers, and there is usually more than one when there are multiple defendants or if the case is complicated, have to be paid at an hourly rate. In one sample of 45 cases that went to trial in North Carolina the average defense cost per case was estimated to be $34,500.[3] The costs varied, of course, with the complexity of the case. In about 20 percent of the cases, the total costs per major defendant were under $10,000 but in about 9 percent of trials the cost exceeded $100,000. Approximately 47 percent of the costs were incurred during the discovery stage of trial and the remaining 53 percent were incurred in trial preparation and the trial itself.[4]

We do not have comparable data on plaintiff costs, but they are probably higher. My examination of the insurance company files uncovered the fact that frequently doctors who reviewed cases and even testified at trial for the defendant did not charge for their time, offering the reason that they are glad to just help a fellow physician in trouble. It should be no surprise, as my interviews with plaintiff lawyers confirmed, that this is not a benefit ordinarily enjoyed by plaintiffs. While plaintiff lawyers work on a contingency fee basis rather than on an hourly fee like defense lawyers, the time they spend on the case must ultimately be figured into their percentage of the award, if any. Because the litigation costs are so high, many plaintiff lawyers who specialize in malpractice indicated that they will seldom consider taking a case unless the expected damage award exceeds $100,000.

Professor Frank McClellan, in his book on medical malpractice, makes the following statement:

> The cost of evaluating and litigating medical malpractice cases compels plaintiffs' attorneys to reject some meritorious cases because the money that could be recovered does not justify the cost of the suit or the risk of losing. Assessing the merits of any case usually costs at least $2000 (as of 1991), and most cases will require an expenditure of $5000 to $10,000 before counsel can be sure that the case is meritorious. If the case goes to trial, costs may exceed $50,000, and expenditures of $75,000 or more are not extraordinary.[5]

McClellan probably had in mind cases with very large damage claims. In cases with smaller claims plaintiff lawyers will retain fewer experts and cut costs in other ways. Nevertheless, the figures provide some rough indication of plaintiff costs. However, although plaintiffs are technically responsible for these costs, most do not have the resources to finance them. Instead, the costs are born by the law firm and later deducted from the settlement or jury award—if the plaintiff is successful.

Another aspect of medical negligence cases involves malpractice insurance. When a lawsuit is filed against a physician, the physician's liability insurer is required to set aside a reserve against its assets in the event that the physician is found liable. The amount of the reserve is based on the insurer's estimated damage award or settlement and the expected litigation costs. The reserve will remain on the insurer's books until the case is closed. As will be seen in the case studies that follow, insurers frequently change these amounts in response to information uncovered during discovery.

Four Case Studies

Having presented this overview, I can now turn to studies of cases that failed to settle and went to trial. Keep in mind that these case synopses are from the defense perspective and are derived from notations in the insurance company files. Nevertheless, I believe they help demonstrate some major themes in the life history of malpractice cases.

Case 1: Cosmetic Surgery

In February 1982, the 62-year-old female plaintiff underwent elective cosmetic surgery, and a spinal accessory nerve was severed during the operation.

February 1985: A claim is filed against the physician alleging that the nerve was negligently cut and that the patient was not informed of the risks of the operation.

March 1985: Investigation by defense attorneys concluded that defendant is "secure" regarding the "failure to inform" claim.

May 1985: Plaintiff has not yet found an expert willing to testify on her behalf.

September 1985: Defense attorney's report on depositions of various witnesses states that the plaintiff is "nervous and neurotic" with a "poor recollection of treatment." However, the report also observed that the main defense expert did not perform well during his deposition.

October 1985: Defense team is still having problems proving that the doctor followed the proper procedures. The notation indicates that the defense lawyer believes that there is a serious need to find better defense experts.

March 1986: Plaintiff identifies an expert, and the deposition of the expert causes defense counsel to conclude that he is a good witness for plaintiff.

September 1986: Defense attorney reports that he is having trouble finding witnesses to support the defendant. Defense confidence in the case declines, and a settlement is considered.

March 1987: Plaintiff attorney offers to settle for $50,000. However, in the meantime, medical records adverse to the plaintiff's case have been uncovered: she complained about her symptoms *prior* to the alleged negligent operation. Defense counsel now estimates that the chance of a defense victory is 75 percent, with a verdict in the range of $25,000 to $75,000 if the plaintiff wins. Defense counsel recommends refusing settlement.

April 1987: After a three-day trial, the verdict is for the defendant.

Case 2: Baby Dies

In March 1985, a woman, 26 weeks into pregnancy, had vaginal leakage and her physician sent her home to bed. The physician advised her to check herself into the hospital when labor began, and if labor did not begin in two weeks to call him again. Ten days later the woman was admitted to the hospital, and a cesarean delivery was performed. The mother had herpes and other infections that would have jeopardized the health of the child if vaginal delivery had been allowed. The baby died four days later.

May 1985: Plaintiff's attorney requests hospital and physician files for review of medical error, and these are given. The physician's liability insurer begins its own investigation of the physician's performance.

August 1985: The preliminary investigation concludes that due to the mother's health problems the baby may have died in any event. A decision is made to deny the plaintiff's claim.

September 1985: Defense attorney report: the problems on liability are that physician did not do a speculum exam; he instructed the patient to make hospital arrangements instead of doing them himself; and he should have monitored the patient more closely given the mother's known health problems. On damages, the evidence tends to show that in any event the baby would likely have died of infections transmitted from the mother.

December 1985: The plaintiff files a lawsuit against the physician.

April 1986: Further evaluation causes the defense attorney to conclude that the defendant's liability is questionable; the insurer's reserve in the case is consequently reduced from $150,000 to $50,000.

July 1986: Upon the results of further discovery suggesting a stronger probability of defendant liability, the insurer's reserve is returned to $150,000.

January 1987: Plaintiff demands $150,000 for settlement. Defense attorney tells the insurer that a local family physician "despises" the defendant physician.

February 1987: Further discovery leads to an assessment that a jury "will not like" the defendant. A decision is made to offer $75,000 to the plaintiff for settlement, but the actual offer made by defense counsel is $50,000.

The insurer obliquely inquires of plaintiff counsel whether the plaintiff will accept a $100,000 settlement.

April 1987: The plaintiff attorney says the plaintiff will accept no settlement for less than $150,000. Defense counsel and insurer reject the offer and prepare for trial.

May 1987: At trial the jury returns a verdict for the plaintiff and awards $100,000.

Case 3: Breast Implant

In August 1981, a 37-year-old female had a breast implantation. Complications resulted, and she was treated by the surgeon through June 1983.

November 1983: Plaintiff's attorney contacts the surgeon and informs him of potential lawsuit because of his failure to recognize and treat the complications, which caused further damage to the breast and resulted in substantial pain and suffering.

January 1984: The insurer's investigation of the case concludes that it is likely that there is defendant liability because of the defendant's failure to treat the problem in a timely fashion. The insurer's reserve is set at $20,000.

May 1984: At a private meeting the plaintiff's attorney outlines the case to the defense attorney and asks for a $300,000 settlement. The plaintiff attorney notes that the statute of limitations is running out and that he will have to file a suit soon or forfeit the claim.

June 1984: The defense attorney informs the insurer that a finding of liability is likely, and he estimates that the claim is worth $50,000 to $75,000. He is "optimistic" that the case can be settled without filing a suit.

August 1984: The defense attorney offers a $40,000 settlement. (He has authority to settle for $50,000.) The plaintiff counters with a demand of $150,000 and negotiations fail.

Plaintiff files suit.

August 1984: The defense counsel is concerned about liability, and the insurer sets a reserve at $85,000. The plaintiff files a damage demand of $450,000 with the court.

October 1984: Defense counsel concludes that it is probable that a jury will find the defendant liable and that it would be best to settle the case for as much as $50,000. However, he informs the insurer that settlement is unlikely.

March 1986: Discovery that continued through 1985 revealed that the plaintiff may have suffered injury to her breast that was unrelated to the surgery.

June 1986: Defense counsel has found experts willing to testify on the defendant's behalf and also notes that the plaintiff was recently involved in a barroom scuffle and may be charged with assault. Defense counsel wants to try the case.

February 1987: Defense counsel still believes liability is possible but recommends that unless the plaintiff moderates her demand on the amount for settlement the case should go to trial.

The trial begins. During the trial the judge relays a revised offer of settlement from the plaintiff to the defendant, but the lowest offer was $110,000. Since the trial was going well—the plaintiff appeared "untruthful" and the expert witnesses for the plaintiff were "damaged" by defense experts—the defense declines to settle. Verdict is for the defendant.

Case 4: Phlebitis

In September 1981 a 43-year-old registered nurse underwent a hysterectomy and had problems after surgery, including a swollen leg.

October 1984: A suit is filed against eight doctors (some associated with an OB-GYN clinic and others with a urology clinic) alleging failure to diagnose and aggressively treat the thrombophlebitis, a painful and potentially dangerous swelling of the leg. The plaintiff claims that it resulted in pain and suffering, lost wages, and increased medical expenses.

December 1985: The plaintiff seeks monetary relief of $500,000.

April 1987: A revised complaint seeks $750,000 and punitive damages against one physician.

November 1987: Although two reviews by medical experts have been conducted for the gynecologist defendants, a new review by a vascular surgeon hired by the defendants says the defendants could have been "more aggressive" with the diagnosis of phlebitis; that is, they could have diagnosed and treated it more quickly.

January 1988: The defense receives the plaintiff expert's report concluding that the defendants were negligent in diagnosis and treatment.

April 1988: Plaintiff's current settlement demand is $525,000. Three new experts for defendants now say there was no breach in the standard of medical care.

June 1988: A defense counsel report indicates that there may be a conflict of interest between the gynecologist and urologist because the urologist made a correct diagnosis initially but the gynecologist did not take cognizance of it.

August 1988: A medical examination of the plaintiff conducted by a physician hired by the defendants reveals that the plaintiff has a permanent disability, but the extent of the disability is difficult to estimate. Another expert hired by the defendants concludes that there was no negligence; rather, the disability was caused by a complication resulting from the plaintiff's obesity.

January 1989: The plaintiff maintains her demand of $525,000 to settle.

April 1989: Two defendants receive a demand of $35,000 each from the plaintiff and decide to settle for that amount.

August 1989: Defense counsel for one defendant concludes that the

case is defensible but "foggy" and advises the insurer that a settlement of $50,000 or less would be "a good idea."

September 1989: The liability insurer concludes that the liability of the
urologist is doubtful, but that there is "questionable" liability
against the gynecologists because of their delay in diagnosis. The
insurer concludes that a settlement in the range of $50,000 to
$75,000 would be advisable, but the plaintiff maintains her de-
mand for a $500,000 settlement.

September 1989: The plaintiff demands $175,000 to settle, but the
insurer rejects any settlement over $100,000.

Another defendant settles for under $15,000.

The plaintiff makes an offer of settlement of "$125,000 to
$175,000 plus costs of $17,000" just prior to trial. The remaining
defendant rejects the offer.

September–October 1989: A two-week trial results in a verdict in favor
of the remaining defendant.

Lessons from the Cases

The four case studies help to illustrate that the litigation process often
involves substantial complexity and investment of time and resources. Most importantly, they show that there is often a great deal
of uncertainty in the process for both plaintiff and defendant. A
"strong" case for one side may suddenly evaporate when new facts
are uncovered or when the reports of medical experts are taken into
consideration. The studies also show that the estimates of case
strength may reverse again at any time as still more information is
uncovered. Settlements by some of the defendants may further affect
how the case progresses.

It should be remembered that these cases are illustrative of the
roughly 7 to 10 percent of cases that go to trial. The remaining cases
are resolved when the evidence produced during discovery indicates
that the plaintiff's case is weak (or at least the legal obstacles are
formidable) and dropped or, alternatively, the developing evidence
shows that the plaintiff has a case, prompting the defendant and the
liability insurer to seek a settlement. These four studies, however,
also show that the plaintiff and defendant may be quite far apart in
their estimates of liability or the amount of damages.

7

The Litigation Process: Putting the Case Studies into Context

The four cases reported in chapter 6 portray only a portion of the events in the life of those cases, but they help to illustrate a number of points, the most general of which is that the process from which trials emerge is lengthy, full of uncertainty, and often in flux. This chapter identifies a number of important elements in the litigation process and their role in causing cases to be tried before a jury rather than settled. The analysis that follows depends heavily on further analysis of insurance files, interviews with plaintiff and defense attorneys, and interviews with representatives of liability insurers. It is a sketch. More extensive treatment of the litigation process is contained in lawyer and professor Frank McClellan's book, MEDICAL MALPRACTICE: LAW, TACTICS, AND EVIDENCE.[1]

The Genesis

As I reported in chapter 6, the average time from filing a suit to trial in North Carolina was approximately 26 months, but in a few cases this time ranged up to about 60 months.[2] However, as the baby death and breast implant cases show, the functional life of the case predates the filing of the formal lawsuit. A medical incident occurs. Sometimes the health care provider recognizes that a lawsuit could result and notifies the insurer immediately. Other times the provider may not be aware of the lawsuit until a plaintiff attorney requests copies of the medical records. Sometimes the defendant learns about a suit only after receiving a subpoena. On other occasions the doctor may immediately inform his or her insurer that an injury has occurred during treatment, and the insurer may engage a defense attorney to undertake preliminary research even before it is known whether the plaintiff will eventually file a claim. Alternatively, the insurer may just sit back and await a response from the plaintiff. In a few instances, where the liability is obvious and a suit is likely, the insurer may even contact the patient immediately and attempt to arrange a settlement, perhaps before the injured patient has even considered consulting an attorney.

We do not know a great deal about the genesis of a lawsuit from the patient's perspective. We do know that only a small percentage of claims arise from the number of negligent medical injuries that occur. The best estimate is that between one in ten and one in six persons who are negligently injured seek compensation. Professor Paul Weiler and his colleagues involved in Harvard University's landmark study of medical malpractice in the state of New York concluded that for every seven to eight patients who suffered an injury caused by medical negligence only one filed a claim.[3] Professors Marlynn May and Daniel Stengel studied a sample of 175 patients who were dissatisfied with their medical care but did not file a lawsuit and 65 patients who did file a malpractice lawsuit.[4] Persons who sued were likely to talk about their injury and seek advice from friends and relatives, including friends or acquaintances who were doctors; they were also more likely to have previous litigation experience.

Although their study was limited to malpractice cases involving birth injuries and emergency room injuries and did not consider a sample of injured persons who did not file lawsuits, Professor Sloan and his colleagues uncovered a number of interesting findings about patients who sued their medical providers.[5] There was no indication that patients were less likely to sue a doctor with whom they had a long-term as opposed to a one-time relationship. While seeking monetary compensation was a significant motive for filing a malpractice suit, the researchers also uncovered the fact that noneconomic motives were important. Sometimes the patient felt that the doctor had not communicated adequately with them, some sought revenge, and others sought more information about the type of care they and other patients received. Sloan et al. also uncovered the fact that some patients' first awareness that they had been injured through negligence occurred when medical personnel other than their own doctors, for example, another doctor or a nurse, made an offhand comment that they had received substandard treatment.

For some eventual plaintiffs, the decision to consult a lawyer may occur shortly after the medical incident; but for others the process of developing the perceptions needed to form a grievance and to decide to seek legal counsel may occur months or even years afterward. The potential plaintiff may then consult an attorney, perhaps one who has performed other services for them. In a few instances this attorney may handle the case, but often he or she refers the patient to someone who specializes in personal injury litigation. The latter attorney may decide to handle the case but frequently makes a referral to an attorney who specializes in medical malpractice.[6]

In any event, once the patient consults a lawyer a process of evaluation, selection, and patient education begins. The lawyer may decide almost immediately that physician liability is unlikely or that the potential value of the case will not warrant the expenses incurred and decline to take the case. While most malpractice attorneys informed me that their general rule is to not take cases with a potential value of under $100,000 because the costs of litigation make such cases financially unviable, these lawyers acknowledged that they frequently broke the rule when liability was so clear that they believed they could obtain an early settlement without undue litigation costs and with relatively small investments of their own time and effort.

If the lawyer decides that the case may have merit and is worthy of further inquiry the process of plaintiff education begins. The patient learns about the contingency fee structure, which is often graduated depending on whether the case is settled early, settled later, or proceeds to trial. One lawyer, for example, charged 25 percent if the case could be settled without actually filing a lawsuit, 33 percent for a lawsuit, and 40 percent if the case went to trial. Plaintiffs also learn about litigation costs, including the costs of experts. These litigation costs are technically the responsibility of the plaintiff, and in some cases the lawyer may insist upon some "up-front" money to cover them. In most instances, however, the lawyer agrees to cover the expenses and deduct them from the final settlement or award. If the case results in no settlement or award, the lawyer will lose his or her investment. At this point, the lawyer also begins the education of the potential plaintiff about the psychological costs of the litigation process. He or she is told that the process may be drawn out over months or years and that there is no certainty of success. The lawyer also advises the plaintiff about the discovery and trial process, including the fact that the defendant has the right to examine the plaintiff's prior medical records or psychiatric history, including details as intimate as sexual behavior and that the suit may even expose the plaintiff's spouse to the discovery process. The prospect of trial and cross-examination is also discussed.

This education process not only begins to inform the plaintiff about what lies ahead but also helps the lawyer to evaluate what kind of witness the plaintiff, and often the spouse, will be. Plaintiff lawyers frankly told us that this is an important consideration in their decision to take cases. Of course, the education and evaluation processes only begin in the initial meetings; they continue throughout discovery and may affect decisions to settle or go to trial. The case studies presented in chapter 6 show that defense lawyers are also highly sensitive to the performance of their own witnesses and those of the other side.

The Records and the Experts

If the plaintiff's lawyer decides that the case appears to have merit, the next step is to seek a review of the medical records. Unless faced with a statute of limitations deadline, the lawyer frequently makes this request without filing a lawsuit. Some physicians will resist providing the records. In recent years, however, insurers and defense attorneys have tended to advise the doctor to cooperate on the grounds that further investigation may convince the plaintiff that there is no medical negligence, thus avoiding a lawsuit. In any event, the plaintiff can obtain the records by filing a suit.

Once the records are obtained, the next step is review by medical experts to determine if "standards of care" were breached. Plaintiff lawyers who specialize in medical malpractice often have a list of physicians who are willing to review cases for a fee on the condition that they remain anonymous and not be called as experts for trial. If the reviewing expert indicates negligence was involved, a search begins for experts willing to testify for the plaintiff. Sometimes such an expert is located before the suit is actually filed and sometimes the search begins afterward.[7]

Three basic types of expert testimony are used in medical negligence cases: testimony on causation and the "standard of care"; testimony on the extent of the plaintiff's injuries; and testimony about the economic, psychological, and social consequences of the injury.[8] Evidence on the standard of care is essential in almost every case because the plaintiff must prove that the standard was breached before the health care provider can be found liable.[9] The standard of care is defined as the standard of practice in treating a patient that is established by the medical profession. Technically, the standard requires that "the physician have knowledge of and perform with a degree of skill and care, accepting modern developments, that an average member of the profession would offer his patients."[10] These standards may vary as a function of the type of practice in which the doctor specializes and the practices of doctors in the local community.[11]

Evidence on the extent of the plaintiff's injuries may overlap extensively with the causation and standard of care evidence and be tendered by the same experts. This evidence may be relevant to questions concerning how much of the patient's condition after the injury was due to a prior medical problem and, if negligence is found, how much of the economic loss and pain and suffering should be ascribed to the prior condition and how much to the negligent injury. The third type of evidence involving economic damages sometimes requires the testimony of an economist skilled in estimating past and future economic damages or that of a rehabilitative or palliative care specialist who can indicate what medical needs the plaintiff will have in the future. The latter two types of evidence may not be essential for the case and, particularly in cases with less severe injuries, the plaintiff may simply rely on the jury's commonsense judgment rather than pay for these additional experts.[12] However, testimony that the defendant violated the "standard of care" is required if the plaintiff is to prove defendant liability.

Therein lies the frequent problem for plaintiff lawyers, namely, finding medical experts willing to testify in open court against fellow physicians. It is particularly rare to obtain a plaintiff expert in the same community as the defendant physician because of close professional, social, and economic ties in the physician community.[13] A doctor who testified against a colleague might find him- or herself socially ostracized and suffer economically as well because other physicians would not make referrals. In several of the closed claim files that we examined, there were notations that other physicians "despised" a doctor charged with malpractice; and in one instance there was a notation that most believed he "was probably guilty." However, the plaintiff attorneys in these cases never found local physicians who were willing to testify. These pressures extend outside the local community, though perhaps to a lesser degree; and physicians and other groups appear quick to label plaintiff experts as "hired guns."[14] Aside from the direct social and economic pressures, a further problem is the tendency of many physicians to deny the concept of negligence in medical error. As part of the New York Medical Malpractice Project, a sample of 47 physicians was surveyed about their attitudes toward medical errors. Almost all conceded that "doctors make mistakes," but most were unwilling to label such mistakes as negligence.[15] These attitudes predispose potential plaintiff experts to be unwilling to testify.

Despite these difficulties plaintiff attorneys usually do find credible, reputable experts. After all, the 50 percent or more of cases that result in settlements with plaintiffs are based on an insurer assessment that the case against the defendant can probably be proven in court. However, it is also clear that the plaintiff runs risks in finding experts and assessing them. Sometimes the credibility of a seemingly good expert is called into question only late in the litigation process. For example, in one insurance file, the notations indicate that just one week before trial the defense counsel uncovered the fact that the primary plaintiff expert had been dismissed from a university research position for falsifying data. In a trial before a judge that I observed in its entirety, a similar unraveling of the credibility of a plaintiff expert occurred on the witness stand—much to the surprise and dismay of an experienced plaintiff's attorney.

On the whole, however, experienced plaintiff malpractice attorneys do manage to find reputable experts. One of the state of North Carolina's most successful malpractice lawyers has three nurses on his staff who help him screen and develop cases. He also has developed consulting relations with doctors who provide assessments and advice for his cases.[16] Another lawyer informed me that one approach is to read the published articles of doctors that contradict the claims of defendants and then appeal to them on grounds of substance and principle. However, it must be said that these experts are also induced by fees of up to $300 per hour or more. Not infrequently in many malpractice cases this places a financial constraint on the number and types of witnesses that can be called. In some major trials, the plaintiff may call only one live witness and present others only through videotaped depositions. Videotapes reduce costs considerably because there is only the deposition appearance and no trial appearance or additional travel costs. However, one impression from juror interviews that I conducted is that this type of testimony was often less persuasive than live witnesses. In one trial, to reduce costs the plaintiff called one expert and then argued the remainder of the case by confronting the defendants and defense experts during cross-examination with writings in leading medical texts that contradicted their assertions.

In contrast to plaintiffs, defense attorneys typically have substantially less difficulty in finding either reviewing experts or experts for trial. Because of a sense of besiegement and a closing of ranks due to the belief that doctors should not be held legally responsible for honest mistakes, many colleagues are often willing to assist defendant doctors. The closed claim files indicate that as many as three or four reviews of records may be obtained in some cases. Reviewers were typically paid about $300 for the review rather than $300 per hour, and many of them refused the check from the liability insurer with a statement such as "glad to help out." Similarly, at trial, defendants typically call more experts. In fact, both the court records and the closed claim files indicate that a problem for plaintiff attorneys prior to trial is the number of expert witnesses. Sometimes the defendant(s) list(s) as many as ten or more experts. Deposing the other side's experts is crucial to knowing what will be said at trial and how to counter it, but doing so requires much time and often considerable travel expense as the plaintiff attorney may have to travel to distant locations to depose those experts. Often plaintiff attorneys have to make strategic decisions about which defense experts are the most important and limit depositions only to those experts; the remaining experts are either asked to respond to written interrogatories or are ignored until they take the witness stand at trial.

Because of the abundance of local experts to review the case and testify, a danger for the defense is that their experts may provide an unrealistic view of the merits of the case. In one closed claim file, for example, the defense attorney had obtained three reviews from in-state experts that strongly supported the defense. The claims adjuster was suspicious of the opinions of "the same good old boy network" and insisted upon an assessment from a more objective expert outside the state. That expert concluded that there was clear negligence and so a fifth reviewer was obtained who also concluded negligence. Without this skepticism, the defense might have taken a case to trial with a sense of confidence that was not justified by the facts.

The data from court records reflect this imbalance in availability of experts. When defense attorneys made motions for dismissal of the case or requested sanctions against a plaintiff attorney, the arguments frequently revolved around either the failure of the plaintiff to name an expert witness or an inadequacy in the type of expert witness that was named. When plaintiff attorneys sought court intervention, it was often on the grounds that the defense had named a lengthy list of experts to be called at trial simply to burden the plaintiff with the costs of deposing those experts.

There were some exceptions to defendants' ability to obtain experts. In several of the North Carolina insurers' files that I examined, it appears that defendant physicians had such a bad reputation in the medical community that none of their colleagues would even undertake to review files or otherwise assist the defense (but presumably would not have been willing to testify for the plaintiff).

On balance, however, defendants in medical negligence cases appear to have a considerable edge in assessing the merits of their cases and getting experts to testify at trial. Experts are more willing to assist the defense. They charge less than plaintiff experts. When there are multiple defendants and multiple liability insurers some of these costs may be spread among the defendants. We did not obtain a great deal of data on the number of experts called by plaintiffs and defendants at trial; but from trials that were observed the number of defense experts who testified on the issue of negligence exceeded the number of plaintiff experts by approximately four to one. It must also be remembered that the defendants themselves are also technically experts who testify about the propriety of health care procedures even if they are not considered experts for purposes of the trial and are clearly "interested parties."

The Plaintiff's Role

In theory, the plaintiff is in charge of the case, and the attorney follows his or her commands. However, studies in other personal injury contexts have shown that the lawyer presents the options from which the client makes decisions and, in effect, controls decision making.[17] This appeared to be true of North Carolina malpractice plaintiffs. Sloan et al. drew a similar conclusion from their interviews with Florida malpractice claimants.[18] There are individual cases where medical malpractice plaintiffs take an active role in their cases, but these tend

to be exceptions. Plaintiffs are one-time players in the arcane processes of malpractice litigation.[19] Many, probably the vast majority,
have had no prior litigation experience, and they do not know what to
expect. Moreover, they are often sick or injured, angry at the doctor,
or desperately in need of money. These factors may create problems
for their lawyer because the lawyer must explain to the plaintiff why
he or she must undergo a physical exam from still another doctor,
why past psychiatric or sexual history is relevant and why the other
side has a right to discover it, why this information may be disclosed
in open court, why it is taking so long to get the case resolved, and
why an offer of settlement should be refused. It is the plaintiff's
attorney who talks to the plaintiff's medical experts about matters of
causation and proof, who deposes the opposing experts, and who
negotiates with the attorneys for the defendants. In consequence, it is
the plaintiff's attorney who creates the "reality" of the case and its
prospects and recommends decisions about dropping the suit, settlement, or going to trial.

In two different trials that I observed the defendants made modest offers of settlement in the middle of the trial. In each, I overheard
the plaintiff attorney discussing the offer with his client, or rather
conveying it to the client. The attorney essentially said, "they've
made an offer of X dollars but I don't think we should take it because
we are doing well." In both cases, the communication was very brief,
and in both cases the plaintiff immediately deferred to the attorney's
judgment.[20]

Throughout the litigation process, plaintiff morale is a crucial
factor. The plaintiff's lawyer, in most cases, has the job of keeping
morale from flagging and preparing the client for the rigors of trial.
The insurance files reveal plaintiffs who insisted on either abandoning trial or on making further settlement attempts even when the
defendants were in a difficult position. In one extreme instance, the
insurers were prepared to make a settlement exceeding $100,000
when the plaintiff insisted, against her attorney's advice, that he settle the case for $15,000 because she "needed the money." There are, of
course, cases in which plaintiffs insist on trial against the advice of
their lawyer; but it is my hypothesis, based on interviews with plaintiff attorneys, that in far more instances the plaintiff, due to risk
aversion, pressures the attorney to settle at a discounted rate.[21]

The Defendant's Role

Some writers speculate that physician defendants play an active role in medical negligence cases but offer two conflicting theories about the direction of influence. The first is that doctors seek trials and reject settlement in an attempt to get formal vindication of their medical competence. The second is that they insist on settlement as quickly and quietly as possible to preserve their public reputation and to put the matter behind them.[22] In fact, each theory is probably correct for subsets of cases. Each theory is too simplistic when viewed with respect to the actual realities of the litigation process.

Physicians belong to a powerful profession and are used to having control over their own lives and those of their patients. At the same time, a siege mentality surrounds medical malpractice suits and is nourished by physicians and their professional societies.[23] When a lawsuit is filed, the physician's reputation may be jeopardized, not only in the community from which the physician draws his or her patients and income, but also among his or her colleagues. There is little question that in most instances physicians feel both threatened and outraged by a malpractice lawsuit, and their initial reaction may be to seek vindication.[24]

Gross and Syverud have argued that the desire of doctors to protect their reputations is a primary cause of trial cases.[25] In the sample of California cases that they studied most malpractice liability insurance contracts contained a "consent to settle" clause that gave the doctor the right to veto any settlement and provided that the insurer remain responsible for any legal defense costs and any judgment that is within the limits of the policy. Gross and Syverud documented the fact that doctors did veto settlements in over 17 percent of cases that eventually went to trial. They concluded that doctors may insist upon trial to vindicate their reputation even when the insurer would be willing to settle for a sum that in many instances would be less than trial costs.

In some cases, doctors may indeed push for trial, but Gross and Syverud's thesis is not satisfactory for a number of reasons. The vindication motive can only account for a small proportion of trials. First, if doctors consistently argued for trial on the assumption that they would win, despite evidence of liability, then a larger percentage of cases that go to trial should result in plaintiff wins because the cases would be proceeding with merits in the plaintiff's favor. In Gross and Syverud's cases, however, plaintiffs won only one case in four. Second, if the potential plaintiff award exceeds the liability policy's limits, the doctor could end up incurring substantial financial costs. Third, unlike California, in most of the North Carolina liability policies there is no consent to settle clause. The insurer has the contractual right to settle the dispute despite the doctor's wishes. Fourth, whatever the doctor's desire for vindication, the process of discovery usually injects a dose of hard reality if negligence has occurred. If the insurer obtains several reviews by physician peers that there is a high likelihood of a jury concluding negligence, the doctor faces a serious risk that he or she will lose at trial. This will have the opposite result from what the doctor desired; rather than vindication, he or she will face newspaper headlines that proclaim his or her negligence. Depositions, with cross-examination by the opposing attorney, may also cool ardor for a public trial. Additionally, the prospect of substantial time away from the doctor's medical practice to prepare for and engage in trial reveals to the physician the fact that vindication has substantial psychological and financial costs.[26] Finally, as I showed in chapter 4, a lot of settlements occur, even in California; this suggests that doctors do not routinely seek trial.

In brief, some physicians may want to settle and avoid more publicity. Others may seek a trial for vindication. The response of the physician may depend on individual personality, the degree of ambiguity about liability, and the reality checks provided by his or her defense lawyer and liability insurer. In considering the vindication motive, it is also useful to think about whether the concern for reputation involves medical peer perceptions or patient perceptions because each has very different consequences. My own observation is that doctors in research hospitals, who are involved in secondary and tertiary medical care, are primarily concerned about their reputation among their peers. They want vindication, and a trial is seen as a mechanism for getting it. In contrast, sole practitioners and doctors otherwise engaged in primary care, while they are concerned about peers, are even more concerned about community knowledge of the case since it has potential adverse consequences for their practice. They may be more prone, in the end, to want to settle the matter quietly. This is only a hypothesis; I have no systematic data to substantiate it.

The bottom line is that there is no single type of physician response to a malpractice suit; and the responses may change over the
course of the life of the lawsuit. In any event, doctors' responses are
heavily shaped by the attorneys, those hired by the insurer or their
own personal attorneys, who convey to them the reality of the law
and the evidence as it develops in the litigation process.

The Liability Insurer

Liability insurers are the hidden defendants in most malpractice
cases, yet their role is central to the litigation process. Regardless of
whether they are investor-owned companies, physician-owned companies, or self-insured hospitals or clinics, insurers have common
characteristics in that they are "repeat players" and are concerned
with balance sheets at the end of the fiscal year.[27] The insurer decides
which defense attorneys are hired and helps determine which and
how many reviewing experts to use. Insurers also influence the
amount of time the defense attorney spends on the case. In short,
insurers keep close tabs on the progress of the litigation. One major
North Carolina liability insurer on occasion actually bypasses defense
attorneys during the settlement process and directly engages in negotiations with the plaintiff's attorney. The defense attorney's role on
such occasions is restricted to conducting discovery, keeping the insurer informed on the legal merits and procedural status of the case,
and preparing for trial in the event that settlement talks fail. Defense
attorneys are not comfortable or happy with this practice since it
removes their personal control of the case and may compromise their
professional obligations to the doctor defendant. However, since the
insurer is the hiring agent and is paying the bills they accede to the
insurer's demands. Recall also the fact, described earlier, that some
liability insurer contracts have provisions that give the insurer rather
than the physician defendants the power to decide how and when
cases are terminated.

My discussions with head claims adjusters for liability insurers
and my examination of adjusters' notes in the closed claim files lead to
the following conclusion: if insurers decide that the defendant is liable, they will attempt to settle the case for as little as possible and as
quickly as they can. However, if they make an assessment that there

is no defendant liability or that plaintiff demands about the settlement amount are unreasonable, they will move for trial as quickly as they can. There are exceptions to this general rule, but it describes the predominating dynamic in defense strategy.

As repeat players, liability insurers know that they will incur a substantial number of cases in which they will have to pay indemnity. They are also highly sensitive to transaction costs, that is, the expense involved in defending lawsuits. It does not make economic sense to spend money defending a case that will be lost at trial, particularly if the reviewing experts indicate liability. Going to trial runs the risk of a larger award than is warranted plus additional litigation costs. Data from a number of studies indicate that settlements, especially early settlements, are financially more advantageous to insurers than trial.[28]

It is sometimes claimed that insurers settle nonmeritorious suits for smaller amounts rather than incur the expense of continuing to defend the litigation.[29] This assertion naively ignores the fact that, as repeat players, insurers must uphold a reputation of toughness and principle. Otherwise, they believe they will be "blackmailed" in increasing numbers of cases by unscrupulous plaintiffs (and their lawyers) with questionable negligence claims. As a consequence, they believe, they will end up with increasing economic losses. Although this is a guiding principle of liability insurers, several claims managers pointed out examples where exceptions might be made. Assume that the insurer estimates only a 20 percent chance that the defendant would be held liable at trial but that this estimate is shaky and the potential exposure is very large if the trial is lost. In this case, the insurer might rationalize making a modest settlement. Nevertheless, the claims managers insisted that such examples are relatively rare.

Another claim made by some plaintiff attorneys who I interviewed is that insurers drag their heels and delay settlement as long as possible as part of a strategy to make the litigation process so economically and psychologically oppressive that the plaintiff will press to settle for less than the case is actually worth.[30] Perhaps this occurs in some cases, but it must be recognized that such a strategy is not cost-free to the insurer. Insurers must set aside an estimate of reserves to cover each claim, and there is a substantial bureaucratic and fiscal need to clear the reserves. Second, dragging out the case also increases transaction costs for the insurer. Here too, money is not unlimited. The claims files contain many notes exchanged between adjusters and head claims managers and between adjusters and defense attorneys that express concerns about escalating litigation costs.

Defense Attorneys and Conflicting Defendant Interests

My earlier discussion of plaintiffs described the plaintiff attorneys as the key player in moving the case forward. The fact that the liability insurer ultimately calls the shots on litigation strategy in many cases does not mean defense attorneys are unimportant in the litigation process. They provide the legal information, depose witnesses, file motions, and counter tactics of the plaintiff attorney. Since negotiations are carried out in the "shadow of trial" defense attorneys provide the information on which decisions on settlement or trial ultimately depend. They also conduct the majority of settlement negotiations with the plaintiff attorney. The closed claim files contain notes bearing on the defense attorney's reports on the progress of the case and estimates of success at trial; for example, "We have an excellent case. [The plaintiff attorney] is a nice guy but has a reputation of not preparing, and juries in this county are usually pretty conservative."

Defense attorneys are also in crucial positions when the interests of their client conflict with the position of the insurer or with other defendants. The latter was exemplified in the phlebitis case, described in chapter 6, in which some defendants settled leaving others to fight alone. In multiple defendant trials defense attorneys coordinate their cases to the maximum extent possible, but decisions on overall strategy cause conflict among them. Conflicting defendant interests, such as a decision to settle, may put defense lawyers at odds with one another.

Conclusions

Trial cases are the residue of a complicated winnowing process involving the interrelated decisions of many actors involved in the lawsuit. They are the result of negotiation and settlement attempts that have failed. The issues discussed in this chapter provide background for the next chapter, in which I develop hypotheses about the selection process.

8

Hypotheses on Case Selection and Their Meaning in Understanding Jury Verdicts

Based on the materials discussed in the preceding chapters, I am led to conclude that cases that proceed to trial *tend* to be cases in which the evidence of defendant liability is weak. Although the North Carolina data supporting my conclusion are indirect this tendency is nevertheless reflected in several ways and corroborated by other research findings. The most important fact is that defendants won four out of five cases that went to trial. Another piece of evidence is that there were prior settlements from some defendants in a substantial percentage of cases that went to trial. Because the remaining defendants did not settle, this itself leads to an inference that the case against them was weak. Still another piece of evidence is the fact that liability insurers and defense attorneys informed me that generally they attempt to settle cases where liability is clear and to fight cases where it is not. The adjusters' notes and other information in the closed claim files appear to corroborate these statements. My conclusion is further supported by the conclusions of researchers, discussed in chapter 4, who have examined malpractice cases in other states and used different methodologies.[1]

A final piece of evidence derives from a survey of both plaintiff and defense attorneys in 25 of the trial cases in our 1987–89 data set. I asked the attorneys in these cases whether expert evidence on damages was introduced at trial and by whom. The survey revealed that in 16 cases, or 64 percent, the plaintiff called an expert on damages, but the defense did not counter with its own expert; in five of the remaining cases, or 20 percent, neither the plaintiff nor the defendant called a damages expert; and in only four, or 16 percent, both called experts. We know from the insurers' files that in many instances the insurers do obtain estimates of damages. Frequently, they do not call their own experts on damages for fear that the jurors will perceive them as admitting liability. However, taken in conjunction with the other evidence, the survey results suggest that the primary reason defendants did not call expert evidence on damages is because the case was fought on the grounds of liability.

Although plantiff's cases in North Carolina tend to be weak, I do not mean to imply that in every trial the plaintiff has a weak case. Plaintiffs do win cases. In some trials the issue may actually be amount of damages rather than liability, even if the defense case is fought on grounds of liability. Some of the cases reported in chapter 6 indicated that the defense team believed that there was a good chance that the defendant would be found liable but a substantial disagreement existed between plaintiff and defendant as to what the case was worth.

The conclusion that plaintiff cases tend to be weak still leaves unanswered the question of why plaintiff attorneys take these cases to trial rather than drop the suit. As I showed in chapter 3, they ultimately do just that in roughly 40 percent of North Carolina malpractice cases. Let us then consider a number of hypotheses that might explain the propensity of plaintiffs to proceed to trial against the odds.

Expected Value

Author Peter Huber, among others, has made the charge that plaintiff lawyers are willing to play the odds in order to get the "big win" that will compensate for a number of losing cases.[2] Stated simply, plaintiff lawyers can afford to lose four cases out of five because they more than recoup their losses in the fifth case. This theory, known by economists and social scientists as the "expected value" theory, is based on multiplying the total amount of damages awarded to plaintiffs at trial by the odds of winning (in North Carolina the odds are 20 percent).[3] As reported in chapter 3, the expected value of each trial case was about $70,849. Assuming that expert and other plaintiff litigation costs are as low as $15,000, a conservative figure, the net would be $51,000.[4] Assuming a contingency fee contract awarding the plaintiff attorney 40 percent of net recovery, the lawyer would earn $20,400. This is not a small sum, but if one considers not only the week or more of 12- to 14-hour days devoted to trial preparation and time in court, but also the many hours spent in screening cases, reviewing records, obtaining experts, deposing witnesses, researching law, and attempting to negotiate a settlement, the plaintiff attorney's hourly rate is not very attractive.[5]

In any event, I have my doubts that lawyers expressly calculate expected values. Lawyers tend to be very case-specific in their logic and reasoning about cases, and they do not tend to view cases in the aggregate as the expected value theory would suggest. The expected value theory may have some credibility only if we assume that many malpractice plaintiff attorneys are willing to work for modest wages.

In for a Pound, in for a Penny

My reversal of the old English adage to label this hypothesis is meant to characterize the fact that a very large portion of the plaintiff attorney's hours and efforts is expended in selecting and developing the case for trial. The case studies in chapter 6 showed that determinations of both liability and damages change throughout the litigation process for defendants, and this has to apply at least equally, if not more so, to plaintiffs. Sometimes plaintiff attorneys may realize late in the game that the case is weak, but so much time, money, and effort have already been expended that they decide to go to trial anyway. Several plaintiff attorneys that I interviewed justified their decision by saying that at this point they just decide to "roll the dice," that is, take the chance that the jury will see things their way.

Asymmetric Reliability in Estimates of Negligence

Cases may also proceed to trial because the information available to plaintiffs causes them to be overly optimistic about their chances of success. This asymmetric reliability hypothesis draws insights from the theory of Priest and Klein on the selection of cases for trial.[6] Their theory states that settlement discussions are based upon predictions, using the available evidence of what the likely outcome will be at trial. Priest and Klein predict that cases that go to trial will, on average, be cases where there is ambiguity about the evidence and likely outcome. On average, the theory suggests, plaintiff win rates should hover around 50 percent. The theory is predicated on several assumptions, namely, that (a) the evidence in most trial cases is close and the verdict could go either way, *(b)* the parties are equally good at predicting trial outcomes, and *(c)* the parties have equal stakes in the case. The Priest and Klein theory has not fared well in some recent empirical tests largely because of findings that plaintiff win rates in certain categories of cases are significantly skewed away from 50 percent.[7] Indeed, in an early article explaining the theory, Priest and Klein noted that in their own data medical malpractice cases tended to have low plaintiff win rates. However, their primary explanation of the discrepancy was based on an assumption that plaintiffs and defendants in medical malpractice cases have different stakes in the litigation process.[8] A far more plausible explanation, in my view, is the relative imbalance of information between plaintiff and defendant.

First, as has already been described in chapters 6 and 7, the evaluation of legal liability involves considerable ambiguity and uncertainty. Furthermore, as the discovery process progresses, the apparent advantage may shift to the defendant, then back to the plaintiff, and perhaps back again to the defendant—or vice versa. This was illustrated in the examples in chapter 6, and research by Farber and White further documents the problems in evaluation of the merits of the case.[9] Recall from chapter 4 that those authors studied 252 malpractice cases against a large self-insured hospital. The hospital asked its own experts to evaluate whether the standard of care was violated with respect to three criteria: whether correct treatment was provided; whether adequate care in administering treatment was not provided or was not provided quickly enough; and whether the harm suffered by the patient was causally related to the treatment. Even though these evaluations were made for internal reasons, in over 30 percent of the cases, the reviewers did not agree. Furthermore, the evaluations did not take into account information about the law, evidence that the plaintiff or plaintiff experts might give, or any number of other factors that might develop later in discovery. In many cases, these other pieces of information might increase the ambiguity severalfold. The inability of doctors to make reliable estimates of negligence in malpractice cases has been found in other studies as well.[10]

Second, from the discussion in chapter 7 it seems apparent that plaintiffs are usually disadvantaged in the information that they receive, at least relative to defendants.[11] Defendants have access to more reviewers and more experts. In cases with multiple defendants the opinions can be pooled.

Nonspecialist plaintiff attorneys would appear to be at a particular disadvantage, but even specialist attorneys face difficulties. Their reviewing expert may give an opinion that the standard of care was breached, but as the case studies in chapter 6 and the Farber and White study illustrate, experts may differ in a substantial number of cases. Due to financial constraints, including the comparatively greater cost to plaintiffs in hiring reviewers, it may not be feasible for plaintiffs to get a second or third opinion. Consequently, the plaintiff's lawyer proceeds to trial on the assumption that his or her expert's opinion is reliable when in fact it may not be. In contrast, the defendant lawyer has a more accurate estimate of negligence because he or she has pooled the opinions of multiple experts. The plaintiff's attorney will probably learn about these contrasting opinions when the defendant's experts are deposed during discovery. However, the opinions may be dismissed as biased because they are from the other side's experts and will not be perceived as being as good as the plaintiff lawyer's own handpicked expert. None of this is to say that the defendant's estimate is always correct, only that across many cases it is more likely to be correct than that of the plaintiff.

More systematic data bearing on the imbalance of information related to the asymmetric reliability hypothesis are required, but the possibility that plaintiff lawyers may labor under overly optimistic and unreliable information seems very plausible. Indeed, a recent theoretical article by Keith Hylton is built around this notion.[12]

Strategic Bargaining Errors

Samuel Gross and Kent Syverud, drawing on prior research, have recently argued that the information hypothesis proposed by Priest and Klein is too simplistic.[13] While predicted trial outcomes may determine an attorney's overall strategy, other dynamics of the settlement process also play a crucial role. These other factors include how much should be offered in the negotiation process, whether and how quickly an offer from the other side should be answered, when a party should make an outrageous demand, and how one should evaluate a threat to go to trial. Negotiation is a two-player (or more, since there are often multiple defendants) process, and failures to settle may result from miscalculations and misjudgments. However, even if we accept the basic logic of Gross and Syverud's alternative theorizing the problem arises of understanding how it explains the low plaintiff win rates.

The asymmetric reliability hypothesis just described argues that one-sided and unreliable information obtained by the plaintiff's attorney may cause him or her to make strategic bargaining errors. The North Carolina insurers' files indicate that in many instances both the insurer and the defense attorneys feel that plaintiff demands are not realistic. A substantial number of cases in the files indicate that the defense team made an initial assessment that liability was improbable. Thus, no offers of settlement were made. However, often the plaintiff persisted in lengthy discovery and proceeded to trial. In a number of other cases, the insurer's review indicated that liability was likely, but the plaintiff's demands were never in the range of settlement. For instance, in a case involving a negligent prostatectomy, the plaintiff's original demand was for over $5 million. However, the settlement discussions involved much lower figures, and the eventual lowest offer of settlement was $175,000. In contrast, the insurer set loss reserves at only $40,000, and at trial the jury returned a verdict of only $20,000.

Escalation of Commitment

There is a substantial body of psychological literature that examines how and why decision makers persist in their commitments to failing courses of action.[14] This phenomenon is labeled "psychological entrapment." In entrapment settings, the problem is not that an initial decision on a course of action was necessarily wrong or irrational. Rather, decision makers persist in throwing good coin after bad despite a changing situation or new information suggesting that the original decision was wrong. Although all of the psychological dynamics are not known, it appears that an initial decision to commit substantial resources to a course of action, along with successive decisions to commit more resources to turn things around, locks decision makers into a mind-set that keeps them from abandoning a lost cause.

Recently, researchers have attempted to apply insights from psychological entrapment research to the negotiation process, and two studies have examined how lawyers may become overconfident in judging the merits of their case.[15] There are some direct parallels to the psychological situation in which plaintiff attorneys operate in malpractice cases. First, consider some of the characteristics of psychological entrapment situations in which parties became committed to failing courses of action: (1) a large reward can only be obtained upon completion of the project, with no or few rewards before completion; (2) the actor is personally responsible for the expenditure of money and effort; (3) the initial investment is high and, relatively speaking, the costs of continuing are low; (4) the probability of obtaining the goal is uncertain, but there have been some signs of possible success; (5) the decision maker feels personally accountable for a negative outcome and therefore puts greater effort into turning things around; and (6) the actor becomes more committed as he or she approaches the goal.

Now consider what we know about malpractice litigation. Plaintiff attorneys carefully screen their cases and pride themselves on separating "good" cases from "bad." Once good cases are chosen, the attorney puts substantial professional effort and financial investment into the case. Uncertainty always exists; it may increase or decrease several times during the course of discovery. After many months of developing the case, the trial is in sight. Any negative information about the merits of the plaintiff's case can be undervalued or rationalized away. Additionally, the attorney may remember previous cases in which a losing cause was won. Any settlement with some of the defendants may increase optimism about prevailing over remaining defendants.

I have no systematic data bearing on the dynamics of psychological entrapment of plaintiff lawyers, but it seems to me that it is a plausible hypothesis and that it is consistent with the "roll-the-dice" comments made by plaintiff attorneys. It is also consistent with comments made by attorneys who stated that they were also occasionally motivated to take cases to trial to protect their reputations as tough bargainers, even though they knew the odds were against them. The escalation-of-commitment hypothesis thus should probably be viewed as supplementing the hypotheses concerning the asymmetric reliability of estimates and strategic bargaining.

Plaintiff Pressure and the Contingency Fee Arrangement Hypothesis

Professors Gross and Syverud have hypothesized that plaintiffs, and not their attorneys, may be responsible for weak cases proceeding to trial.[16] Their argument is that under contingency fee arrangements—and most malpractice cases proceed on this basis—the plaintiff incurs no financial costs if the case proceeds to trial since his or her lawyer is not paid on an hourly basis. While acknowledging that plaintiff attorneys screen cases before taking them, Gross and Syverud speculate that if subsequent research and discovery show the case to be a likely loser, the attorney is constrained from dropping the suit for a number of reasons. One obstacle is that if the plaintiff insists on going to trial, the lawyer may feel obligated to do so out of a sense of personal and professional responsibility. If the case is close to trial, the judge may not permit the attorney to withdraw. There is also a risk that the abandoned client will complain to the state bar or file a legal malpractice suit. A final obstacle, Gross and Syverud speculate, is that the lawyer may acquire a reputation as a "quitter," thereby jeopardizing his or her ability to attract future clients.

The hypothesis that the lawyer feels a sense of personal responsibility does have some ring of credibility. The lawyer is dealing with an injured person who has been nurtured throughout the months or years of discovery. Without question, a psychological bond frequently develops between client and attorney. In referring to the case lawyers will speak of "our case" or say "we believe." In some cases, the attorney may feel obligated to follow the case to a conclusion simply to provide a sense of finality and legitimacy. After losing a case one lawyer said, "The jury has spoken and they did not see the case our way."

On the other hand, there are serious problems with the Gross and Syverud hypothesis that personal and legal responsibility explains why weak cases go to trial. First, in most cases the attorney is in control. As described earlier, the plaintiff attorney generally creates the perception of legal reality for the client. Most attorneys have the skills to convince the client that the case should be dropped or settled for a lesser sum if they become convinced that the case will likely lose at trial. In fact, my data from both the court files and the insurers' files indicate that plaintiff attorneys frequently abandon cases late in the discovery process. For example, in the 1984–87 data set only about 47 percent of cases that were eventually abandoned had been dropped within 12 months, and after 18 months had passed more than 25 percent still had not been terminated. Similar patterns were observed in the 1987–89 data set. Thus, the hypothesis that plaintiff attorneys fear being perceived as quitters conflicts with the factual reality that they quit all the time, sometimes quite late in the litigation process.

Second, plaintiffs incur many costs in proceeding to trial. There are substantial psychological costs to entering the public arena of the trial. And although the law firm usually bears the cost of witness fees and other expenses, some plaintiffs in cases in our sample assumed these obligations. They escalate dramatically if the case goes to trial.

Although I do not believe that the Gross and Syverud hypothesis can explain much about why cases go to trial, it clearly was present in a few of the cases in our studies. In the death of a 79-year-old woman who allegedly died as a result of improper thyroid and antibiotic medication, the plaintiff attorney wanted to settle the case for $10,000, but the members of the deceased's estate rejected this figure. In fact, they considered and then rejected an offer to settle for $30,000, even though their attorney told them it was the very best he could hope to get and that their chances at trial were poor. As the trial began the judge tried unsuccessfully to persuade the heirs to accept the $30,000 settlement. The jury deliberated for 25 minutes and returned a verdict for the defendants. In another case, the court file contained a letter to the judge from the plaintiff's attorney apologizing for the fact that he could not get his client to settle for a reasonable figure and, therefore, felt obligated to go to trial. However, these cases appeared to be the exception, not the rule. Typically, plaintiff attorneys, not plaintiffs, decide whether or not to proceed to trial.

Conclusion

Various sources of data indicate, albeit circumstantially, that many cases that go to trial tend to have evidence bearing on liability that favors the defendants. This chapter has attempted to put forth hypotheses explaining why the cases are not dropped by the plaintiff. Although I have focused on the plaintiff side to attempt to explain the low plaintiff win rates, it is important to recognize that plaintiffs do win some trials; and this is likely due to defendant misjudgments of the case.

My discussion of the various hypotheses involves mostly educated guesses and reasonable conjecture rather than the systematic evidence that I prefer. Unquestionably, the subject requires more research. Nevertheless, the chapters in part 2 serve several purposes.

They acquaint the nonattorney reader with the procedural processes that lead to jury trials. They show the high degree of uncertainty that attends malpractice litigation, with respect to both settlement and trial. And, finally, they suggest that many of the cases selected for trial may have an inherent tendency to favor defendants; that is, the quantum of evidence supports a finding of nonliability. It needs to be said again that my data do not allow us to estimate what percentage of trial outcomes is due to characteristics of cases and what percentage is due to how jurors perceive and react to trial evidence. Nevertheless, the findings strongly suggest that some of the verdict outcomes reflecting plaintiff win rates of 30 percent or less may be ascribed to weak cases. This conclusion establishes the context for understanding the evidence that is presented to jurors. We can now turn to the behavior of juries.

3. Liability

9

Malpractice: Behind a $26-Million Award to a Boy Injured in Surgery

by Steve Cohen

Two days before Christmas 1989, a New York City jury delivered its verdict in a medical malpractice case after only four hours of deliberation. On hearing the decision, one lawyer burst into tears, and another stormed out of the courtroom cursing a "jury out of control." The plaintiff, a 16-year-old boy, was awarded $26 million—the second-largest malpractice verdict in the United States that year and one of the biggest in New York history. I was a member of that jury.

When my wife heard about the award, she called it obscene. I understood completely. How could I condone such inflated awards? What did they accomplish beyond enriching the lawyers, who get as much as a third of the total? Didn't these megasettlements lead to redundant and unnecessary medical procedures, soaring costs, and a deterioration of the bond between doctor and patient?

Perhaps she was right, but for the 10 people—6 regular jurors and 4 alternates—who heard *Melis v. Kutin, Harper, and St. Vincent's Medical Center*, this case was a soul-searching experience. As individuals, we were aware of the bigger issues. In 1989, around 36,000 malpractice suits were filed in the United States. Almost 60 percent of all

Reprinted from NEW YORK 23 (October 1, 1990): 41–49.
I have taken the step of including this article (which appeared in the October 1, 1990 NEW YORK magazine) as a book chapter because it provides some unique insights into the collective mind of the jury. *Melis* is one of the cases that made national news headlines in 1989 because of the size of the verdict. It is not a typical malpractice case in some respects, but it provides grist for the chapters that follow.

doctors of obstetrics and gynecology have been sued. More than one state is experimenting with no-fault systems and severe limits on awards. But, as jurors, we were there to hear one case and decide it on its merits—within the bounds of the system as it exists.

What follows are my recollections of the case, bolstered by those of my fellow jurors. As an alternate, I did not participate in the final deliberations—I didn't get to vote on the verdict or monetary award. But I did spend seven weeks sitting in an unheated Manhattan courtroom listening to the testimony, sharing in the hallway gossip, and ready—even eager—to replace a principal juror if one got sick.

That chance never came. But three weeks after the trial, I invited the entire jury to my home, where they re-created the deliberations and shared their reactions to the trial. Finally, in an effort to tie up the loose ends and answer the questions that are outside the purview of a trial, I interviewed the principals in the case.

The jury was made up of seven whites and three blacks. There were eight women and two men: two retired teachers, a community activist, several marketing executives, a flight attendant, and a secretary. As a vice president at Playboy—with an Ivy League degree and a wallet full of snapshots of my toddler son—I was not alone in my certainty that I would be a terrific juror. During the first week of the trial, however, we were terrified. We were being asked to pass judgment on people—perhaps ruin the doctors' reputations—and decide how the rest of a teenage boy's life would be spent. We were terrified, also, because we were confused. We heard dozens of new medical terms—and we knew we were going to be asked to decide what had really happened in an operating room nine years before.

The case—in state supreme court—involved a boy named Stephen Melis, who, in 1980, at the age of seven, went into St. Vincent's Medical Center for an operation to correct a hereditary lung problem. The doctors were scheduled to remove a portion of Stephen's right lung, which was unable to expel phlegm and left Stephen vulnerable to infection. During the surgery, something went wrong. Precisely what happened, why, and the extent of Stephen's injuries were the crux of the case.

The boy's lawyer was Thomas Moore. He was in his mid forties and spoke with an intensity that flushed his face and made his jaw clench. He dressed in muted, custom-made suits but always wore an oversize belt that wrapped halfway again around his marathoner's body.

A confession is in order. As jurors, we heeded—at least in large part—Judge Stanley Sklar's daily admonitions not to discuss the case until all the evidence was presented. Not once in the seven weeks of trial was there discussion in the jury room about the case. There were, however, frequent comments—typically in the hallway—about the lawyers' performances and foibles.

There was no warmth between Moore and the jury as he began his opening argument. But we listened very carefully as he described complications that had set in during the surgery and ultimately caused brain damage to Stephen.

Three lawyers formed the defense team. James Rosenblum was the lawyer for the surgeon. He looked to be in his late thirties, dressed like an ad for Brooks Brothers, and spoke very softly. Lewis Rosenberg, who represented the anesthesiologist, appeared to be in his late forties, dressed in tweeds, and sported a large white mustache. William Goldstein represented the hospital. In his mid thirties or so, Goldstein looked like a college football player whose hair and weight had grown beyond the coach's limits.

The three lawyers all insisted that the medical care given Stephen had been proper. There *had* been a complication, they said, but when it occurred, the doctors and the hospital had reacted with extraordinary swiftness. Indeed, Rosenblum said, when the boy's heart slowed dangerously, his client, the surgeon, even took it in his hands and massaged it until it began working on its own.

The two lawyers for the doctors made one other point: though Stephen does have problems, they are not terribly serious nor are they necessarily the result of this operation. We would hear testimony, Rosenblum told us, that Stephen was a good student, played hockey and basketball, and spoke two languages.

The plaintiff's case was presented first. Moore called as his lead witness one of the defendants, the surgeon, Dr. Neil Kutin, who looked to be in his forties. Moore told us that he was calling him to the stand as a hostile witness—he was being questioned against his will. The battle began: "Doctor," said Moore, "there came a time that you knew that Stephen suffered brain damage."

"No," replied Dr. Kutin.

I understood almost nothing about the medical issues yet, but I did realize that the surgeon was challenging the very premise of the plaintiff's case.

The questioning proceeded awkwardly. Moore would ask a question, and one of the defense lawyers would jump up shouting, "Objection!" Judge Sklar would rule in Moore's favor. Moore would often rephrase the question, and the witness would insist that he couldn't understand what was being asked. The question would be repeated and objected to again.

Hour after hour, day after day, we sat in the jury box growing frustrated. We were witnessing a play that made no progress, a dance that had no rhythm. When Moore finally finished, there was no cross-examination. As laymen who'd experienced the legal system through the filter of *L.A. Law* and *Perry Mason*, we jurors knew the decision not to cross-examine meant one thing: the defense was confident that Moore hadn't damaged Kutin.

Moore's next witness—also hostile—was Dr. R. Bruce Harper, the anesthesiologist. In his early forties or so and gaunt, Dr. Harper responded to questions with terse answers and a bemused look. The examination of him was equally laborious.

Finally, after more than a week, Moore called a hostile witness—Dr. Robert Hicks, the chairman of the anesthesiology department at St. Vincent's—who acted as if he relished Moore's inquiry. He gave precise, simple answers to questions. Dr. Hicks's hospital—where he'd spent the last 33 years—was on trial, and it was clear that he was a tough boss who brooked no second-rate performers.

Moore asked Hicks the same question he had asked the other two doctors: whether Stephen Melis had suffered a cardiac arrest in the operating room.

"No doubt about it," he responded instantly.

Even Moore seemed shocked. Both Harper and Kutin had emphatically denied that a cardiac arrest had occurred. "What caused this cardiac arrest?" Moore asked.

At last, the full picture was painted: using his hands to give us a sense of scale and action, Hicks explained that during the surgery Stephen was dependent on the healthy left lung to breathe. But, Hicks said, blood somehow leaked into the left lung and clogged it, preventing Stephen from getting oxygen. Without oxygen, Stephen's heart stopped.

The defense lawyers cross-examined the witness for hours but couldn't get him to modify his testimony.

At one point, seemingly out of the blue, Rosenberg asked Hicks whether Dr. Evan Bloom, a first-year resident anesthesiologist assigned to Harper for the Melis operation, had in fact administered the anesthesia. "Dr. Bloom is in no position to give anesthesia," Hicks bellowed. "The patient would have lasted about five minutes had he given anesthesia."

Finally, Moore stood for one last question: Was this cardiac arrest avoidable?

If the doctors had prevented blood from going into the other lung, Hicks replied, this boy wouldn't have suffered the cardiac arrest.

For the first time in the trial, there seemed to be a bit of clarity. A witness didn't hedge or hide behind semantics; cause and effect were explained. As jurors, we relaxed a bit at last: there was someone we could believe.

From the first day, Irene Melis, Stephen's mother, had been sitting impassively in the courtroom. The day after Hicks testified, she took the stand. She appeared to be in her mid forties and dressed conservatively in clothes that I guessed she had made herself. Sitting next to her husband—who had the saddest eyes I had ever seen—she exuded a stoicism that I assumed she'd acquired in caring for a handicapped child. (I learned later that she was in her late thirties. I also learned after the trial that this middle-class family from Tenafly, New Jersey, was struggling to pay for therapy for Stephen—their medical insurance covered only half.)

Moore's questions for her were gentle and brief. She spoke with a touch of a Greek accent, and we learned about Stephen's troubled lung and the therapy she'd had to administer to him at home since he was an infant. There were limitations on her testimony about her other son, but some information slipped through. We learned that the older brother—who I heard later was a thriving college student—suffers from the same hereditary condition for which Stephen had had surgery.

Rosenblum, Kutin's lawyer, took the lead in the cross-examination. He, too, began gently, "Did you give a history to the doctors that Stephen's hobbies include playing basketball?" he asked.

"Stephen cannot play basketball. He's trying to believe that he's playing basketball," the mother said.

"Did Stephen ever play soccer?"

"Maybe he tried."

Rosenblum then reviewed a deposition that Stephen had given where he talked about playing soccer, and he asked Mrs. Melis if she ever tried to challenge that testimony.

"No, I did not."

"Do you recall Stephen being asked [during his deposition] whether he got dressed by himself?"

"No."

The jury was beginning to get disturbed by what it saw as a pattern of apparent contradictions. Moore was trying to make a case that this young boy was severely handicapped, but there were depositions, school records, and medical histories that seemed to refute that. Even John Melis, the father—who testified in tears—admitted that he had tried to treat his son as if he were perfectly healthy.

After the parents testified, Moore called his first expert witness, Dr. Luke Kitahata, a professor at Yale University School of Medicine and the former director of Yale's Department of Anesthesiology. Moore asked Kitahata if he had an opinion, with a reasonable degree of medical probability, as to whether there were departures from accepted medical practice in this case?

"Yes, I do."

"What is your opinion?"

"Yes, there were deviations."

For nearly six hours, Moore led him through extraordinary testimony. The professor was teaching his class, and we—the jury, the judge, even the lawyers—were his students.

Kitahata agreed with Hicks that a cardiac arrest had occurred and that the brain, without oxygen, had sustained damage. For two days, Moore asked Kitahata about the use of the anesthesia agents, about monitoring and tests, about care in the recovery room. Over and over, Kitahata said there had been departures from proper medical care, and there had been carelessness.

The defense lawyers spent a day on their cross-examination. Two weeks before the actual surgery, the doctors had done an exploratory procedure—a bronchoscopy—and Rosenberg at one point asked Kitahata if he'd examined the medical records from that operation. Kitahata said he hadn't.

Rosenberg then asked if Kitahata shouldn't have examined the records before giving his testimony.

Kitahata replied that he was aware of the preoperative report and seeing the record from two weeks earlier would have been helpful but not essential.

The defense lawyer seemed to have a good point. I went home that night proud of what I was beginning to understand but worried that I had put too much faith in Kitahata's testimony.

The next morning, in the jury room before court began, one of the jurors said she wanted to send a note to the judge, asking if we could get out a bit early. Tomorrow was Thanksgiving, and she had family coming to visit. As we lined up to be led into the jury box, it suddenly occurred to me that we would see Stephen in court today. I whispered my deduction to the woman next to me. "Why?" she asked. "Drama," I said. "What could be more effective with a jury than to see a handicapped boy the day before we leave to be with our own families on Thanksgiving? This is the end of act 1."

In the courtroom, the judge said that he *would* try to get us out early. Moore then called Dr. Leon Charash, a leading child neurologist. Dr. Charash testified that Stephen suffered from brain damage caused by lack of oxygen—the result of the cardiac arrest during the operation. Moore turned to the judge and asked to call Stephen Melis into the courtroom; he wanted to have Dr. Charash examine Stephen for the jury.

The defense lawyers were on their feet objecting—they didn't want the jury to see Stephen. But that just raised a question for us: if his injuries were as slight as the defense had been insisting, why the resistance? The judge agreed that it was proper for Stephen to appear at his own trial, and the rear doors to the courtroom were opened.

A handsome 16-year-old boy dressed in gray trousers and a stylish crewneck sweater walked in, followed—a few protective steps behind—by his father. But the boy didn't actually walk—he shuffled— and his facial muscles seemed a bit unbalanced and strained. When he reached the front of the courtroom, Stephen stood alone for a few seconds, an awkward expression on his face. The tension in the courtroom was palpable, but Charash stepped down from the witness chair and put his hand on the boy's shoulder.

"Stephen," he said gently, "I would like you to walk over to your mother and come back over here."

As Stephen walked the 20 feet across the room, Charash provided medical commentary, explaining the boy's disabilities.

"Stephen, would you run over to your mother for me, please."

Stephen didn't run, but his gait was a bit faster than his walk. It was clearly not an act.

"Stephen, would you hop, please."

"I can't."

He asked Stephen to walk heel to toe.

Stephen just stood there.

Charash showed us Stephen's atrophied legs and demonstrated that the boy's reflexes were quite exaggerated. He added, "I don't want to embarrass Stephen, and he understands that."

Then the doctor asked Stephen to perform some calculations in his head: how much is $10 minus $6.58? . . . what is three-fourths plus one-half? Stephen got the answers wrong. When it was over, his father led him out.

Charash explained that because of the brain damage, Stephen suffers from seizures, along with gross and fine motor impairment. This has led to such practical problems as an inability to button his shirt. He can't stand for long periods. Because of the seizures, he'd be at risk working with machinery or cars.

Moore concluded by asking Charash whether, given Stephen's constellation of problems, the boy would be commercially employable.

"I think more likely than not he will not be commercially employable."

On cross-examination, Rosenblum said, "Doctor, do you know, are there any medical records in 1989 that indicate whether or not Stephen can play any sports at all?"

"There may be," Charash said. "When I asked him three years ago, he said, 'I do fine.' He will say he does fine with everything. He is a boy that has a certain image of what he would like to be."

At another point, Charash said that Stephen's parents had a similar attitude—they tend to look at their son through rose-colored glasses.

Most of the jurors had begun to cry. But we were also angry. The defense lawyers, it seemed, had been trying to put one over on us, claiming that Stephen was a normal teenage boy with a few minor handicaps. We had seen him now, and Charash had put his problems in context. He had also given us some understanding of why some of the medical records said that Stephen engaged in sports. The parents desperately wanted to believe that their son was like other—normal—

children, and they encouraged others to give him the hope to try. As we adjourned for Thanksgiving, I realized that this indeed had been a dramatic conclusion to act 1.

When we resumed several days later, there was a noticeably different attitude in the jury box. While we still didn't feel any warmth toward Tom Moore, there was no underlying distrust, no suspicion that he was exaggerating a young boy's infirmities for his own one-third cut.

Moore called several more expert witnesses. The first was an economist who gave us some projections about Stephen's lost income and the expense of various therapies. Then a psychologist detailed a series of emotional and psychological problems from which Stephen suffers and said that Stephen's IQ had deteriorated as a result of the operation. He also explained that, though Stephen attends a regular public high school, the staff makes special accommodations for him, such as untimed tests.

The defense then began its case; James Rosenblum called his client, Kutin, as his first witness. Under Rosenblum's guidance, Kutin described the scene in the operating room. The jury listened sympathetically to this obviously dedicated surgeon. We could almost see him taking Stephen's heart in his hands and performing open-heart massage. The same thought occurred to each of us: How could this man have committed malpractice?

During Moore's cross-examination, Kutin again denied that a cardiac arrest had taken place. He insisted that Stephen had been without a pulse for less than 30 seconds before his open-heart massage took effect.

"I am asking you, doctor," said Moore, "did you see on the anesthesia record that the patient was pulseless for 10 minutes?"

They had been too busy saving the boy's life to keep good records, answered Kutin.

Moore then shifted to a point that had been raised only briefly before: he asked why Kutin's postoperative report, dictated immediately after the procedure, listed Dr. Evan Bloom, the first-year resident, as having given the anesthesia. Kutin responded that Bloom's name must have been picked up by the transcription service.

At that moment, the jury sensed that something strange had just happened, but we weren't sure what it was. Doctors Harper and Kutin had testified that Harper had given the anesthesia to Stephen.

Suddenly, we were hearing that the surgeon in charge had dictated a report immediately following the operation that said the anesthesia had been administered by Bloom. And we hadn't forgotten what Hicks had said: that if Bloom—who was in his second month as a resident—had administered the anesthesia, the patient would have been in trouble.

The defense then called the first of about a dozen of its own expert witnesses, Dr. Samuel Schuster, associate chief of surgery at Boston's renowned Children's Hospital. Speaking easily and articulately, Dr. Schuster insisted that there was no evidence that a significant amount of blood had leaked into the boy's left lung. The cause of the complication, continued Schuster, was the body's natural reaction to the surgery. The boy had bucked—coughed—on the endotracheal tube that was delivering oxygen; thus, there had been a temporary problem. But the treatment was proper.

After several hours of direct testimony, Moore began his cross-examination. "I assume you utterly disagree with Dr. Hicks's saying that there was a cardiac arrest in this case. Is that correct?"

"I found no evidence that there was an actual cardiac arrest."

Moore walked a few steps away from the witness stand and had asked his next question when Schuster suddenly said, "Would you face me when you talk to me?"

Moore's jaw dropped, and his face darkened, "You cannot hear me, doctor?"

"Sometimes. I would appreciate it if you would just face me."

"Did anybody tell you to say that?"

"Absolutely not."

Stalemate. Schuster was not about to be intimidated by Moore.

Aside from the battle of wits, though, I was concerned about the certainty with which Schuster had insisted no malpractice had been committed. Had Kitahata been wrong, or more likely, had I put too much credence in his testimony?

Moore then turned to an apparent conflict in testimony between Kutin and Harper. Kutin had said the complication occurred after he had finished cutting and suturing the bronchus, Moore pointed out, while Harper had said in a postoperative note that the complication occurred considerably earlier. Moore asked what Schuster thought of the conflict.

Schuster responded that he thought it was unimportant.

The jury sat dumbfounded. The two doctors had given fundamentally different descriptions of what happened in the operating room, and this witness was saying the conflict didn't play a role.

Moore probed a bit more, and what he got Schuster to admit seemed incredible to the jury: Schuster had disregarded Harper's account of the operation. Meanwhile, Schuster had begun to argue with Moore over definitions of the most basic medical terms. It was clear he didn't want to get caught in a contradiction. But it was also clear that the jury had seen something quite extraordinary: Moore had destroyed the testimony of the defense's lead expert witness.

We were starting to see the trial not only as *Melis v. Kutin* but as lawyer versus lawyer, and we had become captivated by Tom Moore's skill. More important, we were beginning to believe him and to doubt the defense lawyers. The defense seemed unable to offer a coherent picture of what had happened in the operating room and that was because the surgeon and the anesthesiologist were blaming each other. One of the jurors whispered to me, "Have you noticed that Kutin and Harper don't talk to each other? They won't even look at each other."

The scenario was the same with most of the other expert witnesses for the defense: A reasonable proposition put forth under direct examination was destroyed by Moore's cross-examination. One of the expert witnesses had a particularly strong effect on us. Dr. Joyce Spinello—the administrator of vocational rehabilitation at the Rusk Institute of New York University Medical Center—testified that in her opinion, Stephen was commercially employable. People with handicaps like Stephen's are placed in jobs, she said. In fact, she added proudly, she had three specific recommendations for Stephen even if he didn't get a college degree: a mail clerk, a copy machine operator, or behind the reception desk at a hotel.

Dr. Spinello said she had examined Stephen's records, but the jurors could not imagine she was talking about the same boy we had seen. How would Stephen function at a hotel reception desk? His speech was slow and impaired, and he was physically awkward. Hotels are concerned with image and speed of customer service. The jury was convinced it was unlikely that Stephen would be hired—or would last—in such an environment. We went through the same analysis with regard to Stephen's prospects as a mail clerk or copy machine operator; by this time, Tom Moore didn't have to do it for us.

Soon after the Spinello debacle, the defense called Dr. Evan Bloom, the first-year anesthesiology resident. On both direct and cross-examination, Bloom insisted that—aside from being there—he hadn't participated in the operation and remembered virtually nothing about it.

Finally, the defense rested, and summations began. The lawyers for the defendants went first. James Rosenblum had moved away from the position that Stephen was a healthy, normal boy. But in his summation, he failed to explain plausibly what had happened in the operating room. Lewis Rosenberg raised several points about Kitahata's testimony that made us question some of the professor's conclusions. But he, too, failed to come up with a credible alternative scenario. The hospital's lawyer, William Goldstein, reiterated that the burden of proof was on the plaintiff; that, of course, helped the doctors.

As jurors, we admitted to one another that we'd been looking forward to Moore's summation, and he didn't disappoint. He patiently sketched a picture of what had happened that summer day in 1980 as that little boy lay on the operating table and the surgeon transected the bronchus. Stephen's heart slowed—indeed stopped—and all hell broke loose in the operating room, Moore said. Yes, the surgeon did take Stephen's heart in his hands, massaged it, and got it working again. And, yes, the anesthesiologist responded with drugs he thought appropriate. But, he reminded us, we had heard from doctor after doctor that that cardiac arrest should never have happened.

Why did it happen, and why did all hell break loose in the operating room? Moore argued that Harper, contrary to his and Kutin's testimony, wasn't administering the anesthesia; the second-month resident, Dr. Bloom, was.

We were shocked: Moore was trying to tie up all the loose ends with this final twist to the drama.

Bit by bit, Moore reviewed the evidence that convinced us it was no coincidence that Bloom's name appeared in the official hospital records as the doctor who administered the anesthesia. It appeared not only on Kutin's postoperative report but on the official hospital log and on the circulating nurse's operating room notes as well. Three separate records by three separate people saying the same thing, Moore said.

Moore then put a blowup of a familiar chart on an easel. He pointed out that throughout the trial, we had repeatedly seen and heard about the anesthesia record kept by Harper during the entire course of the surgery. Harper had testified that he personally kept this record, making the periodic notations.

"This is all Dr. Harper's handwriting," Moore said. "If you have any doubt, just look at his handwriting in the chart and you will see clearly. He said it was and it is. There is no doubt about it."

Moore then unwrapped a three-by-four-foot package that had been hidden behind the jury box. In it was a blowup of another medical chart—the anesthesia record kept during the bronchoscopy procedure done two weeks before the main operation. It was performed by the same team, Doctors Kutin and Harper, and, as Moore reminded us, it was a relatively simple exploratory procedure. The chest never had to be opened.

Moore placed the second chart next to the first, and it was apparent it was written in a totally different handwriting. During the first, simple bronchoscopy procedure, Moore explained, Harper had the resident make the notations in the chart. But during Stephen's open-chest operation, as gases were being administered, manual ventilation of his lungs was being performed, and medications delivered, Harper, according to his testimony, had also made the notations in the chart.

Moore argued that the doctor's story was simply not credible. Harper was free to make the notations in the chart, Moore claimed, because Bloom was giving the anesthesia.

The effect was stunning. The bronchoscopy chart had been in the record all along but had never been brought to the jury's attention. Moore had waited until the end of his summation before producing it—a smoking gun just like we had seen dozens of times on *Perry Mason*.

After charging the jury—explaining the law—Judge Sklar gave it a 20-page list that detailed 18 questions of liability (Did blood leak into the left lung? were the monitoring devices and drugs appropriate?) and responsibility.

For seven weeks, the jurors had lived with this case and yet had been unable to talk to one another about it. Once they were in the jury room their frustration exploded. One of the jurors was in tears; she was terribly uncomfortable examining such complex questions in a group. Another was furious with her. Chaos seemed imminent. Haleemah Shakir, a 50-year-old woman who worked as a community arbitrator in Harlem, offered a suggestion. Instead of trying to analyze the entire case, she proposed, the group should go point by point through the judge's questions. That way, the jurors would be able to see how far apart they were on specific points.

As the forewoman, Eunice de Sanchez, began reading each question, the group was amazed: they were in agreement on every point—including the contention that Dr. Bloom had administered the anesthesia. In the end, the jury accepted Moore's scenario completely. In less than two hours, all questions of liability were resolved. By lunchtime, the jury had allocated responsibility: 50 percent to Harper; 30 percent to Kutin; and 20 percent to the hospital.

The tougher questions then had to be confronted: how to compensate Stephen and how to put a dollar value on his lost earnings, his need for continuing treatment, and his pain and suffering. Nicolette Abysalh, a Wall Street analyst, placed a pocket calculator on the worn wooden table and took charge. First, she asked, is it fair to assume—as Moore's expert witness had testified—that Stephen's lost earnings would have been similar to those of an "average" college graduate? The jury immediately agreed that it was not. Though Stephen might not have become a million-dollar-a-year investment banker, he clearly had a promising future before the surgery. Therapies and supervisory care were the next issues to be resolved. It was quickly agreed that Stephen was going to need physical, speech, occupational, and psychological therapy throughout his life. Again using the economist's estimates of costs, the jury assigned a figure.

The last issue was the toughest: calculating Stephen's pain and suffering. In his closing remarks, Moore had suggested a figure—he said he offered it simply to give some basis on which to begin a debate, but it no doubt represented Moore's most optimistic hope. That figure was $8 million. But Moore didn't count on one thing: the jury's anger. For seven weeks, the jury had sat in that courtroom listening to the defense lawyers belittle Stephen's problems. We saw the doctors refuse to acknowledge Stephen's handicaps or to accept responsibility for them. To the jury, at least, it seemed that the doctors had made mistakes, refused to admit them, and then tried to cover them up.

In less than 10 minutes, the jurors agreed on an award. All told, they had deliberated less than four hours.

In court again, the forewoman stood to read the verdict: "We find for the plaintiff, Stephen Melis." As she finished the third of the 18 counts, I noticed that Moore was in tears. It was another 15 minutes before she got to the money: "We award Stephen Melis $2.5 million for lost wages; $2.79 million for the various therapies; $1.5 million for supervisory care; and $19 million for pain and suffering."

In the hallway outside the courtroom, the jurors cried and embraced Mr. and Mrs. Melis. Tom Moore told us that the award would probably be reduced by the judge or on appeal. Nonetheless, he said, it was gratifying.

A few weeks later, in the course of writing this article, I called the lawyers in the case. Each of the defense lawyers raised the same points: How can society afford such outrageously huge malpractice awards, forcing hospitals like St. Vincent's to pay for these sums by abandoning valuable programs?

One of the lawyers—who asked not to be quoted by name on these points—complained bitterly that the jury had been overly influenced by Tom Moore. He said the solution to the malpractice crisis may be to take it out of the hands of jurors. He continued to insist that Bloom had not administered the anesthesia and that the paper trail leading to him was the result of record keeping errors.

I wondered what would happen to the doctors. Would they lose their homes and their careers as one of the lawyers suggested? Each of the lawyers tried to discourage me from writing about the case, saying that these dedicated doctors had suffered enough. I listened, promised nothing, and agonized more than a bit.

Then I stumbled on a few surprises. The doctors' careers are not over: despite the malpractice verdict, they probably won't be reviewed by any medical accrediting boards. Perhaps most startling, they might not even see a rise in their malpractice insurance premiums—which usually go up only when there is a recurring pattern of malpractice or egregious behavior.

The doctors will not lose their homes. (Although plaintiffs, by law, can go after the defendants' personal assets, they rarely do.) In New York, the law says that the defendant with the deepest pocket has to pay what the codefendants cannot. Because each of the doctors in this case was said to have had only $1 million in malpractice insurance coverage—and St. Vincent's is largely self-insured (though backstopped by the Catholic Archdiocese of New York)—the hospital would have to pick up the bulk of the award. Despite my several attempts to question hospital officials, St. Vincent's refused to comment on the case.

A fortnight ago, nine months after the verdict, Judge Sklar ruled on a defense motion to overturn the verdict and reduce the award. He sustained the verdict—actually, 17 out of the 18 particulars—but reduced the award to $4.8 million. Now the case goes to the appeals courts, where the defense will try to reduce the amount further, and the Melises will try to have the original amount largely restored.

Meanwhile, I have struggled over whether or not the jury got carried away with its award for pain and suffering. Wouldn't $5 million have compensated Stephen adequately and still have sent a message? I worried that each huge award in a malpractice case simply drives up the cost of medical care for all of us. And I worried that lawsuits discourage good doctors from practicing.

But I worried only until I realized that the medical profession was failing to adequately regulate, monitor, and punish doctors who commit malpractice. And I decided that at the moment the only thing that would prod the medical profession into reforming its own ranks was more $26-million verdicts.

10

Postscript to *Melis v. Kutin*

A jury's verdict is not the final word in a civil case. It does not become a judgment until the presiding trial judge reviews the verdict and pronounces it as satisfying the law's requirements. The judge may conclude that all or part of the jury's verdict on liability was inconsistent with the trial evidence and set the verdict or parts of the verdict aside or order a new trial. Similarly, the judge reviews the damage award and, through the legal devices called *additur* (i.e., add) and *remittitur* (i.e., reduction), increases or decreases the amount of the award. Of course, after judgment is pronounced, either of the opposing parties may appeal the decision for review by a higher court.[1]

After the verdict in *Melis v. Kutin*, the defendants moved to set aside the verdict or, if they lost on that issue, to reduce the $25,790,000 award. The trial judge, Justice Stanley Sklar, reviewed these motions.[2] His response enables us to begin considering the issue of jury competence with regard to both liability and damages.

The Review of Liability

St. Vincent's Medical Center argued that the evidence showed that the assignment of a first-year anesthesiology resident, Dr. Bloom, to the operating room had no bearing on the outcome of the surgery and, therefore, that the jury's finding that this assignment was a proximate cause of Stephen Melis's injuries was "against the weight of the evidence." Justice Sklar, however, noted that an expert for the plaintiff testified that, given the nature of the surgery and Stephen's underlying lung condition, the accepted standard of medical care would require a more experienced anesthesiologist to assist in the operation. Although defense experts testified to the contrary, Justice Sklar concluded that the jury was free to reject their testimony. Justice Sklar denied St. Vincent's motion to set aside this finding.

St. Vincent's also argued that the jury's finding that the hospital violated the standard of care because it did not have a replacement anesthesiologist in the recovery room was against the weight of the evidence. St. Vincent's claimed that if there was a departure from practice, Dr. Harper, not St. Vincent's, held the responsibility. Justice Sklar, however, noted that he had instructed the jury on vicarious liability and that it was reasonable for the jury to conclude from the evidence that the absence of an anesthesiologist in the recovery room exacerbated Stephen's problem. This motion was also denied by Justice Sklar.

St. Vincent's further claimed that the evidence did not support the conclusion that, in view of the seizures, blood gases, and Stephen's appearance, Dr. Hicks departed from accepted practice when he extubated Stephen in the recovery room. Dr. Hicks had contended that Stephen's condition was consistent with that of a normal patient awakening from anesthesia. The evidence was conflicting, but Justice Sklar concluded that because the law required giving the plaintiff "the benefit of every inference which could reasonably have been drawn from the proof presented," the jury properly could have concluded that Stephen was injured by the premature extubation.

Dr. Kutin also challenged the verdict. He asserted that there was not enough evidence to support the jury's findings that he had failed to occlude a large air leak in Stephen's bronchial tube during the surgery, to suction blood from the left lung, to ensure proper ventilation of breathing before Stephen left the operating room, and to reinsert a breathing tube when blood gas measures suggested there were problems. All of this was determined to have contributed to the injury. Justice Sklar systematically reviewed each of these findings and concluded that the jury could have reasonably decided these issues from the evidence. For example, the plaintiff's expert witness testified that the air leak and the blood leakage into the lung were substantial contributing factors to Stephen's cardiac arrest. Furthermore, the medical records showed that no blood was suctioned until problems had already developed; and some of the defense witnesses themselves admitted that the standard procedure in the event of an air leak is to stop it with a finger in order to prevent that cardiac arrest. In short, Justice Sklar concluded that the jury acted reasonably in finding that the events were a proximate cause of Stephen's injury and that Dr. Kutin departed from accepted medical practice when he did not take preventative steps in response to the signs of Stephen's distress.

A final issue involved the vicarious liability of St. Vincent's with respect to the acts of Dr. Harper. St. Vincent's Medical Center claimed that the issue should not have been submitted to the jury because, according to the law, Dr. Harper was not an employee but rather an independent contractor. Alternatively, St. Vincent's argued that the weight of the evidence did not support a claim that he was a hospital employee, and therefore Justice Sklar's instructions to the jury on this issue were erroneous. The plaintiff's rebuttal argument, however, claimed that since Stephen and his parents did not personally solicit Dr. Harper's services, as they had those of Dr. Kutin, Dr. Harper should be considered to be assigned by the hospital. In addition, Dr. Harper was scheduled by the hospital, was required to follow the hospital's rules and regulations, and provided a service integral to the hospital's surgical operations. Sidestepping the issue of whether he had incorrectly instructed the jury on the issue, Justice Sklar concluded that since Dr. Harper was an independent contractor with the hospital, billed independently for his services, did not share his fees with the hospital, and retained sole professional responsibility for making judgments about a patient's welfare, the evidence under law established in prior legal cases did not support the jury's verdict that St. Vincent's was liable for the acts of Dr. Harper. The finding of vicarious liability on this issue was set aside.

Justice Sklar, therefore, supported the jury's verdict on all liability issues except vicarious liability.

Review of Damages

Justice Sklar then reviewed the $25,790,000 damage award. Damages are typically divided into two main categories, economic damages and noneconomic damages. Within each category there may be multiple subparts. Economic damages are those relating to the money needed to compensate the plaintiff for such things as past and future lost wages, medical bills, palliative care, and rehabilitation or retraining. Noneconomic damages involve compensation for such matters for which there is no metric other than subjective human judgment.[3] Thus, the amounts awarded for past and future pain and suffering, emotional distress due to disfigurement or loss of enjoyment of life's amenities, or loss of sexual and emotional consortium (companionship or pleasure) with one's spouse are all forms of noneconomic damages. Both types of damages figured in Stephen Melis's award.

Consider, first, the economic damages. The jury awarded $2,500,000 for Stephen's impairment of earning capacity based on its judgment that he would have a work-life expectancy of 43 years. The economist called by Stephen's attorney testified that if Stephen had graduated from college and gone to work at age 22, Bureau of Labor statistics indicated he would have a work-life expectancy of 35.9 years. The economist's best estimate was that Stephen would earn $593,539 plus $138,295 in fringe benefits for a total of $731,834. The economist also estimated that Stephen would have earned $912,776 if he worked to age 70, as many people do. Justice Sklar agreed that under New York law the jury could disregard statistical tables on work-life expectancy and decide on a work-life of 43 years. However, based on that figure, the financial estimates provided by the economist could lead only to an award of $830,000. Hence, Justice Sklar reduced the award of future earnings from $2,500,000 to $830,000.

The jury also awarded $1,890,000 for physical, occupational, and speech therapy over Stephen's lifetime. However, the plaintiff's evidence involved an estimate of only $729,693. In reply to the defense motions to set aside the verdict, the plaintiff conceded that the award on this matter exceeded expert opinion. Justice Sklar reduced the award to the latter amount.

The plaintiff, through expert evidence, claimed $207,000 for future psychotherapy to help Stephen adjust to his condition throughout his life. The jury awarded $900,000. Stephen's attorneys conceded that an award over $207,000 was excessive, but they argued for it nonetheless. Justice Sklar noted that the evidence showed that Stephen had continued to resist this form of therapy as a child and that there was inadequate testimony on whether he would seek it as an adult or how often. Consequently, the $900,000 award on this matter was set aside in its entirety.

At trial, Stephen's attorneys made a claim for the supervisory care that he would need during his waking hours because of his judgmental and locomotion problems, his difficulty in dressing, and his susceptibility to seizures. Estimates of the cost of this care ranged from $2,897,929 to $3,446,651. The jury awarded only $1,500,000 but, nevertheless, the defendants claimed that the award was not supported by the evidence. In reviewing this component of the award, Justice Sklar observed that the defense attorneys had no trouble cross-examining the plaintiff's expert on this issue and called two of their own experts to rebut the plaintiff's expert. On the evidence, it was reasonable for the jury to give money for supervisory care and in an amount less than the plaintiff claimed. The $1,500,000 award was allowed to stand.

The final damage issue was the past and future pain and suffering component for which the jury awarded $19 million. The plaintiff attorneys conceded that the figure was excessive, but they argued that $8 million was a reasonable figure. Under New York case law, judges can review the pain and suffering award in relation to prior cases. Justice Sklar reviewed some of these cases, and he concluded that the award was excessive to the extent that it exceeded $1,750,000. It is not precisely clear how he arrived at this figure, but among the various cases that he cited the largest pain and suffering award allowed by an appeals court was in *Sastoque v. Maimonides Medical Center* (1990).[4] This was a medical malpractice case involving a brain-damaged infant in which the plaintiff was given $1,750,000.

St. Vincent's made a final request. It asked Justice Sklar to reduce the total award to "present value," that is, to award only the amount that would be necessary to generate the needed revenue over Stephen's life span if the money were placed in an interest-bearing account today rather than award the full amount in a lump sum.[5] Justice Sklar concluded that this matter was the proper subject of legislative, not judicial action. The award was not reduced.

The damage award issues are summarized in table 10.1. It compares the sums requested by the plaintiff, the amounts awarded by the jury, and the final award allowed by Justice Sklar. The plaintiff had requested a total award of between $12,567,427 and $13,297,091 depending on which estimate of the costs of supervisory care was chosen. The jury almost doubled this request to $25,790,000. Justice Sklar's judgment was approximately one-third of the plaintiff's original request and less than one-fifth of the jury's award.

Outcome

Justice Sklar's judgment stated that unless Stephen's father, acting as the natural guardian, accepted the reductions within 30 days after notification, he would grant a new trial to the defendants on the awards for pain and suffering and impairment of earning ability.

There was one additional development in the case. Justice Sklar's judgment, as just described, was published on October 10, 1990. Steve Cohen's article in NEW YORK magazine was published later that month. The defendants responded by filing an additional challenge to the jury's verdict.[6] They claimed that the article showed that the jurors had violated Justice Sklar's admonition not to discuss any aspects of the trial until they had been instructed on the law and begun their deliberations. Cohen's article says,

> As jurors, we heeded—at least in part—Judge Stanley Sklar's daily admonitions not to discuss the case until all the evidence was presented. Not once in the seven weeks of trial was there discussion in the jury room about the case. There were, however, frequent comments—typically in the hallway—about the lawyers' performances and foibles.

In responding to the defense motion, Justice Sklar concluded that the jurors may have made minor comments about the trial, but the

TABLE 10.1.   Components of Award in *Melis v. Kutin:* Plaintiff, Jury, and Judge

Component	Plaintiff Evidence ($)	Jury ($)	Judge ($)
1. Impaired earning ability	731,834[a]– 912,776[b]	2,500,000[c]	830,000[c]
2. Physical/occupational/speech therapy	729,693	1,890,000	729,693
3. Psychotherapy	207,971	900,000	0
4. Supervisory care	2,897,929[d]– 3,446,651[e]	1,500,000	1,500,000
5. Pain and suffering	8,000,000	19,000,000	1,750,000
Total	12,567,427– 13,297,091	25,790,000	4,809,693

[a]Based on work-life expectancy of 35.9 years.
[b]Based on work-life expectancy of 48 years.
[c]Based on work-life expectancy of 43 years.
[d]Estimate based on cost of a personal counselor.
[e]Estimate based on cost of a household worker.

article indicates that the jurors did not discuss the case itself. Justice Sklar also took issue with defense contentions that the article showed that the jurors were improperly influenced by their anger at the defense during their deliberations. Justice Sklar rejected this characterization, saying that the article showed that "the answers to liability questions were far clearer [in the jurors' minds] than the defendant's had hoped."[7] Furthermore, the Cohen article indicates that the jurors drew distinctions and did not find liability on all of the questions that were put to them.

Perspectives from Melis

In many respects *Melis* is not a typical case. Few malpractice trials last as long as seven weeks. As we have seen in prior chapters, very few result in verdicts even approaching $26 million. The case was exceptionally complicated. It involved damaging testimony against a doctor from the head of one of the hospital's own departments, an event that occurs in few malpractice trials.

The case does draw attention to a point that is often overlooked in debates about the jury. The jury verdict is usually scrutinized by the judge as to both the issues of liability and damages before judgment is entered.[8]

Justice Sklar's review of the jury's decision on liability can give solace to supporters of the jury. He concluded that the jury reached reasonable decisions on every liability issue except vicarious liability. (And the instructions he gave them on the latter may have been responsible for misleading them.) It should also be emphasized that reaching a "reasonable" decision based on the evidence does not mean the answer was clear-cut or unambiguous. Cases go to trial in large part because both sides believe there are grounds for seeing the case their way.

A further matter relating to jury competence should be addressed. Jury critics often characterize "the jury" as a group of uneducated persons who, as some critics have claimed, did not have the ability to make up a good excuse to get out of jury duty.[9] However, one would have to go pretty far to characterize the *Melis* jury as stupid or uneducated. As Cohen relates, the jury contained two retired teachers, a community activist, several marketing executives, a flight attendant, and a secretary; and Cohen, who could have easily been one of the regular jurors rather than an alternate, has an Ivy League degree. Most jurisdictions in both federal and state courts have reduced or eliminated statutory exemptions from jury duty, and many have instituted "one day–one trial" or "one week–one trial" jury conscription with the result that executives, accountants, professors, and other professionals frequently serve on juries. In many states, doctors, lawyers, and nurses also serve on juries. North Carolina is one such state, and as will be shown in the case studies discussed in subsequent chapters, some well-educated people have served as jurors in North Carolina medical negligence trials.

Critics of medical negligence juries can also find solace in *Melis*. Justice Sklar unequivocally judged the jury to have gone overboard on the damage award. Even the plaintiff's attorneys conceded that the jury went beyond the evidence on some issues. Cohen's article suggests that even the jurors felt the $19-million pain and suffering award was probably excessive. One may take the view that they were sending a message about what they perceived to be egregious behavior on the part of the defendants, that possibly the pain and suffering awards actually contained a de facto "punitive" component against the defendants.[10] If this was so, the jury went beyond the instructions it was given.

Judicial review corrected the jury's errant ways in this case. In part, this was because New York, like some other jurisdictions, requires the jury to respond to each contested issue on a special verdict sheet.[11] Other states, including North Carolina, require only a general verdict on the matter of damages, that is, the total sum undifferentiated as to components. Judicial review, as occurred in *Melis*, is severely constrained in general verdict jurisdictions because the judge cannot differentiate the components. It should also be noted that while New York courts review the pain and suffering award for proportionality in relation to other cases, in other jurisdictions, state legislatures have placed limits, or "caps," on the amounts that can be given for pain and suffering.[12]

Melis deserves a final comment with respect to the adjusted judgment rendered by Justice Sklar. Reasonable people can still argue that the $4.8-million award is too high or too low, considering the circumstances. Is $3,059,693 too much, too little, or about right for economic damages? What about $1,750,000 for pain and suffering? There is, of course, no correct answer. In fact, there are no correct answers for either the liability or the damages issues. There is only human judgment. *Melis* sets the tone for my consideration of these matters in relation to juries in North Carolina and elsewhere in the United States in the following chapters.

An Introduction to the Liability Controversy

A team of researchers under the guidance of Dr. Thomas Julian of the Department of Obstetrics and Gynecology at the University of Minnesota undertook an intensive study of 220 obstetrics cases that resulted in malpractice claims.[1] Each case was reviewed by five obstetricians. The purpose of the study was to identify risk factors that can lead to injury and malpractice suits. Using criteria set by the American College of Obstetrics and Gynecology, the experts who reviewed the cases concluded that "common obstetrical risks were often not recognized or not recorded in medical records."[2] In fact, the risks were recognized and recorded only 54 percent of the time. Julian et al.'s reviewing experts also concluded that the attending physicians correctly managed the risk factors only 32 percent of the time. The study also concluded, however, that lawsuits occurred in more than 30 percent of cases in which the risks were appropriately managed. Generally similar findings have been found in other studies of obstetrics malpractice cases.[3] A major study of medical injuries in New York State indicated that about 1 percent of hospital patients were victims of negligence.[4] Of these, about 25 percent died and another 3 percent suffered major permanent disabilities.

The significance of these studies for our present purposes is to remind us that medical negligence does occur, and the consequences can be horrendous. However, equally important, the studies also remind us that lawsuits are brought when, perhaps, there has been no negligence. The task of the legal system—and in a significant percentage of the cases, the task of juries—is to determine which cases are and which are not the result of negligence on the part of the health care provider.

This chapter revisits concerns about the competence and biases of

juries on the matter of liability. It then presents an overview of the
trial context in which jury decisions are made.

Concerns about Jury Competence and Bias

Recall some of the statements made by critics that I introduced in
chapter 1. The 1988 report of the American Medical Association's Specialty Society Medical Liability Project summarized concerns about the
competence of the jury:

> Juries are not optimally suited to decide the complicated issues
> of causation and duty of care. Under the best of circumstances,
> the determination of professional liability is not easily made by
> laymen.
>
> With respect to the major elements of liability—duty of care
> and causation—the parties almost always must present expert
> testimony, which the jurors cannot evaluate independently.
>
> [J]uries can never be as effective at deciding these cases as
> specialized hearing officers because jurors are exposed to the
> medical issues only once and thus they cannot develop an institu-
> tional memory to aid them in deciding a specific dispute. This not
> only impairs their ability to decide each case, but it also leads to
> inconsistency in verdicts across cases.[5]

Concerns about juror emotions and sympathies are closely inter-
twined with the concerns about competence. The North Carolina Hospital Association, for instance, said:

> There is no way to predict how a jury will rule on a particular set of
> facts. . . . [T]oday juries often make awards regardless of the
> "fault" of anyone—out of sympathy for an injured person. More
> and more the public attitude is that insurance will compensate the
> injured party and the defendant will not sustain any loss. . . ; too
> often juries appear to award on [the] basis of emotion as opposed
> to facts and/or realistic evaluation of case circumstances.[6]

In his book Health Care Law and Policy, Professor Clark
Havighurst argued that juries do not understand the experts and fall
back on emotions:

Although it is customary in our adversary system to regard a jury trial as a "black box" the outcomes of which (on nonlegal questions) are granted a powerful presumption of legitimacy, realism compels recognition that juries are often poorly positioned to choose reliably between the well argued, but often highly confusing theories of the two sides' experts. As a result they often fall back on such irrelevancies as the witnesses' demeanor and style of presentation or sympathy for the plaintiff's plight or the defendant's reputation.[7]

And Professor Stephen Sugarman, referring to juries in both malpractice and products liability cases, said:

Jurors selected at least in part for their ignorance about the topic at hand are asked to decide extremely difficult scientific issues. . . . Of course, the jury is aided in this process by the testimony of experts. What that means in practice is that it must resolve a dispute between sophisticated witnesses, whose scientific credibility the jurors are unlikely to appraise.[8]

Sugarman makes the further claim that the problem occurs "in nearly every medical malpractice and product design defect case coming to trial. . . ."[9]

These opinions can be best understood in the context of the evidence juries hear and the decisions they are required to make.

The Jury's Task: An Overview

In his exceptionally lucid discussion of medical liability, MEDICAL MALPRACTICE: LAW, TACTICS AND ETHICS, experienced trial lawyer and professor Frank McClellan observes that a doctor cannot be held to be negligent simply because he or she made a mistake in judgment or failed to do something that resulted in an injury to a patient.[10]

Rather, the legal criterion by which medical negligence is judged is the standard of medical practice. In many areas of personal injury, such as an automobile accident, a defendant's negligence is judged in terms of whether he or she exercised the prudence and care that a "reasonable person" would have exercised under similar circumstances. By contrast, in medical malpractice cases the legal guideline is whether the physician's treatment of the patient comported with the standards of professional practice followed by other physicians in the same field of medical practice in that community at the time that the injury occurred. In other words, what would a reasonable doctor under the particular circumstances have done? Thus, under the law, a general practitioner living in a rural community might be held to a less rigorous standard of treatment than a neurosurgeon practicing in an urban teaching hospital. The latter has access to more technology and updates in medical developments and through training should know more than the general practitioner. The standard also varies according to the health provider's specialty. For example, podiatrists or osteopaths will be held to the standards of their particular field and not the standards of general medicine.

The use of the standard of practice criterion has two interrelated consequences. First, under the law, the jury is not allowed to second-guess the doctor's decision after the fact by applying its own judgment of "reasonableness" as it would, for example, in an auto negligence case. Second, the jurors learn about the standard of practice through the testimony of medical experts. At trial, the plaintiff and defense experts typically differ in their respective interpretations of the standards of care. The jury has to decide between these conflicting opinions. These opinions sometimes involve complex medical technicalities and are dependent upon specific case facts. Furthermore, even though the defendant physician is not legally treated as an expert on these standards for purposes of his or her own case, in reality the defendant's testimony also conveys important information about the standard of care.

The doctrine of informed consent also plays a significant role in some medical negligence cases.[11] Many medical procedures entail significant risks of injury. Iatrogenic injuries—those that occur as a result of treatment—are not unusual events under even the very best treatment conditions. For example, many useful drugs have side effects in some patients. Likewise, an angiogram, which assists in the diagnosis of a heart ailment, is statistically expected to injure a certain number of patients. The procedure requires inserting a catheter through a femoral artery in the groin area and threading it up into the heart or areas near the heart. Sometimes the procedure can kill the patient even when absolutely no negligence is involved. Physicians have a positive obligation to fully inform the patient of all of the risks of a medical treatment before agreeing to undertake it, but the risks are present. Physicians may also be liable if they do not inform the patient of the risks of refusing medical treatment.

Res ipsa loquitur, another legal doctrine meaning, roughly, that "the facts speak for themselves," may be relevant in some cases where there is no direct evidence about how an injury occurred.[12] A medical sponge or other instrument left in a body cavity after an operation would be a simple example of a case in which the doctrine applies. In other instances, an expert may testify that if a medical procedure had been carried out properly, the injury could not have occurred despite the absence of direct evidence bearing on how it occurred.

At trial an issue may involve a dispute over whether the injury was a result of a normal iatrogenic risk or negligence. In other instances, the dispute may revolve around the extent to which the injury is separate from the effects of the ailment that caused the patient to seek treatment in the first place, from the consequences of treatment for another ailment, or from failure of the patient to follow the physician's advice. Consider a few examples. Obese or diabetic patients are more prone to serious reactions during or after surgery. The patient may claim that the injury was due to negligence, but the doctor may contend that the result was a consequence of the prior health problems. A patient may claim that a malformed breast after cosmetic surgery was due to a negligent operation. The doctor may assert that it resulted from her failure to follow his advice about self-care during postsurgery recovery and her failure to appear for the scheduled follow-up visits.

A further consideration in assessing the context out of which jury verdicts are rendered is the panoply of possible forms of negligence. These include failure to diagnose diseases, failure to give timely treatment of that disease, misdiagnosis, improper medication, failure to obtain informed consent, and failure to inform the patient of the risks of not undergoing medical treatment.[13] More than one element, sometimes many of them, may be present in a single medical negligence case. Even in those cases with a single defendant and a fairly straightforward injury, the attorney for the plaintiff may present several theories of liability and argue to the jurors that even if they believe that the evidence does not support theory A, they still must consider theories B and C. When the case has multiple defendants who provided different aspects of treatment, or when there are multiple injuries, some of which may have been present prior to treatment, the difficulty of deciding liability may increase substantially.

All of the above kinds of problems often result in expert medical testimony that goes beyond simply defining standards of practice. The experts give opinions about the contribution of the preexisting illness, the magnitude of the injuries that the plaintiff suffers, and the prognosis for future health problems.

Conclusion

Although extremely brief, this overview of liability issues suggests that it is difficult to define a "typical" medical malpractice case because of the possible combinations and permutations of the factors that may be at issue at trial. It also would seem to bolster the prima facie arguments of jury critics that liability decisions are beyond the competence of laypersons. However, before accepting this last conclusion consider the case studies and other data presented in the next three chapters.

12

Are Trials Always Technically Complicated? Three Case Studies

While chapter 11 may leave the impression that trials can be so compli-cated that laypersons cannot hope to understand the issues or render an informed judgment, this view may be misleading. I want to at-tempt to document an alternative opinion—that jurors can render informed judgments—through three case studies. These case studies tell us about jurors' understanding of the issues in a trial and some-thing about their attitudes as well. These three studies also begin to move the concept of the malpractice trial from the abstract to the concrete, so that claims about complexity and juror competence can be judged on their merits. The trials occurred in North Carolina be-tween 1987 and 1990. Each trial was observed from beginning to end. Afterward, the jurors were interviewed about their understanding of the evidence and their attitudes toward the trial and its participants.

Case 1: Urinary and Rectal Incontinence

Factual Background

In July of 1981, a urologist, Dr. U., who had been treating Mrs. F., referred her to a teaching hospital for a series of complex tests to evaluate her bladder strength and capacity. Mrs. F., then 47 years old, was plagued with severe urinary incontinence that increased succes-sively after the birth of each of her four children. In addition to two previous bladder operations, Mrs. F. had undergone a hysterectomy and a radical mastectomy and had received drug therapy for a thyroid condition, severe depression, and bladder problems. After several months of treatment for her urinary incontinence, including the use of caudal blocks to the nerves that serve the bladder, she was recommended to Dr. N. Dr. N. proposed a surgical procedure known as a sacral rhizotomy: cutting the S-3 nerve from the spine to relieve the pressure that accompanied the incontinence. Following the operation, Mrs. F. continued to experience urinary incontinence and subsequently developed rectal incontinence; the latter resulted in the necessity of a colostomy in 1984. Later in that same year, Mrs. F. brought suit against the urologist, the neurosurgeon, and a neurosurgery resident (the resident was dropped from the suit before trial). Mr. F. sought damages for loss of consortium with his wife.

The Legal Issues

There were three primary issues around which the trial revolved. First, was Dr. U. negligent in diagnosing the plaintiff's condition and recommending the sacral rhizotomy? Second, was the plaintiff's injury, rectal incontinence, the result of Dr. N.'s negligence in performing the sacral rhizotomy? Third, was the plaintiff fully informed of all the potential risks and complications of a sacral rhizotomy? The main arguments of the plaintiff's attorney were that the defendants were negligent because they had not fully exhausted all conservative modes of therapy before recommending an operation as irreversible as a sacral rhizotomy, and they had not obtained informed consent because they had not fully explained the risks of the rhizotomy.

The Trial Evidence

The plaintiff's attorney began the trial by calling the two defendants as the first witnesses. Dr. N., the neurosurgeon, was questioned about the sacral rhizotomy procedure and the surgery report. Early emphasis in the examination of Dr. N. focused on the surgery report that stated that the patient's problem was "interstitial cysticitis." Dr. N. stated that the report was written by the medical resident and that it was wrong. Dr. N. conceded that this diagnosis also appeared in follow-up reports more than a year later and, furthermore, that he had repeated the interstitial cysticitis diagnosis in a sworn deposition in 1985. Speaking directly to the jury, Dr. N. said he had not prepared for the deposition and had made an error during that testimony.

The examination of Dr. N. then turned to the rhizotomy procedure. The testimony was very technical but it was accompanied by charts, X rays of Mrs. F., and examples of the instruments used in the operation. Much of the examination centered on whether, instead of just cutting the S-3 nerve, Dr. N. might have severed another nerve instead. Dr. N. conceded that this was possible but remote since he had conducted numerous tests both before and after the surgery. However, under aggressive questioning by the plaintiff's attorney, Dr. N. conceded that there was no evidence of a cystoscopy (the visual examination of the interior of the bladder performed under anesthesia) in the preoperative records that he reviewed, and he admitted that there should have been.

On the morning of the second day of trial, the defense attorney offered the plaintiff $25,000 to settle the case, with the hint that perhaps a settlement amount might go somewhat higher. The plaintiff attorney conveyed the offer to Mrs. F. with the recommendation that she should refuse it. She did and the trial continued.

Additional examination was directed to the issue of whether Mrs. F. had been informed of the risks of the operation. Dr. N. testified that Mrs. F. knew that one of the consequences of the surgery would be that she would have to catheterize herself four to six times each day for the rest of her life to void urine and that there was a substantial risk of repeated urinary infections from this process. Dr. N. stated that she had nevertheless agreed because of her embarrassment over the incontinence. Mrs. F. was also warned of possible numbness in her pelvic region. Dr. N.'s preoperative medical notes stated that he had discussed these risks with her and that she signed a consent form in 1982. Dr. N. also offered the opinion that Mrs. F.'s rectal incontinence may have been the result of a spastic colon since prior to the surgery she had alternated between constipation and then, due to laxatives, diarrhea.

The plaintiff's second witness was Dr. U., the other defendant. Most of Dr. U.'s testimony revolved around his diagnosis of Mrs. F.'s problem and the issue of whether her urinary problem resulted from stress or urge incontinence. The type of incontinence might lead to different treatment options. The jury was repeatedly tutored, ad nauseam some jurors would later say, in the reading and interpretation of cystometrograms and their implications for the diagnosis of stress versus urge incontinence. Dr. U. also related that after Mrs. F.'s colostomy but before she filed suit she had visited his office "anxious to be declared disabled." Dr. U. testified that he told her he could not comply; although he was sympathetic to her many problems, he did not feel her disability met the disability criteria of the Social Security Administration.

The plaintiff's next witness was a urologist who was a professor from an out-of-state teaching hospital. His evidence focused on the diagnosis, the issue of urge versus stress incontinence, and his claim that a sacral rhizotomy was too extreme when more conservative modes of treatment had not been tried. In cross-examination, however, he was shown a letter bearing on the interpretation of the cystometrogram. He conceded that the letter had not been shown to him and that it might change his opinion somewhat. He continued to maintain the position, however, that Dr. U.'s diagnosis was open to question and that other treatment options should have been explored. The plaintiff also introduced a videotaped deposition by another highly qualified urologist that basically supported the opinion of the first plaintiff urologist.

Testimony by Mrs. F. followed. She was not highly articulate about her understanding of medical matters. She testified to her prior health problems and her presurgery frustration and embarrassment over her incontinence, which had become progressively worse. Mrs. F. also described her postsurgery problems (including the colostomy), her difficulties with the colostomy bag, and her need to visit a coleorectal surgeon every several months to have excess fecal material manually removed from her rectal area. She also acknowledged that she had been willing to undergo a surgical procedure that would require lifetime self-catheterization. However, she was absolutely adamant about one matter: "I would never, never have agreed to the operation if I had known that this horrible thing would happen. I would not have traded bladder for bowel control—under no condition." In response to a question from defense counsel, she first denied then admitted that she had some fecal incontinence prior to the surgery.

Mr. F. was also called as a witness. He testified about their marriage and sex life before and after the surgery. He was nervous and embarrassed, mumbled, and was noticeably relieved when his brief testimony was over.

The defense evidence consisted primarily of the testimony of two urologists, one of whom was employed at the same hospital as the neurosurgeon. The first returned to the cystometrogram again and, as the defendant urologist had testified earlier, systematically tutored the judge and jury in its interpretation and its implications for the diagnosis. Both defense experts offered the opinion that Mrs. F.'s treatment and the referral for a sacral rhizotomy fell within standards of professional practice.

No experts were called on the issue of damages. In final arguments, the plaintiff attorney suggested that an award in the range of $400,000 to $500,000 would appropriately compensate Mrs. F. for the injuries resulting from loss of bodily functions.

The jury returned after 55 minutes with a verdict in favor of the defendants.

The Jurors' Responses

Within the next two weeks, 7 of the 12 jurors were interviewed, either in their homes or over the telephone. All interviews lasted between 40 and 70 minutes. Four of these jurors had college degrees, including the foreperson who had a background in biology and had previously been employed as an autopsy technician.

The jurors overwhelmingly thought the plaintiff had been informed of the risks of the surgery but that she either did not understand the risks or ignored them. They believed that the defendants had considered all other forms of treatment and had settled on nerve surgery as a last resort. All thought that the plaintiff had failed to prove that the surgery was improperly performed. The plaintiff's lack of an expert neurosurgeon to prove this last issue was critical, and two jurors speculated that cost may have been a factor in explaining why the plaintiff did not have such an expert.

The jurors felt that they understood the difference between urge and stress incontinence and the ambiguity inherent in reading a cystometrogram. In fact, the foreperson and two other jurors demonstrated considerable sophistication about the medical issues during the interviews and ascribed this knowledge to the clear and repetitive tutoring of the trial witnesses. In the end, however, the stress versus urge incontinence dispute was viewed as inconsequential because, whatever its clinical reason, the incontinence was severe and the plaintiff had assumed the risks. The ambiguity in reading the cystometrogram favored the defendants because it made the diagnosis seem more reasonable.

Some jurors made reference to the "distance" from North Carolina of the plaintiff's experts, and one juror specifically stated that an outsider was not capable of testifying about how North Carolina doctors and the hospital should operate.[1]

In varying degrees of explicitness all of the jurors were critical of the plaintiff. Several observed that she did not file a lawsuit until after Dr. U. refused to certify her as disabled. They also saw her testimony as "coached" by her attorney. And three of the jurors said a turning point for them was the day that the plaintiff testified. Mrs. F.'s testimony was scheduled to begin after a 15-minute morning recess. She appeared in different clothes than she was wearing before the recess. About a half hour into her testimony her attorney asked why she was wearing different clothes. She said that an accident had occurred and, in response to a follow-up question, she testified that this incident exemplified her present condition. However, the jurors were very skeptical. As one juror stated: "She sat in that courtroom for four days without a problem and then just before she testifies. . . . Come on! We're not fools. The whole thing was faked."

In the end the deciding issue for the jurors was whether Mrs. F. was informed of the risks of the surgery. Her past medical history, her willingness to undertake a surgical procedure requiring self-catheterization, the defendant's evidence, and the records indicated that she had been informed. Furthermore, in the jurors' view, if she did not understand, it was not the doctors' fault. In the jury room, only a few jurors indicated they were "undecided," and after less than 30 minutes of discussion the vote was unanimous. The jurors remained in the jury room another 25 minutes "just for appearances and to have a cigarette."

Case 2: The Brain-Damaged Baby

Factual Background

In January 1986 Mrs. P., living in a small town, had a normal menstrual period and began taking oral contraceptives. However, in April she discovered she was pregnant, and in May visited Dr. H., a pediatrician who had delivered her previous two children. Based on the date of her last menstrual period and a physical exam, her delivery date was estimated to be November 3. In subsequent prenatal visits, the fundal height of her uterus, an indication of fetal size and gestation, was found to be 4 centimeters larger than expected. On October 8 during a routine visit she was estimated to be 36-weeks pregnant but a routine vaginal exam revealed her cervix to be dilated to 4 centimeters, which was more than normal for 36 weeks. The exam also revealed that her baby was in a "footling breach presentation," that is, bottom first and with feet extended toward the birth canal. A footling breach delivery has a high risk of umbilical cord compression resulting in deprivation of oxygen during delivery. Dr. H. informed Mrs. P. that if the baby did not turn it would have to be delivered by cesarean section at 40 weeks or whenever her membranes ruptured. He did not discuss the dangers to her or the baby in detail, he later testified, because of his concern that she would be unduly upset. Mrs. P. was sent home with instructions to call Dr. H. or go to the hospital emergency room if her membrane ruptured.

Mrs. P.'s membrane ruptured at 3:45 A.M. the next morning. Dr. H. was called, and Mrs. P. was rushed to the hospital, with Dr. H. arriving within an hour. A brief attempt to use an external fetal monitor was abandoned when no fetal pulse was detected. The baby was still in the footling breach position, and cervix dilation was 6 centimeters. A cesarean section was ordered; but in preparation for surgery Mrs. P. was not given oxygen or placed in the knee-chest position, treatments used to reduce and monitor fetal distress. The operation occurred 30 minutes after Dr. H.'s decision. The male baby was born blue and had low respiratory and heart rates but was revived by a pediatrician. Unfortunately, the child was born with severe, permanent brain damage as a result of hypoxia caused by compression of the umbilical cord. At birth, the child weighed nine and one-half pounds, and Dr. H.'s own reports listed him as a term infant, the product of a 40-week rather than 36-week pregnancy.

At two years of age medical evaluations revealed that the child was severely retarded and would never be able to use his arms or legs or be able to sit in a chair without support. He will never talk, will have limited ability to communicate by other means, and is blind and deaf. Furthermore, no doctor was willing to testify under oath that it was unlikely that he would have a life span shorter than 72 years; and thus the jury was told to assume he would live to that age.

The Legal Issues

The plaintiff claimed Dr. H. was negligent in four ways.

First, by relying primarily on her last menstrual period he failed to properly date her pregnancy. He did not take into account the unreliability of this dating technique when oral contraceptives are used, and he ignored the evidence in prenatal exams that consistently showed the fetus to be larger than expected.

Second, he should not have sent Mrs. P. home on October 9 given the dilation of her cervix since statistics indicate that over 90 percent of women in this condition deliver within 24 hours. In addition, footling breach babies are 20 times more likely than headfirst babies to have umbilical cord prolapse, which can compress the cord and shut off the blood supply to the fetus, resulting in oxygen deprivation.

Third, Dr. H. should have obtained informed consent before sending her home. She had the right to be told of the risks of not going immediately to the hospital.

Finally, Dr. H. failed to provide adequate care in the hospital. Mrs. P. alleged that Dr. H. knew the fetus was in distress but failed to adequately monitor it, to provide oxygen, to place Mrs. P. in the knee-chest position, or to manually decompress the cord by pushing it upward in the uterus.

The defendant asserted that the care Mrs. P. received was acceptable within the standard of care for an obstetrician practicing in that semi-rural community. He relied on her report of last menses and claimed that the standard of care did not require additional diagnostic tests such as ultrasound to reconcile the discrepancy with fundal height. He also argued that under the standard of care he was not required to admit her to the hospital on October 8 because some women have cervical dilation at 36 weeks. Further, it was unnecessary to inform Mrs. P. of the risks of returning home because it would unnecessarily worry her.

Finally, Dr. H. justified his treatment at the hospital on the grounds that he monitored fetal status by physical exam and proceeded to the C-section as quickly as possible. The alleged failure to administer oxygen was not addressed, but he claimed that he did know from the physical exam that the cord was pulsating and therefore that compression was not complete. He did not position Mrs. P. in the knee-chest position because she was being prepared for surgery and any change might exacerbate the cord compression, as might an attempt to manually reposition it.

The Trial

Both parties agreed to an abbreviated private two-day trial before an eight-person jury. Mrs. P. and her husband had an immediate need for money. Dr. H. and his insurer feared that if liability were found the damage award could far exceed coverage, and Dr. H. was very concerned about limiting media attention. The trial agreement stipulated that whatever the jury's verdict, the plaintiff would receive at least $300,000 and no more than $1.5 million. However, the defendant's trial strategy was based solely on liability, and the jurors were completely unaware of the high-low agreement during trial and in the weeks following their verdict.

The plaintiffs began their case by calling two obstetricians. These experts' testimony was addressed to the plaintiff's theories of negligence and supported the contention that Dr. H. was negligent with respect to each of the four claims. Next, the child's father testified about his son's disability. This was followed by a videotaped deposition of a psychiatrist who testified about the child's long-term health care needs and outlined a "Cadillac" plan for that treatment. Next, Mrs. P. testified about the events, about her son, and about her emotional distress. The final witness was an economist who calculated the costs of the health care plan for the child in Mrs. P.'s community ($5.3 million) plus estimates of lost wages ($2.7 million) for a total of $8 million in damages. Finally, the plaintiff's lawyer called Dr. H. as a witness. He gave the impression of being a very sincere person who argued that his services in all respects were within the standard of care, that he had rushed to the hospital, made a timely decision, and began the cesarean section as fast as humanly possible, and that he was heartbroken about the outcome even though it was not his fault.

The defense began its case by calling two obstetricians who maintained that the treatment was within the acceptable standards of care. The defense next called a neonatologist who presented evidence regarding the onset of seizures in the newborn infant. He offered an opinion that the seizures indicated that the hypoxic (oxygen deprivation) injury occurred approximately 12 hours before delivery, while Mrs. P. was asleep, and thus supported the defense contention that the injury was not caused during the delivery phase of birth. Three other physicians gave brief testimony to the effect that Dr. H. had followed accepted medical standards in treating his patient.

In rebuttal the plaintiff attorney called a pediatric neurologist who did not agree that the seizures following hypoxic injury always occur about 12 hours after the injury. He maintained that the injury was caused by umbilical cord compression during birth. The plaintiff attorney then recalled Mrs. P. and one of the obstetricians for clarifying testimony and read to the jury parts of the testimony of two of the defense experts.

Following final arguments and judicial instructions, the jury deliberated one hour and forty-five minutes and returned a verdict in favor of the plaintiff, with a damage award of $8 million.

The Jurors' Responses

The jurors were interviewed as a group immediately after their decision and individually by phone one week later. The interviews indicated that the female foreperson was chosen after a female teacher declined the job. The first vote on the causation of the child's injury was unanimous. The initial vote on whether Dr. H.'s treatment violated the standard of care was seven to one, but after some deliberation it became unanimous. The jurors were very apprehensive about awarding such a large sum for damages, but since the defense did not present evidence on the matter they eventually decided they had to rely on the only damage estimate they had been given; indeed, the judge instructed them to decide all issues only on the evidence at trial.[2]

In the posttrial interviews the jurors, particularly the women, believed that they had a good understanding of the issues. The mothers on the jury were quite familiar with the concepts of fundal height, dating from the last menstrual period, and cervical dilation. Most felt Dr. H. should have been suspicious of his dating. Two mentioned that ultrasound, which was used by their own or their daughters' doctors, was common and should have been used. Many felt that Dr. H. should have admitted Mrs. P. for observation on October 8, and some even believed he should have done a C-section at that time. None of the jurors expressed any fault with Dr. H. for the care provided at the time of delivery. He had done his best; the negligence occurred prior to her entry into the hospital. The jurors also felt Dr. H. violated the standard of care with respect to informed consent, but they held widely varying opinions on the importance of the issue. Some did not like deciding against the doctor on this issue, but they felt that the law was clear and that they had to follow it. With respect to the issue of whether the injury could have occurred 12 hours or more prior to delivery, as the defense contended, the jurors felt that the plaintiff's evidence was much stronger.

Finally, the jurors almost unanimously expressed great concern over the magnitude of the $8 million award, but felt they had no choice but to follow the judge's instructions and decide on the basis of the uncontested evidence of the plaintiff's expert. Several mentioned their concern over how the award would affect Dr. H. financially and its impact on his practice. All viewed him as a concerned and caring physician who, regrettably, had been negligent.

Case 3: Death from Ruptured Bowel

Factual Background

Mrs. T. had inoperable cancer that was treated with radiation and chemotherapy. She also had numerous other ailments such as asthma, bronchitis, and pain from chest surgery. As a primary consequence of the radiation and chemotherapy, the 65-year-old woman suffered constant and extremely severe pain from shingles, a viral infection of cutaneous nerves. After consultations at two other major hospitals around the country, she was referred to Dr. F., a neurosurgeon teaching at University Hospital, who would determine if she was a suitable candidate for experimental surgery—a rhizotomy—which is a severing of nerves that could alleviate the pain from the shingles.

Upon admission to the hospital Mrs. T.'s vital signs were all good, but she complained of constipation and requested the laxative that she had brought with her. (There was no later disagreement that the constipation preexisted the hospital admission and was a direct consequence of the many drugs she took for her problems.) When it did not work and she still complained of severe stomach cramps, a resident doctor ordered an enema, which was administered by a nurse, but Mrs. T. could not hold the liquid. At about 2:00 P.M. another doctor noted that she was in extreme pain. Shortly after, her stomach began to swell, X rays were taken, and she was rushed into exploratory surgery. The surgeons found large quantities of both impacted and loose fecal material in her abdominal cavity. She died of an acute peritoneal infection shortly thereafter.

The next morning Dr. F. expressed his sorrow to Mr. T., calling the death "a catastrophe." The body was returned home to be buried and the matter was ended until several months later when Mr. T. received the death certificate. It listed the cause of death as "accidental." Mr. T. contacted an attorney who obtained the autopsy report conducted by the hospital. That report described the cause of death as perforation of the sigmoid colon and rectum. A companion report by the medical examiner for North Carolina stated that Mrs. T. died from a puncture wound from an enema tip. A lawsuit for wrongful death was filed against the hospital and Dr. F., the neurosurgeon. The case went to trial in late July 1987.

The Legal Issues

The plaintiff's estate, through her husband and three children, asserted that negligence was the cause of Mrs. T.'s death on two grounds. First, the nurse who administered the enema, an employee of the hospital, was negligent and proximately caused the death. Second, regardless of how the death was caused, the hospital, through residency doctors and other employees, failed to provide reasonable care. The plaintiff further argued that the doctrine of *res ipsa loquitur* allowed the conclusion that if death was caused by the enema, negligence could be inferred. The neurosurgeon was also alleged to be negligent because, as the admitting physician, he had overall responsibility to ensure that the hospital provided care consistent with accepted standards. The surgeon who conducted the exploratory operation was initially named as a defendant but was dropped from the suit before trial.

The hospital argued that the conclusion of its own pathologist and that of the North Carolina medical examiner notwithstanding, Mrs. T.'s death was caused by a "rock hard" impacted fecal stool that perforated necrotic, or dead, tissue as a result of her straining attempts to void her bowels. The necrotic tissue resulted from her cancer and other illnesses and the medicine that was used to treat it.

The neurosurgeon supported the hospital's position. He asserted, however, that although he was listed as the admitting physician, Mrs. T. was in the care of other hospital personnel who were to examine her physical health before he could consider whether his own treatment was feasible. Furthermore, he claimed that he had checked on her condition through the reports of other hospital staff and that until the crisis resulting in her rush to surgery he was assured that there were no problems.

The Trial

The trial lasted 10 days and involved 22 witnesses. The first plaintiff witness was Mr. T., who described the events leading to his wife's death. In particular, he angrily charged that, as his wife's distress increased, he tried to get help but the hospital staff ignored his pleas. However, in cross-examination he conceded that in a pretrial deposition he had said that several doctors and nurses had attended his wife. The cross-examination also forced the reluctant admission that his wife's oncologist and a psychiatrist who had treated her for depression had estimated she had only a 4- to 8-month life expectancy at the time of her hospital admission.

The next witness was the hospital pathologist who signed the death certificate. She was a reluctant witness who gave the appearance of being under pressure to exonerate the defendants. But she was caught in the bind of thereby conceding that she had produced a sloppy and erroneous pathology report. Cross-examination documented a number of matters helpful to the defendants. The hospital pathologist was only a resident at the time and was relatively inexperienced in autopsies. She had based her conclusion of accidental death on the temporal relation between the enema and the death without reviewing slides or knowing about the extent of Mrs. T.'s pain before the enema was administered. The pathologist's testimony also produced a factual error that was critical to the issue of how the bowel rupture had occurred but was never corrected by either side. The bowel perforation was estimated to be 14 to 19 centimeters from the anus. The judge interrupted the examination to ask for a translation to inches, and the witness said about 10 or 11 inches rather than 7.5 inches, which is the correct conversion. The larger figure made it less likely that the enema caused the perforation.

The following witness was a nurse who, cross-examination

revealed, agreed to testify for the plaintiff before reading the records. She offered the professional opinion that hospital record keeping in Mrs. T.'s case was inadequate. She further attempted to demonstrate how an enema insertion could violate standards of nursing care.

The nurse was followed by the main plaintiff witness, a retired surgeon whose present sources of income were primarily from testifying as a plaintiff's expert witness. His lengthy examination and cross-examination resulted in often imprecise reasons for his conclusion that the tear in the bowel was due to a puncture by an enema tip.

The young physician who ordered the enema and was the attending physician during the crisis was called. Plaintiff attorneys effectively questioned him about missing notes relating to Mrs. T.'s treatment and left the impression that he might have destroyed them, particularly when they forced him to admit that he had told hospital staff on the day following Mrs. T.'s death that he anticipated a lawsuit.

The plaintiff also called two of Mrs. T.'s children who testified about their relationship with their mother. The plaintiffs also introduced video depositions of another doctor indicating that the medical records showed no evidence of dead bowel tissue.

The plaintiffs closed their case by calling the defendant neurosurgeon, Dr. F., in an attempt to prove that he was the admitting physician and therefore responsible for the treatment and subsequent injury of Mrs. T. However, he created the impression of being a physician who was just willing to try to ease the pain of a dying woman and who was only nominally in charge of her care prior to a determination that she was an appropriate patient for the experimental rhizotomy procedure.

On the seventh day of trial, before the defense began its case, the trial judge ordered a directed verdict in favor of the neurosurgeon. The jury was informed that as a matter of law Dr. F. was no longer a party to the suit.

On the same day, unknown to the jury, the defendant hospital offered the plaintiff $30,000 to settle, with an indication that the amount could be raised to $50,000. Its rationale for the offer was that the two autopsy reports, the first produced by their own doctor, seriously harmed their claim of no negligence. The trial judge was involved in the discussions and pushed hard for a settlement. The plaintiff would not consider less than $100,000, and the trial proceeded.

The defendants called the nurses and physicians who were associated with Mrs. T.'s care. The thrust of their testimony contradicted Mr. T.'s claim that they had ignored his pleas that his wife was in distress. In addition, the surgeon who conducted the exploratory surgery asserted that other portions of Mrs. T.'s bowel tissue were not live.

The defense also called an independent expert, who testified that an enema tube could not have gotten by the fecal impaction to cause the perforation. A surgeon who reviewed the records and was a very important witness concluded that it was likely that Mrs. T. had other dead bowel tissue and that the hospital pathologist had jumped to a wrong conclusion based on inadequate examination and missing information. Mrs. T.'s oncologist testified by videotape that Mrs. T.'s condition was terminal, that the cancer could have spread to her bowel region, and that the various cancer treatments could also have affected the viability of the bowel.

At the conclusion of the defense case, the plaintiff called another expert, a certified pathologist, who reviewed the records and concluded that the shape of the tear indicated an enema tip was a possible cause. However, in cross-examination he conceded that colon perforation by impacted fecal stool was not an unusual occurrence.

In final arguments the plaintiff's attorney suggested to the jury that a verdict of $750,000 was a reasonable amount for Mrs. T.'s pain and suffering, medical and funeral expenses, and the loss of companionship by Mrs. T.'s husband and children.

After instructions, the judge sent the jury out to deliberate at 2:55 P.M. At 4:30 P.M. they returned a verdict in favor of the defendant.

The Jurors' Responses

Four of the twelve jurors were interviewed in person or by telephone after the trial. The essence of their view was that the plaintiff had not carried the burden of proof. They viewed the primary plaintiff experts, the nurse and the out-of-state surgeon, as "hired guns." Mr. T. and his son were viewed as disingenuous in their testimony and ungrateful. As one juror said, "Dr. F. and the hospital were trying to help a dying woman and did the best they could; there should never have been a lawsuit." The jurors, in response to interview questions, were able to articulate the alternative theory that Mrs. T. died from natural causes rather than an enema wound. They viewed the hospital pathologist as inexperienced and her report as poorly conceived.

Postscript

The jury verdict and the directed verdict were appealed and a new trial that included Dr. F., as well as University Hospital, was ordered. A first retrial in early 1992 ended in a mistrial, after which the hospital offered a settlement. A new trial against only the neurosurgeon began shortly thereafter. The jury deliberated 30 minutes and returned a verdict for the defendant.

Trial Complexity

These three cases are reasonably representative of issues that jurors face in many malpractice trials. Were these issues beyond the intellectual scope of laypersons? I would argue that they were not beyond the intellectual competence of the group ability of 12 jurors. The incontinence case was the most technically complex, but the attorneys and the witnesses taught the laypersons enough about the medical details to enable them to form a reasonable opinion that the diagnosis of incontinence is a difficult enterprise in which doctors may have different opinions. The jurors resolved that ambiguity in the defendant's favor. Moreover, in the end the case really turned on a judgment that the plaintiff was adequately informed of the risks of the operation. She certainly understood that one consequence would be a dysfunctional bladder that required self-catheterization and carried a high risk of recurring infections. Perhaps better plaintiff evidence could have shown that the neurosurgeon did not conduct sufficient testing through caudal blocks or otherwise improperly conducted the surgery. But that evidence was missing, and the jury correctly decided that the burden of proof was not carried. The other two cases, although not without ambiguity or medical detail, were not beyond the scope of the combined judgment of 12 laypersons to understand.

In all three cases, the interviews showed that most jurors had a clear understanding of the adversary process and evaluated witnesses accordingly. Jurors expressed sympathy for both plaintiffs' and defendants' plights; but, if anything, there was a tendency to more closely scrutinize the motivations of plaintiffs and to have more sympathy for the defendants. In the case where the pediatrician was found negligent, the jurors decided the case according to the law that they were given despite their sympathy for the defendant. Although jurors in all three trials expressed frustration over the arcane and prolix instructions they received from the judge, on the whole they understood the concepts of negligence and the standard of care.

Now a question will arise about the extent to which the three cases are typical or atypical of the general run of malpractice cases. I do not have systematic data on this issue and in any event there is plenty of room to argue both about the complexity of these cases and whether the jurors truly understood the issues. Nevertheless, it is instructive to turn back to table 3.1 in chapter 3 and consider some of the 21 cases in which North Carolina juries decided that negligence had occurred. In case 110511, following surgery on the patient's spine, silver nitrate was placed on the wound, causing second-degree burns and scars. In case 125516 a feeding tube was inserted into the patient's lung rather than her stomach, resulting in a partial lung removal; after the patient relapsed, a feeding tube was improperly inserted into the other lung. Case 133752 involved two improper insertions of an intubation tube into the patient's esophagus. In case 155501 the surgeon performed an unauthorized tubal ligation, and in case 159529 a patient was administered 10 times the required chemotherapy dosage. In case 197-708 the physician ignored medical records of Hodgkin's disease and prescribed medicine that was contraindicated for Hodgkin's disease. In case 3-00-810 a patient was given the drug Dilantin over his protests that he was allergic to it. High-risk specialists failed to make a timely appearance in case 3-25-703, resulting in a baby born with severe brain damage. A drug overdose was prescribed in case 3-25-924, resulting in a patient with permanent paralysis and brain damage. In case 3-33-702 surgery was performed on the wrong foot of a child. Many similar examples can be taken from the remaining 80 percent of cases that North Carolina juries decided in favor of defendants.

My own conclusion from the research described in this chapter is that a prima facie argument can be made that there is nothing so extraordinary in many of the cases that most or all of a group of 12 laypersons could not understand them. In some the issue of negligence, or its absence, is pretty straightforward. In others, the primary issue revolves around the credibility of patients versus doctors about what occurred and when. In still others, good lawyers and experts appear capable of educating laypersons about complex matters. I will discuss this matter further in chapter 14 after presenting some systematic empirical data but will first consider some case studies in chapter 13 in which the evidence was complex and confusing.

13

Complicated Trials:
Some Case Studies

Some malpractice cases are more complicated than those described in chapter 12. This chapter discusses cases that I would classify as complicated trials. They each involved highly technical medical issues or procedural complications and resulted in substantial jury disagreement.

Permanent Blindness

Factual Background

In early April 1988, Ms. C., a 26-year-old unmarried mother of a small child, went to the office of a general practitioner complaining of acute mental confusion and headaches. She was referred to Dr. N., a neurologist practicing in a nearby county, who admitted her to the hospital and conducted tests. She was discharged two days later with prescribed painkillers. The notation in her medical record stated that the mental confusion and headaches were improving. When her symptoms persisted she returned to Dr. N. two days later. He conducted a second EEG (electroencephalogram) and sent her home. The next day she reported to the emergency room at her local hospital complaining of distress and "head swelling." Dr. N. was called at home and prescribed strong painkilling medicine. Ms. C. was discharged, but she returned to the emergency room several more times that day for more painkilling injections. The next day she was admitted once again to the local hospital with headaches of unknown origin and put in the intensive care ward. She was released after two days.

Six days later her general physician again referred her to Dr. N. who admitted her to the hospital a third time. The next day, after a spinal tap, she was diagnosed as suffering from herpes encephalitis and treated with Zovirax, a medicine used to control herpes. The next day she was transferred to the intensive care unit because her left pupil was dilated and vision was declining rapidly in both eyes. The following day doctors in the hospital detected severe intracranial pressure, but Dr. N. continued to treat her for viral encephalitis. The patient was having visual hallucinations and her pupils were reactive.

The next day Ms. C. was again transferred to intensive care. A CT (computerized tomography) scan was conducted by Dr. W., a radiologist. Signs of a thrombosis, a blood clot, in the sagittal sinus in the back of the head were present but not reported to Dr. N. Several days later another CT scan showed a clear blood clot, a hemorrhagic infarct, rather than encephalitis. Ms. C. could not see light; the blindness persisted, and six days later the thrombosis was noted. After several additional weeks, when Ms. C. was transferred to another hospital for rehabilitation, the admitting opthamologist stated that the likely cause of the blindness was nerve damage from sustained and markedly elevated intracranial pressure.

Many months later Dr. N. completed a disability form for Ms. C., who is completely blind and has no sense of smell. She also has brain damage that impairs her gait and renders her dependent on a cane for walking. He listed herpes encephalitis as the primary cause of her condition.

In 1991 Ms. C. filed suit against Dr. N. and Dr. W., the radiologist. Her son, now living permanently with Ms. C.'s sister, was also a plaintiff, alleging severe mental stress as a result of the loss of his mother, who he now sees only on weekly visits.

The Legal Issues

The plaintiffs' claim revolved around the theory that Ms. C. had suffered from an undiagnosed sagittal sinus thrombosis, a blood clot in the back of her head, which had allowed pressure to build and damage the optic nerve. The defense theory was that Ms. C. suffered from a viral infection, herpes encephalitis, that was treated properly but unfortunately could not be controlled in time to save her vision; however, the efforts of the medical team did save her life.

The plaintiffs charged that Dr. N. improperly discharged her from the hospital; that he subsequently failed to readmit her at appropriate times; and that he failed to test, diagnose, monitor, consult with other physicians, properly interpret CT scans, order an MRI (magnetic resonance image) or arteriogram, or transfer her to another physician. Further, he failed to use his best judgment and reasonable care.

Dr. W., the radiologist, was charged with negligence in reading, interpreting, reporting, and informing Ms. C.'s other health care providers of the result of the CT scan. As with Dr. N., the claim also stated that Dr. W. failed to use his best judgment and to exercise reasonable care.

The Trial

The trial revolved around a classic battle of experts. The plaintiff called five experts; four were from leading medical schools outside North Carolina. Three were neurologists, one was an opthamologist, and another was a radiologist. The two defendants together had nine experts, all from North Carolina, including neurologists, neuro-radiologists, and radiologists. Three practiced in the same clinic as Dr. N. The plaintiff's pretrial motion to prohibit defense counsel from inquiring into Ms. C.'s past history of illicit drug use was granted. The trial lasted two and one-half weeks.

The plaintiff opened the trial by calling Dr. N. as an adverse witness. Dr. N. had received his original training and had practiced in the Philippines before moving to North Carolina. He testified that his original diagnosis was "muscular headaches," and he treated her on that basis. He conducted a spinal tap on the patient in his first examination that yielded a reading of 210 pressure. Although texts indicate that normal readings are between 180 and 200, Dr. N. testified that 210 was not unusual. He believed that Ms. C. subsequently developed viral encephalitis, which is not treatable; but he treated her for herpes encephalitis, which is treatable, as a precaution, even though he did not know if this was the cause of her problem. He conceded that in her second visit she was vomiting. Dr. N. gave the opinion that sagittal sinus thrombosis, which is rare, developed later, probably as a complication resulting from the encephalitis.

Dr. N.'s records showed no indication of an eye examination in any of Ms. C.'s three visits. In fact, the only record of an eye exam was one conducted by a resident physician after her third admission to the hospital; it indicated florid papilledema, pressure on the optic nerve. The notes of Dr. N.'s nurse indicated that Ms. C. had spots before her eyes and had them closed. In the end, however, Dr. N. could not substantiate whether he had conducted an eye examination and also stated that in his recollection Ms. C. did not complain about problems with her vision during any of the first two visits.

All three of the plaintiff's neurologist experts were, in the later evaluation of the jury foreperson, outstanding witnesses who systematically "taught" the jury about sagittal sinus thrombosis, its implications, and its treatment. These experts testified over many days, but their testimony will be only briefly summarized here. The first expert said that in his opinion all the plaintiff ever had, beginning with the first visit to Dr. N., was sagittal sinus thrombosis. In this condition the blood clot prevents cranial fluids from draining, and the resulting buildup of fluids can sometimes force the brain into the sinus cavity, a brain herniation. In Ms. C.'s case, the fluid put pressure on the optic nerve, which, as a consequence, atrophied and died. This expert and all subsequent experts indicated that the neurologist should always conduct an eye examination in which signs of intracranial pressure can be detected and which can be followed up by other tests. Regardless of the cause of the fluid buildup, steps must be taken to drain the fluid and relieve the pressure.

The second neurologist testified that the diagnosis was not the primary problem but rather that it was the failure of Dr. N. to treat the increased intracranial pressure. In this expert's view, there were multiple signs of pressure: head pain, vision problems, nausea, vomiting, and the spinal tap reading of 210. The 210 reading is significant in the context of other symptoms since a single reading can be ±50 points; hence, it could have been as high as 260.

The testimony against Dr. W., the radiologist, was that he should have diagnosed Ms. C.'s problems from the CT scan. Further, he should have conveyed the diagnosis to Dr. N. and other hospital staff.

While the plaintiffs' experts stated their opinion that Ms. C.'s brain was never forced into the sagittal sinus, defense experts offered the opinion that it was and that her life was saved as a result of the treatment she eventually received. The defense experts, supporting the view of Dr. N., argued that the thrombosis developed much later in the course of the illness, probably close to Ms. C.'s third admission to the hospital. One of the defense experts, an opthamologist from a local teaching hospital, had originally agreed to testify as the plaintiff's expert but reversed himself and testified for the defendants. His evidence was that no intracranial pressure was evident from the spinal tap. Under cross-examination he said that he changed his opinion because of the 210 reading from the spinal tap; he was evasive on the possibility that the reading could have been as high as 260 due to the unreliability of the test.

One claim of the plaintiff, based on the testimony of her own experts, was that other tests, including an additional spinal tap, should have been considered. The defense experts testified that due to Ms. C.'s condition at the later stages of her illness a second spinal tap could have been extremely dangerous. The tap would have reduced fluid in the spinal canal and could have aggravated the thrombosis as the cranial fluid attempted to flow to an area of lesser density, thus causing or aggravating a brain herniation. Cross-examination brought out the fact that some procedures that defense experts claimed were not available in 1988 might in fact have been in use in their own hospital at that time.

The plaintiff called rebuttal evidence with regard to some of the defense testimony. However, in the process the plaintiffs' lawyer appeared, to the jury, to admit that Ms. C. might have had a hemorrhagic infarct, or blood clot, a fact that had not been admitted previously.

No expert evidence was called on behalf of Ms. C.'s son although his aunt, with whom he is now living, testified that he was confused about his maternal relationship and, at times, exhibited stress. The plaintiffs' attorney called no expert evidence on the matter of damages. In closing arguments he spent only a brief time addressing factors to consider and suggested that the jury should come up with its own figures for the impact of the injury and blindness on Ms. C.'s life and its impact on her son. But he did indicate that an award of $5 million or more was reasonable.

The jury deliberations extended over four days. Dr. N. was found negligent, and Dr. W. was found not liable. The jury awarded $2.4 million to Ms. C. Her son received no award.

How the Jury Reached Its Decision

The 12-person jury contained a number of persons with advanced degrees. The person chosen as jury foreperson was a practicing attorney. Other members were a nurse, a person with a Ph.D. in biology, a person with a Ph.D. who worked in a computer lab, a manager at IBM, and two persons who owned small businesses. My understanding of the jurors' reactions to the trial and their deliberation processes is derived from two lengthy interviews with the jury foreperson.

From the very beginning the jury was split on every issue, with some jurors strongly favoring the plaintiffs and others as strongly favoring the defendants. Debate was vigorous among nine of the jurors; but three, who had hardly talked to the other jurors during the trial, said almost nothing during deliberations. At several points during the discussions the jury appeared to be at an impasse to the point that the foreperson was prepared to tell the judge they were a hung jury. The jurors had been allowed to take notes and several did, including the foreperson. Although the judge had admonished the jurors several times that they must not give undue deference to the notes or the opinions of the note takers, the notes ultimately proved crucial in persuading the leader of the pro-defendant faction that she was wrong on a crucial point about some actions taken by Dr. N.

In the end the jury was left with three impressions that weighed heavily against Dr. N.: (a) neurologists should always do an eye examination; (b) the only eye examination of which there was evidence was performed on the third visit, and it was conducted by a hospital resident; and (c) Dr. N.'s testimony that the patient did not complain of vision problems was contradicted by his nurse's notes.

The jury viewed the plaintiff's experts as outstanding. These experts educated the jury in a calm and convincing manner. However, even with this effort, the foreperson did not believe that either side's lawyers simplified the issues enough for the jury to easily digest. The jurors were less impressed by the defense experts, particularly those who were partners of Dr. N. Their testimony was considered to be highly biased. These and the other defense experts tended to be less clear than the plaintiff experts; and some phrased their answers in very particular and technical ways that caused the jurors to disbelieve their testimony. It was viewed as convoluted, compared to the straightforward explanations of the plaintiff experts. The expert who had switched from the plaintiff to the defense severely hurt the defendant's case. The jurors detected a bias resulting from friendship between the expert and the defense counsel, creating the impression that they had worked together in prior cases. During cross-examination this doctor appeared to the jurors to be "hostile," "sarcastic," and "immature."

Further, his explanation that he had switched sides on reconsideration of the spinal tap reading was unconvincing since the other experts on both sides unanimously agreed that the reading was not conclusive proof that elevated intracranial pressure was absent. Worse, in almost the next sentence this expert stated that he would probably have performed surgery to relieve the fluid pressure based on such a reading. The jurors concluded that his testimony indicated that, at the very least, Dr. N. should have consulted with other physicians upon receiving the spinal tap results.

Some jurors continued to believe that Dr. W., the radiologist, should also be held liable. However, other jurors who felt Dr. W. might also have been negligent also felt that the plaintiff had not proved it.

Even months after the trial, the foreperson remained convinced that the decision of liability could easily have gone in Dr. N.'s favor. A single different juror or the absence of the juror notes could, at the least, have resulted in a hung jury. A few additional opinions and observations are critical to understanding the jury's verdict. The jury, in the foreperson's opinion, ignored much of what they were instructed to do. They relied heavily on the notes taken by a few jurors to resolve disagreements. They did not apply terms like "burden of proof," instead opting to decide on the basis of general impressions. Some of the medical records taken into the jury room had been blacked out with a magic marker to prevent consideration of inadmissible evidence, but the jurors held the records to the light to read them. The jurors also speculated about liability insurance and argued on the basis of their own experiences with doctors and hospitals.

I will discuss the jury's deliberations on damages in chapter 20, but two facts are germane to assessing the verdict. First, the jury felt considerable empathy for the coplaintiff, Ms. C.'s son, but felt that a monetary award was inappropriate. Second, after much heated discussion and compromise they arrived at an award of $2,400,000.

Death in the CT Scan Room

Factual Background

In 1988 after an argument with his wife, Mr. H. was involved in a serious motorcycle accident. He was rushed to University Hospital;

Mr. H. was legally intoxicated, with a blood alcohol content of 0.19. His liver was severely lacerated, and two consecutive surgeries were performed to stop internal bleeding. Mr. H. spent several days in the intensive care unit and then was transferred to another floor in the hospital after his condition had stabilized.

Because his doctors suspected an abdominal abscess, a CT scan was ordered. Mr. H. was taken to the CT scan room; his condition was stable, but he was pale and had a fever. As part of the CT scan procedure, barium and contrast dye were ordered so that Mr. H.'s organs would appear clearly on the scan. Mr. H. had taken barium orally earlier that morning; and upon his arrival at the CT scan room, defendant Nurse L. injected Mr. H. with a test dose of contrast dye. When Nurse L. detected no adverse reactions, she administered a full dose of contrast dye.

Nurse L. then put Mr. H. into the CT scan and went into the control room. A large window and mirrors allowed Nurse L. to observe Mr. H. A few seconds after the CT scan began, Nurse L. noticed that Mr. H. had begun to twitch. At 1:00 P.M., she ran into the scan room and checked his vital signs. Realizing that Mr. H. was not breathing, Nurse L. promptly called an emergency code.

Shortly thereafter, defendants Dr. M. and Dr. S. arrived. Mr. H. began vomiting a green liquid, but he remained unconscious. Nurse L. and Drs. M. and S. turned Mr. H. onto his side to prevent aspiration, the sucking of vomit into the windpipe, and continued efforts to revive him. Some minutes later, the hospital's code team arrived. Despite the code team's efforts, Mr. H. died at 1:45 P.M.

As administratrix of Mr. H.'s estate, Mr. H.'s widow brought an action for wrongful death against Dr. S. She also brought an action for severe emotional distress against Nurse L. and Drs. M. and S. The members of the code team were initially included in the latter action but were voluntarily dismissed as defendants during trial.

The Legal Issues

The legal issues of the case were as follows: (1) was Nurse L. properly supervised when she administered the contrast dye? (2) was Mr. H. ventilated properly, that is, was the vomit suctioned from his mouth, was a proper seal obtained with the oxygen mask, and was the airway unobstructed so that the oxygen could reach his lungs? (3) was epinephrine indicated as a treatment at that time for an allergic reaction to the contrast dye? (4) did Drs. M. and S. arrive in a timely manner? (5) what was (were) the cause(s) of Mr. H.'s death? (6) was Dr. S. negligent in administering basic life-support treatment until the code team arrived, and, if so, did Dr. S.'s negligence cause the wrongful death of Mr. H.? and (7) were Nurse L., Dr. M., and/or Dr. S. negligent, and, if so, did their negligence cause Mrs. H. to suffer severe emotional distress?

Procedural Complications

A number of procedural events complicated the legal issues of the case. First, the plaintiff attorney filed a motion to compel discovery on the grounds that the defense was stalling by withholding information and documents. The trial judge granted the motion. Although the defense may not have intentionally delayed discovery, the statute of limitations for the wrongful death claim had expired against all but one of the medical professionals involved. Therefore, Dr. S. was the sole defendant in this action. The only way to sue the other defendants was to bring an emotional distress action against them. Due to North Carolina law, these reasons for bringing two causes of action were never explained to the jury. Second, further complicating matters, the attorneys failed to clearly delineate these causes of action and argued both actions as one case.

A third procedural maneuver, which confused the jury, involved the number of defendants. Initially, members of the code team, as well as Nurse L. and Drs. M. and S., were joined as defendants in the emotional distress action. However, the plaintiffs voluntarily dismissed the code team members from the suit during the middle of the trial. The plaintiff attorney revealed the reason for these dismissals in a posttrial interview: the code team members were joined as defendants only to ensure their presence and testimony in the courtroom. Thus, joining and dismissing these defendants were solely strategic maneuvers, planned by the plaintiff attorney to obtain trial evidence. However, the jurors, unaware of the plaintiff attorneys' strategy, were confused by these unexpected dismissals.

Adding complexity to the jury's truth-finding task, five years had passed between Mr. H.'s death and the trial. At trial many of the witnesses involved in the incident claimed that they could not remember relevant details, such as the exact time that each event occurred and the precise sequence of events. To make matters worse, some of the documentation was missing. Also, many defense witnesses' testimony differed from their depositions, which were taken one year after the incident.

The Trial

The plaintiffs began their case by calling three physicians who testified about the cause of Mr. H.'s death and the likelihood of medical negligence. Each testified that the cause of death was either an allergic reaction to the contrast dye, blockage of the airway by aspiration, the sucking of vomit into the windpipe, or a combination of both. Each expert also stated that, in his opinion, the physicians could have prevented Mr. H.'s death. The experts testified to the following: that Mr. H. had not sustained life-threatening injuries in the motorcycle accident, that Dr. S. did not properly supervise Nurse L., that it was likely that Nurse L. did not ventilate Mr. H. sufficiently, that administering epinephrine would have effectively treated Mr. H.'s allergic reaction, and that ample time had passed between the calling of the code and the arrival of the code team such that Drs. M. and S. should have done more than merely aid in ventilation and take Mr. H.'s pulse.

Mr. H.'s widow and Mr. H.'s parents also testified. The thrust of their testimony was that Mr. H. was not an alcoholic, that his marriage with Mrs. H. and his relationship with his parents were strong, and that Mrs. H. suffered severe emotional trauma as a result of Mr. H.'s death. Two psychologist experts corroborated this last claim. Finally, Mr. H.'s job supervisor and an economist testified regarding, respectively, Mr. H.'s work ethic and the present value of his future earnings.

The defense called the three defendants, Nurse L. and Drs. M. and S., to the stand. In addition, six of the other health care professionals involved in the code alert in the CT room testified. Finally, four medical experts who were not involved in the incident and who had no affiliation with the hospital testified. In all, the defense called 13 medical professionals to testify, while the plaintiff called three.

The defense witnesses argued that a combination of factors caused Mr. H.'s death, including his weakened condition from his internal injuries, an unpreventable and untreatable allergic reaction to the contrast dye, unpreventable aspiration and respiratory arrest, and possible abdominal inflammation. Furthermore, they testified that epinephrine was not required at the time at issue, given the symptoms that were present. They further testified that Dr. S. properly supervised Nurse L. and that Nurse L. effectively ventilated Mr. H. Lastly, they testified that only five minutes had passed between the time the code was called and the time the code team arrived; thus, the defendants only had time to maintain the airway and take Mr. H.'s pulse.

In cross-examination, the defense attorneys pointed out several other factors in Mrs. H.'s life that were possible alternative explanations for her emotional distress, such as her alcoholism, Mr. H.'s alcoholism, childhood family problems, a history of prior abuse by another man, and marital problems with Mr. H. Thus, the defense claimed that, though traumatic, Mr. H.'s death did not cause Mrs. H.'s severe emotional distress. Finally, Mr. H.'s alcoholism and injuries were emphasized to suggest that he may not have been able to earn the salary that the plaintiffs' economic expert projected.

The Jury Decision

The jury returned a verdict of no negligence on the part of Dr. S. regarding the wrongful death claim. However, it could not unanimously agree on the emotional distress claim. A mistrial was declared when a single juror would not agree with the other 11 that the defendants should be held liable.

When the jurors were interviewed by telephone, they gave widely differing reasons for their decisions. They explained that Dr. S. was not found negligent because the wording of the wrongful death claim ("the cause") on the verdict sheet was much stronger than that of the emotional distress claim ("a proximate cause"). One juror stated that Dr. S. was not "the cause" of Mr. H.'s death; nobody really knew what caused Mr. H.'s death. However, some jurors believed that Dr. S.'s negligence *was* a cause of Mr. H.'s death. Another juror thought that, though Dr. S. may have been partially responsible, it was unfair to hold him negligent as the sole defendant.

Regarding the negligence of the three defendants in the emotional distress claim, the jurors again held divergent views. Some jurors believed that approximately 10 minutes had elapsed between the calling of the code and the arrival of the code team and that Dr. S. should have done more than he did to save Mr. H.'s life. Other jurors thought that only five minutes had passed before the code team arrived and that Dr. S. had acted responsibly. Still others indicated that Dr. S. should have known that Nurse L. had given Mr. H. contrast dye and that Dr. S. should have supervised her more closely. One juror even described Dr. S. as "a bit shifty." The 11 jurors who favored finding the doctors liable on this issue said that they resolved their doubts around the connotations of the charge. They decided that "emotional distress" did not seem as harsh as a verdict stating "wrongful death." However, their ambivalence on even this issue was expressed in their reluctance to pressure the one holdout juror into unanimity, and they informed the judge they could not reach agreement.

In contrast to the range of opinions expressed about Dr. S.'s negligence, most jurors concluded that Dr. M. was not negligent for the following reasons: hospital policy did not require his presence in the CT scan room when Nurse L. administered the contrast dye, Dr. S. was the direct supervisor of the CT scan procedure, and Dr. M. seemed intelligent and sincere when testifying. Impressions of Nurse L.'s negligence were also fairly consistent among the jurors. Some jurors stated that Nurse L. did all that she could under the circumstances and that she appeared "earnest." Further, some jurors thought that Dr. S., as Nurse L.'s supervisor, was ultimately responsible; thus, Nurse L. was not negligent.

The jurors could not come to a consensus on the major issues of the case: ventilation, physician supervision, and the appropriateness of administering epinephrine. Regarding ventilation, some jurors believed Mr. H. was not ventilated effectively; others thought either that Mr. H. was properly ventilated or that Nurse L. "did all she could." The jurors were also split on the issue of physician supervision. Some jurors felt that Dr. S. adequately supervised the procedure, while other jurors disagreed. Still others believed that supervision was not adequate but that this was not a cause of Mr. H.'s death. The third issue, concerning epinephrine, remained cloudy and confusing to many jurors, as the plaintiff experts contradicted the defense experts. However, some jurors were convinced that epinephrine was not indicated given the specific situation.

The jurors also expressed various opinions about the effectiveness of the expert testimony. One juror stated that he did not remember any of the many experts in particular. In contrast, another juror remembered each expert explicitly and commented extensively on the knowledge and persuasiveness of each. Finally, some jurors believed that there were too many experts and, as the jurors were not allowed to take notes during trial, they had trouble recalling each expert and his opinion.

Conclusion: What the Case Studies Tell Us

The two case studies just presented as well as the three in the preceding chapter are open to alternative interpretations. Some might argue that the classification scheme is wrong, that one or more of the cases reported in chapter 12 were as technically complicated as the permanent blindness case. It might be argued that the blindness case also hinged primarily on the credibility issues that were central in determining liability. These alternative views can be entertained because almost every medical malpractice case has technical elements of medicine that must be judged by the prevailing standards of care as well as some issues of witness credibility involving the plaintiff, the defendants, and the experts. What I would strongly defend is my argument that malpractice cases do not hinge solely on technical matters that are beyond the scope and comprehension of laypersons.

Further, the case studies help make the point that we must seriously question the claim that plaintiffs always use "hired gun" experts who will testify to anything for a fee and that jurors will uncritically accept their testimony. The main plaintiff expert in the ruptured bowel case, in my opinion, could be classified as a "hired gun"; but I would not so classify the experts in any of the other cases. To be sure, there were some other problems with plaintiff experts. Some testified on the basis of incomplete information. The expert in the urinary incontinence case, for example, offered an opinion that seemed less credible when a defense attorney, in cross-examination, uncovered the fact that the opinion was formed without some crucial information. Whether the information had been inadvertently withheld or was an intentional ploy on the part of the plaintiff attorney, one can argue that the expert should have asked for this information before agreeing to testify in court. Expert witnesses do occasionally get caught up in the adversary process and go out on a limb. However, the case studies also suggest that often the limb also gets sawed off in cross-examination. The interviews with jurors, moreover, suggest that they were far from unperceptive and uncritical of the weaknesses of experts and their testimony.

The case studies also show the other side of the coin, namely, that defendants and their experts occasionally show some disingenuousness. In all five of the cases reported in these two chapters, the jurors were quite sensitive to the possibility that defense experts might be bending the facts to put the actions of the defendants— their colleagues—in the most favorable light.

These reactions of jurors to experts in the North Carolina malpractice cases are consistent with those found by Professor Valerie Hans and her student Sanja Ivkovich.[1] As one part of a larger study of Delaware jurors who decided cases involving business, corporate, and medical malpractice defendants, they conducted an in-depth study involving interviews with 55 jurors. Fully 76 percent of the experts in this subsample of cases were medical doctors. Hans and Ivkovich found that the jurors were concerned about the experts' credentials and motives for testifying and were particularly harsh in their judgments of experts whose testimony was unclear. It should be of no surprise that jurors admitted having more problems with testimony that was technically complex, but the majority of them tried to critically evaluate the content of the testimony and looked for points that seemed illogical or mistaken. Hans and Ivkovich drew the following conclusion:

> the claims that jurors either ignore or accept uncritically expert testimony seem farfetched. We observed a good deal of critical assessments of experts, their credentials, and their motives for testifying. Jurors do not appear to be as naive as some commentators have assumed about the financial and other motivations that may lead some experts to become "hired guns." Furthermore, when jurors are faced with the difficult task of evaluating evidence that is outside their common knowledge, they rely on sensible techniques: assessing the completeness and consistency of the testimony and evaluating it against their knowledge of related factors. For especially complex topics, the jury relies on its members who possess greater familiarity with the subject matter of the expert testimony.[2]

The CT scan room death case study captured another dimension that complicates some jury trials, specifically those involving multiple defendants and interrelated causes of injury, namely, procedural maneuvers that complicate the jury's task. One additional case, presented briefly, will highlight the issue of apportionment of blame among multiple defendants.

Mrs. B., 28 years old, was in labor. There were signs of fetal distress, so a cesarean section was performed. The child was born normal, but Mrs. B.'s uterus was accidentally lacerated during the surgery. The laceration was repaired, and Mrs. B. was sent home with antibiotics. She was readmitted to the hospital a week later with pus draining from her abdominal incision. Several days later there was evidence of abscesses in her pelvis and ovaries. In another two days she was diagnosed as suffering from peritonitis and, due to the infection, her bowels stopped functioning. Her treatment by a team of physicians included a gastroenterologist and, while the gastroenterologist was away on vacation, his partner. The gastroenterologists were in charge of nutrition. Unfortunately, the prescribed intravenous fluids were severely deficient in vitamins and calories so that for almost six weeks, Mrs. B., already critically ill, was subsisting on the equivalent of a starvation diet.

Mrs. B. eventually recovered from the infection but suffers from permanent brain damage. Her speech is slurred and her hearing and vision are impaired. She has ataxia, or brain damage, that severely affects her balance and restricts many activities. She also has impaired memory and is prone to be distracted from even simple tasks.

The legal problem of the case involved the apportionment of causation and negligence, not negligence itself. There were allegations of negligence in the surgery, in the subsequent diagnosis and treatment of the infection, and in the medical care provided by the gastroenterologists. As a result, there were disputes about the cause of Mrs. B.'s brain damage. Two of the treating physicians settled with the plaintiff. One physician, it was alleged, altered medical records, prompting the plaintiff to file a separate suit requesting not only compensatory but also punitive damages. The suit against the two gastroenterologists involved a summary jury trial over the amount of damages they should pay but the defense argued its case partly around the issue of liability.[3]

The jurors who heard the case against the gastroenterologist were prevented from hearing evidence about the actions of the other defendants. In posttrial interviews they expressed considerable confusion about why the other doctors were not on trial and about the issue of causality of Mrs. B.'s injury. This brief case history helps to illustrate two points. First, even if there had been a single trial involving all defendants, causality, and therefore the liability of individual defendants, was very complex. Second, the procedural severing of defendants by itself can complicate the presentation of evidence and the jury's task, even if the technical medical issues are not complex.

Assuming we can categorize cases according to their complexity or noncomplexity, the case studies presented in these chapters do not provide any indication of what percentage of each is represented in jury trial cases. Once again, however, the studies do show the evidential and legal diversity of medical negligence trials, and they produce a profile of how the juries responded to specific issues.

Finally, the case studies provide no standards against which the correctness of the verdicts may be judged, except for the opinion of each reader. My own opinion is that the juries in *Melis*, the three cases in chapter 12, and the blindness case in this chapter made reasonable, defensible decisions. I am not comfortable with the CT scan trial decision because the jury appears to have compromised around the connotations of "wrongful death" and emotional distress rather than around the legally relevant elements of those charges. Their disagreement or even confusion over the difficult evidence about events that occurred in the emergency room in a period of less than 10 minutes is reasonable. A judge would also have been bewildered. Nevertheless, their apparently muddled thinking about the semantic connotations of the two legal instructions does not inspire admiration.

My judgment is not a very good yardstick, however, and the case studies presented are not a random sample but rather were chosen for illustrative purposes. This raises some interesting questions. Are there standards by which the reasonableness of the verdicts can be judged? Could alternative decision makers do a better job than juries? These questions and some other issues related to liability decisions will be addressed in chapter 14.

14

Jury Performance Compared: Doctor Judgments of Negligence and Other Criteria

The case studies presented in the last two chapters together with *Melis v. Kutin* (chaps. 9 and 10) provide us with rich detail about what juries hear and how they go about deciding matters of negligence and liability. They also allow us to draw some personal judgments about how well they perform their task. Yet a number of questions remain. Can we generalize from these case studies? How good are jury decisions when judged by independent criteria? What about the charges that juries are confused or misled by experts or that they give undue weight to irrelevant factors such as the expert's appearance? This chapter attempts to address these questions.

Alternatives to Juries: Neutral Doctors

Unless we assume that doctors never make negligent errors or that they should not be held accountable for negligent errors, then some individual or group must determine whether in a particular case the physician was negligent.[1] Any judgments of jury performance in determining liability must be made from a comparative perspective. If the jury is not to decide causality and negligence, then some other person or persons must make these decisions. Physicians' groups have long argued that the decision makers most qualified to make such judgments are physicians and other health care providers.

For example, the AMA has argued in favor of replacing the jury system with an administrative system that relies very heavily on the judgments of doctors.[2] Their arguments against juries are as follows.

161

The fact finder must make a determination of causation in the face of considerable uncertainty about why illnesses strike particular individuals at particular times. In addition the fact finder must decide whether the patient was treated appropriately whenever experts cannot agree on that question. Lay juries are ill-equipped to resolve the arcane issues involved. Furthermore, juries cannot evaluate independently the expert testimony almost always introduced in malpractice cases to explain the two major elements of liability: failure to meet the appropriate standard of care and causation.

The nature of medical knowledge compounds the difficulties presented as a result of the jury's lack of expertise. . . . Because of the complexity of the issues, judges allow juries to hear medical views that may not be scientifically credible.

Moreover, the process of presenting issues to the jury through questioning of an expert by counsel is not always calculated to educate jurors on the issues. . . .

Even under the best of circumstances, juries can never be as effective as specialized triers of fact at deciding malpractice cases because jurors are exposed to the medical issues only once; consequently, they cannot develop an institutional memory to aid them in deciding a specific dispute.[3]

The AMA's proposed alternative to juries for deciding the issue of liability consists of doctors recommended by state medical societies or similar health care organizations. These experts would be specialists within the accused doctor's field of expertise and would be assumed to be impartial toward the patient and the physician.[4]

A moment's reflection will show a central empirical assumption of the AMA critique and its proposed alternative: doctors would decide cases differently than juries. In fact, in 1992 the Physician Payment Review Commission stated the assumption just that bluntly: "physicians probably apply the standard [of negligence] differently than do juries."[5] A study of New Jersey malpractice cases by Dr. Mark Taragin and four other colleagues allows us to put this assumption to an empirical test.[6]

The New Jersey Study

The Taragin study was based on data obtained from the New Jersey Medical Insurance Exchange, a physician-owned insurance company that provides liability insurance to approximately 60 percent of New Jersey's doctors. The database consisted of 8,231 malpractice cases occurring between 1977 and 1992.[7]

Each claim filed against a doctor was assessed internally by the insurance company according to whether the doctor's actions were consistent with prevailing standards of medical care. The decision was intended to be based solely on medical criteria and not influenced by legal concerns. The evaluation was intended to give a neutral assessment of possible negligence to aid the insurance company in deciding whether to contest liability. The assessment was not "discoverable" and, therefore, could not be learned or used by the patient or by anyone else.[8]

If the physician admitted error to the insurance company, the case was labeled "indefensible—insured admits deviation [from standard of care]." If the physician claimed no error, the company asked a volunteer physician from the same medical specialty to conduct a review of the case. In neurosurgery and orthopedics cases, a panel of physicians reviewed the case. As a consequence, Taragin et al. were able to classify each of the 8,231 cases as either "indefensible," "defensible," or "unclear." The unclear category was used when the reviewing physician could not clearly state whether the standard of care was violated or when a panel of reviewers disagreed about whether it was violated. Fully 62 percent of the cases were classified as "defensible," 25 percent were labeled "indefensible," and the remaining 13 percent were classified as "unclear."

In addition the researchers classified each case into one of three categories according to the severity of the alleged injury. The "low" injury category entailed no, minor, or minor temporary disability; the "medium" injury category involved major injury with temporary disability and minor or major injury with moderate disability; and the "high" injury category involved grave injuries, brain injury with impaired life expectancy, and death. Injury severity was low in 28 percent of the cases, medium in 47 percent, and high in 25 percent.

Jury trials took place in 15 percent of cases classified as defensible, 5 percent of cases classified as indefensible, and 10 percent of cases where defensibility was unclear. Altogether, jury trials accounted for 12 percent, or 988, of the 8,231 cases.

Plaintiffs won 24 percent of the trials, and awards to plaintiffs ranged from $3,281 to $2,576,377. The median award was $114,170. The most striking findings, and the most relevant to my discussion here, involve the comparison of these awards with the insurance company categorization of negligence and severity. Jury verdicts on liability were positively and significantly related to the neutral physicians' judgments of negligence.[9] The severity of the plaintiff's injury was *not* correlated with the probability that the plaintiff would win.

In short, there was statistically significant support for the hypothesis that jury verdicts on liability correlate positively with those rendered by physicians instructed to act as neutral evaluators. In contrast, there was no support for the hypothesis that juries are prone to find doctors liable simply when the plaintiff's injuries are severe.

It is also important to add that Taragin et al. speculated that many of the cases that were classified as "defensible" were probably misclassified, a possibility that makes the jury verdicts appear even more rational.[10] Taragin et al. explained that the physicians' judgments of negligence were made very early in the case and, in light of subsequent information, these initial judgments may have been inaccurate. Taragin et al. also suggest that the "neutral" reviewers may err in favor of fellow physicians and that the insurance company itself may err toward concluding nonnegligence to avoid making unnecessary payments.[11] These last observations by Taragin et al. lead us to consider other research findings about doctors' judgments of liability and the relevance of this research to assessment of jury performance.

Reliability and Bias in Assessing Medical Negligence

The discussion by Taragin et al. of probable misclassification of some cases of negligence by doctors is consistent with my own earlier discussion in chapters 7 and 8 of the problems of getting reliable estimates of when negligence has occurred. If jury performance in determining liability is to be judged against the criterion of doctors' assessments of negligence in these same cases, then we need to consider any reliability or bias problems associated with the criterion itself. Additional studies shed light on the assessments of medical negligence made by doctors.

Professors Henry Farber and Michelle White studied 252 malpractice charges against a single large hospital that occurred and were resolved between 1977 and 1989.[12] Similar to the liability insurer in the Taragin study, the hospital required initial assessments of negligence as part of its decision on whether to contest liability or seek settlement. These assessments were not "discoverable" by the other side, and thus the hospital had no incentive to obtain biased reports. Farber and White's article is not totally clear on this point, but it appears that the assessments in each case were frequently made by multiple health care providers: for example, supervisors of relevant departments, other hospital physicians in the relevant specialty, or outside experts who might appear as experts for the hospital if the case went to trial.[13] The experts were asked to consider: (1) whether correct treatment was provided, (2) whether treatment failed because of inadequate or tardy care, and (3) whether the alleged harm was causally related to the treatment. Based on these assessments the quality of care was classified as either bad quality, ambiguous quality, or good quality.

Only 13 (5 percent) of the 252 cases went to trial, and the hospital was not found liable in any of them. What is more germane to my present analysis, however, is the fact that of all of the 252 cases, almost one-third were classified as ambiguous by the hospital, either because the reviewing experts were undecided about the quality of care or because reviewers disagreed in their assessments. The actual figures were as follows: bad quality care, 31.7 percent of cases; good quality care, 37.7 percent; ambiguous quality care, 30.6 percent.[14]

The thrust of these findings is that even in a context in which doctors were asked to give neutral, unbiased judgments about negligence, in 30.6 percent of the cases they could provide no clear answer.

Further evidence bearing on doctors' ability to judge medical negligence comes from a study that was published in the JOURNAL OF THE AMERICAN MEDICAL ASSOCIATION. Robert Caplan, Karen Posner, and Frederick Cheney asked 112 practicing anesthesiologists to read a selection of 21 anesthesiology cases that resulted in bad outcomes and indicate whether or not the doctor had taken reasonable and prudent care in treating the patient.[15] Although Caplan et al. did not change any of the facts leading to the injury for each case, the adverse outcome was described as either a temporary injury (not serious) or a permanent injury (serious). The type of injury was randomly assigned in the cases given to the anesthesiologists. For each case they were asked to rate whether the medical care was appropriate, less than appropriate, or impossible to judge.

Caplan et al. found that even when injury seriousness was taken into account, the reliability, that is, agreement, between doctors in judging care was only "fair."[16] Furthermore, their anesthesiologist doctors were more likely to conclude that the medical care was less than appropriate when the injury was serious than when it was temporary. Also, compared to temporary injuries the serious injury conditions increased the frequency of the anesthesiologists' saying that the facts were "impossible to judge." Thus, the anesthesiologist raters were susceptible to what social psychologists have labeled a "hindsight bias"—knowledge of an outcome affecting the interpretation of events that led to that outcome.[17] A "hindsight bias" has been demonstrated in other studies of medical decisions, and other medical researchers who have studied doctors' judgments of malpractice have concluded that "expert testimony in malpractice cases is often subjective and biased."[18] Juries might also be affected by hindsight biases, of course, but the important lesson is that doctors' decisions about medical treatment are based, at least in part, on subjective factors.[19]

The other study bearing on physician judgments is the Harvard Medical Malpractice Study.[20] As one part of that study 47 physicians practicing in the state of New York in 1988 were interviewed in considerable depth about their attitudes toward medical malpractice. Based on the survey results the authors of the study drew the following conclusions.

> Physicians tended to equate a finding of negligence with a judgment of incompetence. Thus, although willing to admit that all doctors make mistakes, physicians were often unwilling to label substandard care as negligent and were opposed to compensation for iatrogenic injury.[21]

This finding appears to support the conclusion of Taragin et al. that, as a group, doctors tend to be hesitant to conclude negligence has occurred. And it also directly raises the issue of whether physician judgments are less neutral than those of the 12 laypersons who sit on the jury.[22]

The Florida Study and the Hospital Study

Concerns about reliability and bias in physician judgments notwithstanding, research by Professor Frank Sloan and his colleagues and by Henry Farber and Michelle White yields further support for the Taragin study.[23] Sloan et al. examined a sample of 187 Florida malpractice suits that closed between 1986 and 1989 and that involve birth-related injuries and injuries allegedly resulting from care in hospital emergency rooms. For purposes of the study, independent panels of four physicians reviewed information drawn from insurer files, from interviews with claimants, and from abstracts of hospital charts. These panels rated each case according to whether any of the medical professionals named as defendants in the case contributed to or caused the outcome and whether their actions deviated from the standard of care.

Only 37 of the 187 cases went to trial, but the data showed that the liability ratings of the physician panels were positively related to the outcomes at trial. Plaintiffs won an award in 83 percent of the cases in which the panels decided that the defendant had liability or that liability was uncertain; among cases that plaintiffs lost, 77 percent were judged not liable or uncertain.[24] Sloan et al. phrased their conclusions this way: "[d]efendants thought by the evaluators to have been not liable lost at verdict in less than a fifth of the cases."[25] These findings were not statistically significant, perhaps because of the small sample size.

Farber and White expanded their study of lawsuits against the private hospital that was described earlier in this chapter. Their database in the expanded study involved 465 cases that were resolved by mid-1993. Only 26 of the cases were decided by a jury and plaintiffs won awards in only four. Two of the awards were in cases rated by the hospital's neutral experts as involving "bad" care and two were in cases involving "ambiguous" care. The hospital prevailed in all 13 of the cases rated as having "good" care. The difference was statistically significant. However, there was no relationship between winning and the severity of the plaintiff's injury.

It must be emphasized that both the Sloan and the Farber and White studies involved very small samples of jury trials. Nevertheless, the results of both are entirely consistent with those found in the Taragin study in New Jersey.

The OB-GYN Study

Stephen Daniels and Lori Andrews of the American Bar Foundation conducted another study that gives additional insight bearing on the rationality of jury decisions.[26] From a total of over 1,800 malpractice jury verdicts in 46 jurisdictions in 10 states that were rendered between

1981 and 1985, they identified 364 as OB-GYN cases. In addition to the verdicts they collected information on the severity of the patient's injury, the type of treatment, and class of injury. The type of treatment was categorized as pregnancy, labor and delivery, abortion, hysterectomy, tubal ligation, and cancer. The cases were further categorized as to the class of injury. Class 1 injuries (45 percent of the sample) involved alleged physician acts of commission, that is, a new abnormal condition caused by the treatment. Class 2 injuries (30 percent of the sample) resulted from allegations of incomplete diagnosis or treatment. Class 3 injuries (25 percent of the sample) involved alleged acts of omission resulting in a new abnormal condition caused by incomplete prevention or protection during treatment.

Plaintiff rates of winning at trial were somewhat more successful in OB-GYN cases (36.8 percent) than in malpractice cases generally (32.4 percent), but the injuries also tended to be more severe. Success rates varied according to the type of treatment and the class of injury. The median award (in 1985 dollars) was $390,000.

While any of the differences between severity, injury type, or treatment could be, in whole or in part, a result of how cases were selected for trial, they clearly appear to be contrary to the claim that juries capriciously decide cases. If juries made no distinctions, there should have been no differences. Instead, there were high plaintiff win rates in labor and delivery and in cancer cases, but there were relatively low win rates (and relatively low awards) in hysterectomy and tubal ligation cases, even when the patient suffered severe injuries.

In a further breakdown of their data, Daniels and Andrews identified 23 labor and delivery cases in which it was alleged that the injury was caused by the improper use of oxytocin, a drug dating back to 1910 that is used to induce labor.[27] Medical knowledge regarding oxytocin is well established in the medical profession, including circumstances in which it is contraindicated. Plaintiffs won 14 of 16 cases in which contraindicative use of oxytocin was evident at trial. All 16 cases resulted in permanent injury or death; the two cases that were lost involved grave permanent injury. Plaintiffs lost six of the seven cases in which evidence of contraindicative use was lacking in the case summaries. Daniels and Andrews concluded from their findings that "juries appear to have responded in no uncertain terms to the misuse of an old, established technology whose limitations and contraindications were well known and widely disseminated."[28]

Considering all their data Daniels and Andrews concluded that physicians were more likely to lose cases involving older technologies than those involving specific procedures, particularly when the injuries were severe. However, juries did not overwhelmingly decide in favor of plaintiffs even when the injuries were severe. Moreover, even winning plaintiffs did not receive large amounts of money when they suffered less severe injuries.

Juror Attitudes toward Plaintiffs and Defendants

It is usually alleged that jurors' sympathies lie with injured plaintiffs. Recall from chapter 2 that the former U.S. Surgeon General C. Everett Koop claimed that the parents of a brain-damaged child are likely to find a jury that will give an award, not necessarily because they think the doctor is liable for malpractice but because sympathy for the injured child and the family dictates it. This opinion is shared by others critical of malpractice juries.[29]

The fact that juries find for plaintiffs in only one-third or less of trial cases and that jury verdicts in the New Jersey study and Florida studies generally corresponded with those of doctors and independently of severity of injury raises further doubts about this proposition. Daniels and Andrew's OB-GYN study is also consistent with these findings. In fact, research data raise the opposite possibility, namely, that jurors, or at least some jurors, may be biased against plaintiffs.

During pretrial questioning for jury selection in the North Carolina malpractice trials that I studied, it was not unusual for prospective jurors to state, "too many people sue their doctors" or "it is just going to raise the health insurance rates for the rest of us." Some even explicitly stated that greedy lawyers encourage undeserving patients to sue. While persons who were so explicit in voicing their attitudes were usually not selected to serve on the jury, the same sentiments, in more subtle forms, remained in many who did serve. For example, in the case of the woman who died as a result of a ruptured bowel (see chap. 12), one juror said, "the doctors were just trying to help his wife and he shows his ingratitude by suing them." Another said, "too many people are unfair to doctors."

Interviews with jurors in the case of the woman who suffered rectal as well as urinary incontinence after surgical rhizotomy (chap.

12) strikingly demonstrated how jurors may scrutinize the motives of plaintiffs. Recall that Mrs. F. had sat through several days of trial before it was her turn to testify. The jury had already been apprised that part of her complaint was that she suffered from frequent embarrassing accidents, either from urinary discharge or from the slipping of the colostomy bag, which had to be held in place by a fragile paper tape since she had an allergic reaction to the adhesive on regular surgical tape. Shortly after she began her testimony, the court took a brief recess; but when court resumed, she was wearing different clothes. Upon a query from her lawyer she said an accident had occurred while she was attempting to change the colostomy bag. Neither she nor her attorney made a great deal of the incident other than to say it was typical of her problem, and the questioning proceeded on other matters.

The incident, however, apparently consumed about one-third of the jury's short deliberation time because they saw the incident as contrived. As one of several jurors spontaneously remarked during an interview:

> The whole week she sat there and didn't need to go to the bathroom but then she says she can't go to church because of it. And then she has an accident while testifying. It was just faked.

When I tactfully inquired whether the accident was not fairly typical of what other witnesses had also described regarding Mrs. F.'s problem, the suggestion was strongly rejected. The jurors also focused on the fact that the evidence showed that she began the lawsuit only after her urologist had said she did not qualify as a disabled person: "She asked for disability and he wouldn't give it and maybe that's why she took him to court; [Mrs. F.] wanted money."

The juror skepticism toward plaintiffs that I found in the North Carolina jurors was also found in Valerie Hans and William Lofquist's study of Delaware juries who had decided cases involving corporate responsibility.[30] Four of every five jurors that they interviewed endorsed the view that "People are too quick to sue rather than resolve disputes in some way" and "There are too many frivolous lawsuits today." Only one-third of the jurors agreed with the statement that "Most people who sue others in court have legitimate grievances." After analyzing the jurors' responses to the specific

trials in which they had participated Hans and Lofquist drew the
following conclusion:

> Jurors' dubiousness about plaintiff claims led them to scrutinize
> the personal behavior of plaintiffs, trying to understand their mo-
> tives and to assess the reasonableness of their claims. Seemingly,
> no aspect of the plaintiff's behavior was beyond question. Jurors
> often penalized plaintiffs who did not meet high standards of
> credibility and behavior, including those who did not act or appear
> as injured as they claimed, those who did not appear deserving
> due to their already high standard of living, those with preexisting
> medical conditions, and those who did not do enough to help
> themselves recover from their injuries.[31]

Similarly, Professor David Engle has documented a set of attitudes indicating that many Americans subscribe to the belief that we
should accept misfortune and not blame others.[32] Surveys of jurors
and the general public have found that mass media publicity about
the "insurance crisis" and "irresponsible" jury awards has affected
many citizens, causing them to be concerned about both liability and
damage awards in civil lawsuits.[33]

None of this case study data nor the work of other researchers
refutes the claim that some jurors may indeed be pro-plaintiff.[34] Possibly some juries have a majority of pro-plaintiff members. Nevertheless, contrary to the claims of Dr. Koop and others, malpractice plaintiffs may often bear an extra burden of proof. Juries will sometimes
decide in favor of plaintiffs; but if the evidence is very close the doctor
may get the benefit of doubt.

Juror Attitudes toward Experts

Recall from chapter 11 that another charge against jurors is that they
weigh the evidence of experts on grounds other than probative value.
Critics assert that lay jurors not only fail to understand the evidence,
they evaluate it on irrelevant grounds. Some commentators have
gone even further, claiming that jurors almost exclusively give preference to style and ignore substance.[35]

One of the consistent findings that emerged from the interviews
with the North Carolina malpractice jurors is that they clearly

understood the adversary system. They were keenly aware that there were reasons that witnesses testified for each side. Whether the jurors held these views before the trial began or not, they appear to have developed them during trial. In many instances their perceptions of adversary witnesses solidified when the testifying physicians were questioned about how many times they had testified in other cases, for whom, and for how much per hour. Not surprisingly, questions about the competence of witnesses evoked some jaded comments, for example, "Each side's got its own witnesses and they're trying to win"; "Pay me $300 per hour and I'll testify too—for either side"; "He may have had a big long list of academic degrees, but he's just like the rest—trying to help the lawyer win his case."

In the incontinence case discussed in chapter 12, the jurors clearly pegged the primary plaintiff's witness as a hired gun. In the case of the woman who became blind (chap. 13), the jurors were very aware that several of the defendant's expert witnesses were his partners and close colleagues, and thus they tended to view their testimony as inappropriate and biased. During deliberations the jury also discussed the possible motives of the doctor who had begun as a plaintiff witness but retracted his opinion and testified for the defense. He was judged to be disingenuous, pompous, and self-aggrandizing. Such skeptical views have been documented in other types of trials.[36]

Moving beyond the issue of general skepticism it is difficult to confirm or refute the charge that juries base judgments of witnesses on irrelevant factors. Some researchers in other trial contexts, particularly trials involving complex cases, have concluded that jurors sometimes do rely on general impressions rather than the substance of the evidence.[37] Indeed, some of the individual jurors in the North Carolina malpractice trials exhibited similar tendencies. In one case, for example, a defendant was characterized not only as caring, sincere, competent, and honest but also physically very attractive and "charming."

It also appears that when there are competent experts on both sides, and they offer contradictory or confusing opinions, jurors may resolve the differences by relying on general impressions of character and veracity. However, as Professor Samuel Gross has documented, this is sometimes the way that experienced judges resolve their doubts.[38] For example, he cites *Wells v. Ortho Pharmaceutical Corporation*, a products liability case resulting out of a child's severe birth defect. The case was tried by a judge rather than a jury. Experts for the two sides presented conflicting testimony. In explaining his decision, the trial judge stated candidly that,

> The Court paid close attention to each expert's demeanor and tone. Perhaps most important, the court did its best to ascertain the motives, biases, and interests that might have influenced each expert's opinion.[39]

Systematic studies of the decision making by judges are sparse, but the judge's reaction in the *Wells* case may not be atypical.[40] The fact is that when competent experts disagree and the judge or jury has to decide between them, it is natural, and some would argue not inappropriate, to focus on their demeanor, biases, and motives.[41] In any event, the jury interviews in our malpractice cases found evidence of such behavior.

Summary

Jury verdicts show a positive relationship to "neutral" doctors' judgments of negligence. There appears to be no relationship between the severity of the plaintiff's injury and verdicts for the plaintiff, refuting the claim that sympathy for injured persons causes jurors to ignore the legal issues bearing on negligence. Other studies indicate that doctors themselves are not always able to make clear judgments of negligence, and many doctors hold attitudes that reject the notion of medical negligence—at least with respect to charges of malpractice. Data about juror attitudes also seem to go against the claim that jurors tend to favor patients over doctors; indeed, there may be a tendency in the opposite direction. Our interviews with jurors strongly suggest that they come to understand the adversary system and on the whole evaluate expert witnesses in the light of this perspective.

15

A Summary Perspective
on Liability Decisions

How often do juries "get it right" with respect to their verdicts on liability? It should be clear by now that there can be no definitive answer to this question because, in the end, legal negligence is a matter of human judgment. Contrary to views that have portrayed malpractice as a largely technical matter that can only be determined by doctors, the case studies presented in chapters 12 and 13 make it clear that questions bearing on credibility of witnesses—different versions of events between patient and doctor or between medical personnel—pervade many malpractice disputes. Furthermore, from the examples presented in chapter 12 I contended that an argument can be made on prima facie grounds that not every case is medically complex: operating on the wrong foot or giving 10 times the required chemotherapy dose were two outstanding examples, though not the only ones. This is not to say that technical medical matters are unimportant in malpractice cases. However, it is also clear from the studies discussed in chapter 14 that even when acting in a neutral capacity, doctors themselves frequently cannot agree on the technical issue of whether medical care was appropriate. Furthermore, the selection processes by which cases are chosen for trial tend to ensure that the cases that juries decide contain a high proportion of disputes where the evidence is most ambiguous.[1] Thus, there is often no clear or uncontestable criterion by which jury performance may be judged.

Nevertheless, taken in total the data presented in the preceding chapters clearly contradict assertions that have been made against malpractice juries. The findings that juries decide in favor of plaintiffs in fewer than one case in three and that their decisions on liability are not related to the severity of injury suffered by the plaintiff refute the extreme view that juries are anti-doctor, motivated by sympathies, and ignore the trial evidence. These findings are bolstered by my case studies and juror interviews. The most striking findings, I believe, involve the high concordance between doctors' judgments of medical negligence and jury verdicts that was found in the Taragin et al. New Jersey study and in the Sloan et al. Florida study. If doctors' judgments are the criterion by which jury verdicts are to be judged, as the AMA and others have argued, then it is difficult to argue that juries are incompetent or biased against medical providers.

In concluding the discussion of liability verdicts, I want to briefly consider three additional topics.

A Hypothesis Based on Jury and Doctor Concordance

The high concordance between doctors' assessments of negligence and jury verdicts in the New Jersey and Florida studies leads to a hypothesis that suggests exactly the opposite of what jury critics have claimed, namely, that on the whole juries may in fact be biased in favor of doctors. Recall from chapter 14 that Taragin and his colleagues speculated that even though the insurance company asked the doctors to provide neutral assessments of liability, there would be a tendency for them to err on the side of finding no negligence.[2] This could happen for three reasons. First, doctors are reluctant to find their fellow professionals negligent, a finding that seems supported by the Harvard Medical Malpractice Study Group's interviews with doctors. Second, insurance companies would want to err on the side of finding no negligence in order to avoid making unnecessary settlements. Third, the evaluations are made early in the life of the case before all the facts are known, particularly facts supplied by the plaintiff. If it is indeed true that the "neutral" ratings are biased in favor of doctors and that jury verdicts are positively correlated with them it follows that juries may be similarly biased in favor of doctors. The comments made by many jurors in the posttrial interviews are consistent with this interpretation. Other data about juror attitudes on the matter of damages, discussed in part 4 of this book, are also consistent with the hypothesis.

I want to stress that the hypothesis is only a hypothesis and that it should not be pushed too far. I am inclined to conclude only that there is reason to believe that, on balance, juries have a tilt slightly in favor of doctors. This is not to say that every juror favors doctors—

some indeed do not. I also want to suggest that any bias in favor of doctors can be overcome if the trial evidence favors the plaintiff.

Jury Performance in Other Tort Cases

It is useful here to digress to consider my conclusions about jury performance in deciding negligence in malpractice cases in light of conclusions that have been reached by other authors who have studied jury behavior in other contexts.

Recently, Professors Shari Diamond and Jonathan Casper conducted experimental research on how jurors responded to expert witnesses in a price-fixing trial involving complex statistical evidence.[3] Their subjects were jurors awaiting trial assignment in a Chicago court. The jurors watched a videotape of the trial, and their deliberations were recorded and analyzed. Diamond and Casper's conclusion from their findings was as follows:

> The responses to expert testimony . . . suggest that jurors play an active role in assimilating and assessing testimony. Jurors did not simply adopt the view of a witness they rated high on expertise, using apparent expertise as a peripheral cue to conclude that the expert must be correct. Rather, consistent with deeper processing of information which produces attitude change when the listener is lightly involved, the jurors appeared to consider and evaluate the content of what the expert was presenting and were less likely to be persuaded if they did not feel they understood it.[4]

Casper and Diamond's conclusion captures the essence of how jurors indicated they dealt with the expert testimony in North Carolina malpractice trials.

As part of the classic Chicago Jury Project conducted in the 1950s, Professor Harry Kalven compared the jury verdicts in over 6,000 civil trials with questionnaire data from the presiding trial judge bearing on how he or she would have decided the case.[5] Judges agreed with the jury on the issue of liability in 79 percent of the trials. The remaining cases involving judge versus jury disagreement were split almost evenly between plaintiffs and defendants: 11 percent of the time the jury favored the plaintiff while the judge would have decided for the defendant, and in the remaining 10 percent the judge would have decided for the plaintiff but the jury sided with the defendant. However, even in the disagreement cases most of the time the judges indicated that the evidence was such that arguments could be made that the jury's verdict was as reasonable as that of the judge.

More recently, Professor Perry Sentell surveyed both state and federal judges in Georgia and used Kalven's study as a vehicle for assessing jury performance in contemporary civil cases.[6] Sentell found that the judges said that they agreed with the jury verdicts on liability at rates similar to those Kalven found. Another study conducted by the Federal Judicial Center also surveyed judges. It found that judges believed juries generally were competent when they decided complex civil trials.[7] A roughly similar study by Professors Larry Heuer and Steven Penrod found that judges were no more likely to disagree with the jury's verdict when cases were complex than when they were not, a finding suggesting that trial complexity is not the basis of disagreement.[8]

Finally, Professor Richard Lempert has undertaken a review of a number of actual trials bearing on the ability of juries to decide cases involving complex scientific and technical evidence.[9] The trials involved evidence on antitrust matters, trade secrets, sexual harassment, and criminal charges. In Lempert's analysis, the jury was not always correct, but his overall conclusion is worth quoting.

> Throughout this review strengths of the jury emerge. A close look at a number of cases, including several in which jury verdicts appear mistaken, does not show that juries are befuddled by complexity. Even when juries do not fully understand technical issues, they can usually make enough sense of what is going on to deliberate rationally, and they usually reach defensible decisions.[10]

He further concluded that "we cannot assume that judges in complex cases will perform better than juries."[11]

In short, my conclusion that on the whole juries perform well in deciding negligence and liability in malpractice cases is consistent with researchers' conclusions about jurors' performance in other contexts.

Juries versus Legal Professionals

An alternative to the jury is the judge. Some commentators argue that judges, or lawyers serving as arbitrators, would decide malpractice cases differently—and better—than juries.[12] Unlike juries, judges have training in evidence and experience with many types of cases. They would be better positioned to detect unreliable testimony from experts and to understand the arcane medical issues raised in trial testimony.

Unfortunately, there are no studies bearing on how judges would decide liability in malpractice cases. Justice Sklar's review of the decision in *Melis* agreed with the jury on most of the liability issues, but it is only a single case.[13] Kevin Clermont and Theodore Eisenberg compared verdicts rendered by judges and juries in malpractice trials in federal courts and found that judges rendered more verdicts for plaintiffs than juries, but the differences were likely due to the fact that the judge and juries were not deciding the same types of cases.[14] There is, however, some indirect data from several studies that deserves consideration because it at least suggests the conclusion that judges might not be superior to juries.

Consider, first, a case study of a North Carolina malpractice case that was decided by an experienced senior lawyer in an arbitration hearing. While washing dishes in the late afternoon, Mrs. R. suffered a severe hand laceration below her thumb from a broken glass and went to an emergency clinic. The standard of care in such cases requires the physician to conduct a number of routine tests to determine if there is nerve or ligament damage. The test for ligament damage is a "range of motion" test in which the patient is asked to rotate the thumb. If a ligament is partially cut the patient will experience sharp pain. In such an instance the patient normally would be immediately referred to a specialist in hand surgery. In this case the physician concluded there was no such injury; he sutured and bandaged the wound and sent the patient home. Several weeks later the main tendon in Mrs. R.'s thumb ruptured, causing it to curl back and rendering it useless. Eventually Mrs. R. had to undergo two painful operations in which a ligament from her middle finger was used to replace the ligament in her thumb. Mrs. R. sued the treating physician and submitted a sworn deposition from a hand surgeon stating that if the range of motion test had been conducted, the laceration would have been detected and proper care would have required the emergency physician to immediately refer her to a hand surgeon.

The defendant doctor contested the claim, stating that his medical records showed that the range of motion test had been conducted. At the hearing, Mrs. R. testified that a physician's assistant had begun the examination, but midway through the treating physician appeared, sent the assistant out to do something else, and completed the suturing. Mrs. R. insisted she had never been asked to do the range of motion test but conceded that she was very upset, nearly hysterical at times, during the treatment. The physician, on the other hand, could not clearly remember much about the incident having treated many other patients that day and in the following months. However, his medical records showed that notations on the first three of the six routine tests were in the handwriting of his assistant and the last three, including the range of motion test, were in his handwriting. One scenario favoring the plaintiff's version of events would be that the doctor came into the room in the middle of the tests and, through miscommunication, assumed the assistant had done all the tests when in fact the range of motion test had not been conducted. If this assumption were correct then we might reasonably conclude that the doctor incorrectly wrote the tests into the record. The case, then, pitted the plaintiff's version of events and the sworn deposition of her expert that, if conducted, the range of motion test should have detected the laceration against the medical record and the doctor's recollection of events.

Despite extensive examination and cross-examination of the defendant physician and similar questioning of a qualified defense expert, neither the plaintiff's attorney nor the arbitrator, who engaged in active interrogation of witnesses, asked a crucial and obvious question. It was important to the case and, indeed, might have been dispositive in resolving the dispute: how accurate is the range of motion test in detecting laceration of a ligament? If it is only accurate 50 or 60 percent of the time the answer is not informative, and we are forced to rely on the records and testimony of doctor and plaintiff. However, if the test would detect a laceration 95 to 100 percent of the time then we would be inclined to conclude the test was not performed, as Mrs. R. claimed. The deposition from the plaintiff's expert had stated that the range of motion test was very accurate, but neither the plaintiff's lawyer nor the arbitrator pursued this issue with the defendant or his expert.

The illustrative point of this case example is that the plaintiff lawyer and the arbitrator, both well trained and above average in ability, seemed unaware of what to me, a social scientist interested in reliability of tests, was the obvious and crucial question. And they each seemed surprised and befuddled when I raised it in interviews conducted a week after the arbitrator rendered his decision in favor of the doctor.

The lesson from this case example is that despite many skills, lawyers and judges may often not be more competent than laypersons in assessing issues relevant to the evaluation of expert testimony. Case studies of decision making from Supreme Court justices down to trial judges have documented the fact that judges frequently have great difficulty in understanding scientific evidence, particularly when it involves statistical reasoning.[15] For instance, in *Williams v. Florida* members of the Supreme Court interpreted a classical psychology experiment as concluding just the opposite of what the results implied when they decided a leading case allowing juries smaller than 12 members. Similar errors have been documented in a number of reports and case studies.[16] In a recent experimental study, Professor Gary Wells presented various forms of statistical evidence to both college students and judges. He found that judges exhibited degrees of fallacious statistical reasoning that were similar to those of students and other groups of persons.[17]

In another study Professors Stephan Landsman and Richard Rakos conducted an experiment to test the claim that, because of their training and experience, judges possess a special capacity to control their reactions to biasing evidence, whereas jurors lack this capacity.[18]

In the study 88 judges attending a judicial conference and 104 persons awaiting jury duty were asked to render verdicts on liability in an abbreviated version of a products liability case. Each participant received one of three versions of a case. The final version made no mention of some evidence that was harmful to the defendant's case. A second version presented this evidence with an instruction that it had been ruled to be legally admissible. The third version contained the same harmful evidence, but the judges and jurors were instructed that it had been ruled legally inadmissible and, therefore, must not be considered in reaching their verdict. As expected, in comparison to the no-evidence condition, the harmful evidence significantly increased the number of verdicts against the defendant. However, the hypothesis that, in comparison to the jurors, the judges would be able to ignore the harmful evidence when it was inadmissible received no support. Judges and jurors alike rendered verdicts unfavorable to the defendant in approximately the same proportions as they had in the second condition. In short, the Landsman and Rakos study yielded no support for the proposition that judges have special capacities to set objectionable evidence aside.

The evidence in judicial reasoning is much too sparse to yield any reliable conclusions about the competence of judges versus that of juries. It would be totally improper to reach the conclusion that judges have no special capacities that distinguish them from jurors. Nevertheless, the existing studies do raise questions about judicial superiority, particularly when we consider that the jury is composed of 12 persons, at least some of whom might have the education, experience, or intuitive perspective to "get it right" and convey their knowledge to the other jurors. We must also keep in mind the facts discussed earlier: that malpractice trials frequently involve more than just technical judgments and that, by and large, judges indicate that they usually agree with jury verdicts.

On Balance

Nothing in the preceding chapters should be interpreted as meaning that the determination of medical negligence is an easy task or that juries always make the correct decisions. However, what must be kept in mind is that medical negligence is a legal concept requiring human judgment rather than a scientific or technical concept and that jury performance must be evaluated in comparative perspective. On balance, there is no empirical support for the propositions that juries are biased against doctors or that they are prone to ignore legal and medical standards in order to decide in favor of plaintiffs with severe injuries. This evidence in fact indicates that there is reasonable concordance between jury verdicts and doctors' ratings of negligence. On balance, juries may have a slight bias in favor of doctors.

4. Damages

16

A Prologue to Damages

Now we turn to the second part of the jury's task, determining damage awards. If the jury decides that the defendant is liable, the plaintiff is entitled to damages. The *Melis v. Kutin* case (chaps. 9 and 10) introduced some of the elements of damages, but we now need to be more systematic. It is helpful to think of damages as falling into three main categories: economic damages, noneconomic damages, and punitive damages.[1] The first two categories involve compensating the plaintiff for the injury whereas the latter is intended to serve as punishment for behavior that is willful, malicious, or fraudulent. In the quaint words of the law compensatory damages are intended to "make the plaintiff whole." Being "made whole," however, is a classic example of being easier said than done and is central to the debate about jury incompetence and irresponsibility.

"Economic" damages is the term used to refer to those financial costs that are incurred by the plaintiff as the result of injury. These costs might include such items as past and future medical care, that is, bills already incurred as a result of the injury and those expected to be incurred in continuing treatment, past and future loss of income, and the physical care or education of the plaintiff's children or other dependents. In theory, economic damages can be easily estimated by an accountant or economist. In practice, these estimates are more complicated and open to contention. The calculations, for example, must take into account not only the projected life expectancy of the plaintiff but also estimates of the rates of inflation. If the plaintiff will need continuing medical care testimony from health care specialists and economists will be important evidence at trial. In many instances medical and rehabilitative experts will disagree about the future health care needs of the plaintiff: for instance, whether, as a direct result of the injury, his or her health will improve, remain the same, or degenerate and what medical care will be required. The extent to which the costs of any medical condition preexisting the malpractice injury should be discounted from these estimates will also provoke disagreement among lawyers and their experts. Based on this information the economist must make highly hazardous guesses about rates of health care inflation, which over past decades have generally been higher and less predictable than the general inflation rate.

Then there is the matter of lost income. If the plaintiff is a child, his or her lawyer will argue that a college education had been a near certainty and projections of future lost income should be based on those for someone with a college degree whereas the defendant may argue that a college degree was unlikely. Where the plaintiff, though handicapped, may be capable of earning some income through retraining, both sides may disagree about what the income may be or even whether any future earnings are likely. Similarly, there is great room to differ about what an injured adult's future income would have been, particularly if he or she is self-employed. There are lots of "ifs" in the calculation of economic damages and lots of opportunity for litigants, their experts, and deliberating jurors to disagree.

Frank McClellan, an experienced trial lawyer and professor, states in his book MEDICAL MALPRACTICE that "the sums being talked about [at trial] are likely to astound the jury, at least initially."[2] As he points out, the determination of economic damages requires long-term thinking and detailed analysis that takes into consideration such financial issues as rates of inflation and the reduction of the award to "present value." Projected over decades of life expectancy even conservative estimates of economic damages can total hundreds of thousands or even millions of dollars. The *Melis* case discussed in Steve Cohen's article (chap. 9) is one example. Another is a North Carolina case involving a brain-damaged baby wherein even the liability insurer's economists could not come up with a figure below $2.1 million.

Noneconomic damages involve financial compensation for the injury to the intangible, subjective state of the plaintiff's life. Lawyers and newspaper reporters alike often give this component of damages the generic label "pain and suffering." Noneconomic injuries might include compensation for the physical pain felt by the plaintiff at the time of the injury, physical pain during recuperation, or physical pain that will continue into the future. They can also include emotional pain such as fear, anxiety, or embarrassment over the loss of a breast or a disfiguring scar. Loss of "life's amenities" is another possible component and so are "loss of good offices and counsel" and "loss of consortium."

The term "pain and suffering" has come to have a pejorative connotation in the minds of legislators and the public, namely, "getting something for nothing." In truth, however, the purposes behind the law of damages are not as frivolous as they are often portrayed.[3] Consider a few examples from some of the North Carolina malpractice cases. As a result of alleged negligence on the part of doctors, a nine-year-old child had to have all of her arms and legs amputated at the trunk. A young single mother with a small child lost total vision and her senses of smell and taste. A young man became impotent; a young woman will never be able to have children; a patient's disfiguring facial scar makes strangers react with aversion; brain damage causes a patient to have short-term memory loss, slurred speech, and an ataxic walk that makes her appear drunk. The jury's task in such instances is to award some money to attempt to compensate for the injury even though, of course, in many instances even millions of dollars cannot make the plaintiff "whole" again.

A major problem in conceptualizing components of noneconomic damages is their overlap with economic damages. For instance, consider a plaintiff with a substantial disfigurement resulting from medical negligence. In addition to the emotional pain and embarrassment, the condition may also affect his or her ability to adequately perform certain jobs or gain promotions, particularly in jobs that involve contact with the public. Or consider how a disfigurement or sexual dysfunction might affect a person's marriage prospects or, in the case of a married person, eventually result in divorce. In either instance the consequence may be declining financial status, an economic rather than pain and suffering–related loss. Similarly, the "loss of good offices and counsel" may involve the costs of counseling or psychotherapy for severe emotional problems of the young children of a deceased or gravely injured parent.

The final category of damages is "punitive" damages, also called "exemplary" damages.[4] The purpose of such damages is to punish egregious or malicious behavior to deter others from the behavior or to extract a measure of retribution on the defendant. As documented in chapter 5, in 13 percent of North Carolina malpractice cases, the plaintiff initially asked for punitive damages, but in most instances the claim was dropped before it got to a jury. It seems likely that in many of these cases the claim was made as a tactic of intimidation that was never intended to be seriously pursued. However, a few examples will illustrate why punitive damages might be asked. In one case it was alleged that a doctor lied to the patient about a treatment error, delaying corrective treatment. In a similar case of surgical error it was alleged that the doctor not only lied about the first error but then charged the patient for a second operation on a false pretext that was actually intended to correct the bungled first surgery. In another case a dental patient claimed that when she complained about severe pain during treatment, the dentist swore at her, closed the door, and, against her will, continued drilling. Other cases alleged that the doctor destroyed or altered medical records. Professors Thomas Koenig and Michael Rustad, in research that I will discuss in chapter 21, have shown that nationwide the most frequent malpractice cases in which punitive damages are awarded involve sexual abuse by psychiatrists and sexual assaults on patients by medical providers.[5]

The jury may be asked by the plaintiff's lawyer to consider any number of relevant circumstances in awarding compensatory damages. Experts may be called to offer their opinions on economic, medical, and psychological issues bearing on these claims, and the defense may counter with its own arguments and experts. The judge will instruct the jury to treat such evidence as it does other evidence and arrive at a verdict that is "fair and reasonable" in the light of the evidence.

Juries are often instructed that whatever future compensatory costs they award to the plaintiff should be "reduced to present value." What this means is that the jurors are asked to adjust the award downward to reflect the fact that the plaintiff is getting all the money now rather than when the expenses will be incurred, and thus with prudent investment the interest on the principal amount will increase to cover projected costs.

Instructions to itemize damages into their separate components, as the *Melis* jury was told to do (see chaps. 9 and 10), is not common in most jurisdictions. New York and some other states do require the jury to give itemized damage awards, called special verdicts, but most others, including North Carolina, instruct the jury to consider the components although the jury's verdict is given to the court only as a lump sum called a general verdict.

The crux of the matter is that the jury has many things to consider in arriving at its damage award. Moreover, it typically receives only vague guidance, particularly in those jurisdictions that require only a general verdict. During the trial the plaintiff's lawyer may present evidence, including expert testimony, bearing on damages and summarize these findings during final arguments. The defendant is allowed the same privilege, though, as I showed in chapter 8, in malpractice cases the privilege is often ignored: defendants seldom had experts testify about damages.

At the end of the trial the judge addresses damages as the last part of often lengthy instructions on liability. The jury is told that if it finds one or more of the defendants was negligent it must decide the amount of the award. The instructions may tell the jury about what to assume about the plaintiff's life expectancy: for example, under a North Carolina statute jurors are told to assume that the plaintiff will live to be 72 years old. The instructions call attention to the various components of damages and the state of the law, but they are usually pretty general. For instance, with respect to physical pain and suffering the judge may state the law approximately like this:

> The damages for pain and suffering should include such amounts as you find, by the greater weight of the evidence, is fair compensation for the actual physical pain and mental suffering which were the immediate and necessary consequences of the injury. There is no fixed formula for evaluating pain and suffering. You will determine what is fair compensation by applying logic and common sense to the evidence.

With respect to reducing the award to present value, the instructions—in abbreviated form—may be approximately as follows.

> Damages must be reduced to their present worth. A smaller sum received now is equal to a larger sum received in the future. In calculating these figures you should rely on the trial evidence, including the mortuary tables that indicate the plaintiff's life expectancy.

After instructions, the jury is sent to the jury room to begin deliberations.

17

Spiraling Awards, "Deep Pockets," and Jury Sympathy: The Claims and the Evidence

Claims about Profligate Juries

Some of the claims about the irresponsible and incompetent jury were introduced in chapters 1 and 2, but let us reacquaint ourselves with them as they pertain to damages. There are five main, somewhat overlapping, claims. First, jury awards are said to have risen dramatically over the last few decades, and they are out of proportion to the injuries sustained. Thus, in 1986 the Reagan administration's *Report of the Tort Policy Working Group* claimed that between 1975 and 1985 the average malpractice award increased 363 percent, from $220,018 to $1,017,716.[1] It called the increase "explosive." In 1988 the AMA's Specialty Society Medical Liability Project quoted a Department of Justice report claiming that available data "demonstrate an extraordinary growth in civil jury awards in recent years, particularly in . . . medical malpractice" and called the trend "alarming."[2] Professor Paul Weiler, in his influential book MEDICAL MALPRACTICE ON TRIAL, refers to "spiraling jury verdicts."[3]

Second, it is said that juries typically award more when they perceive that the defendant can afford to pay more. The AMA report, for instance, asserted that even when the injury is the same, doctors are assessed damage awards that are larger than other defendants: "What makes the damage awards in professional liability lawsuits particularly disconcerting is the fact that *identical* juries will command much higher recoveries in malpractice cases than in other tort suits, such as automobile accidents."[4] Similarly, in its annual report to Congress in 1991, the Physician Payment Review Commission stated:

Malpractice injuries seem to be compensated more than comparable injuries arising from nonmedical settings. For example, researchers estimated that median awards for a leg amputation were $199,999 in an automobile accident case, $330,000 in a private property owner case, $687,000 in a product liability case, $754,000 in a medical malpractice case against a physician, and $761,000 in a workmen's compensation case. The disparities may be due to jurors' knowledge that physicians are heavily insured or that the claimant's legal fees must be taken out of the judgment.[5]

As we saw in chapter 1, Weiler made a similar declaration: "juries . . . are more willing to reach into the deep pockets of malpractice insurers to compensate the victims generously—more willing than when they encounter the victims of automobile accidents, for in these cases the insurance premiums at risk are paid directly by the jurors themselves."[6] This first claim about damages is usually labeled the "deep pockets" effect.

The third claim is that the primary center of largess in jury awards involves the noneconomic, or "pain and suffering," component of awards. Weiler, for example, asserted that "the most troublesome feature of large tort verdicts is the amount of damages awarded for pain and suffering, not for direct medical costs."[7] He went on to make the claim that "damages for pain and suffering, broadly defined, now make up nearly 50 percent of total tort damages paid for medical cases, with the largest awards taking the lion's share of this money."[8] Professor George Priest cited figures between 25 and 50 percent and estimated that in Cook County, Illinois, noneconomic losses comprised 47 percent of total tort damages.[9] The AMA, drawing on the same primary sources as Weiler, said that pain and suffering accounted for 80 percent of the total verdict in large malpractice cases.[10] Concern with the pain and suffering component appears to derive from its subjective nature. The authors of the AMA report said, "Because large portions of the awards depend upon subjective and emotional considerations, some injured patients recover nothing, some receive less than fair compensation, and others recover amounts far in excess of their losses, both economic and noneconomic."[11] In conjunction with this claim there has also been the belief that the percentage of the award constituting the pain and suffering component has been increasing over recent years.[12]

The fourth claim is that juries seize the opportunity to award punitive damages against doctors whenever they can.[13] Moreover, it is believed that the amount of the punitive award usually exceeds the compensatory award by many times. Concern with punitive awards in malpractice litigation takes place in the midst of a larger debate about the role of punitive damages in products liability and other cases involving business corporations.[14]

The final major claim is that whatever uncertainties and subjectivity are inherent in determining damages, legal professionals—judges or experienced arbitrators—could do it better than juries. The AMA's proposed alternatives to the tort system wanted to keep the issue of liability in the hands of doctors but proposed that damages should be determined by legal or other professionals.[15] In comparing malpractice damages in the United States with England, Germany, Japan, Canada, and France, Professor Gary Schwartz concluded that pain and suffering awards appear to be much higher in the United States. He explained that "[m]ost of the difference . . . probably results from the American practice of trial by jury."[16]

The claim that judges will be superior to juries consists of two assumptions.[17] The first is that because of their legal training and professional responsibility judges are less susceptible to emotional factors that may influence lay jurors. The second is that judges and other legal professionals have a comparative perspective on pain and suffering that juries do not have. Each jury decides the award based solely on a concept of justice for each individual case. In contrast, judges have a perspective that transcends the individual case. They know about other cases that are comparable to the one they are deciding, either because they have personally decided similar cases in the past or they know how other judges have decided similar cases.[18] In short, it is presumed that jury awards will be more affected by emotional factors associated with the case and in any event that there will be greater variability in the size of the awards.

Empirical Data on "Spiraling" Jury Awards

The problem of concluding that jury awards have been "spiraling" based on verdict reports was discussed in chapter 2. I will summarize those arguments. In the first place, many of the statistics relied on by

various authors were drawn from data sources that are unrepresentative of the universe of jury verdicts. Second, even those researchers
who have used representative verdict data have ignored the problem
of potential changes in the types of cases going to trial. This makes
conclusions susceptible to the problem that I identified as the inability
to determine whether the differences in awards reflect the fact that
juries are deciding cases differently or they are deciding different
cases. Third, by reporting average rather than median awards authors
ignore the fact that the average statistic may be inflated by a small
number of very large awards.

With these problems in mind, Stephen Daniels and Joanne Martin of the American Bar Foundation conducted a systematic study of
jury verdicts rendered between 1970 and 1990 in the state jurisdictions
of Los Angeles, San Francisco, Dallas, and Cook County, Illinois (Chicago).[19] They found no support for the proposition that awards were
skyrocketing. In fact what they discovered was that the patterns of
median awards differed between the four locations over the 20-year
time period. Median awards shifted upward and downward but not
in synchrony with each other. However, the largest shifts in median
awards in all four locations involved cases in the top 25th percentile of
awards. The most dramatic awards in the cases involved very serious
birth injuries. Furthermore, because in 1975 California had placed a
$250,000 cap on the amount that could be awarded for pain and suffer-
ing Daniels and Martin estimated that the large awards were primarily for economic damages.

While the Daniels and Martin study must be qualified by the fact
that we do not know about changes in the processes through which
cases were selected for trial, I believe that those authors are correct in
concluding that their data do not support the view that jury verdicts
are spiraling or skyrocketing. Moreover, their data raise the important
question of whether the actual economic damages sustained by some
severely injured plaintiffs have increased. Professor Weiler captured
this idea in his book:

> The fact that million-dollar malpractice verdicts have become com-
> monplace . . . is not by itself evidence of a malfunctioning litiga-
> tion system. It is equally plausible to infer that this tiny minority
> of accident victims actually suffers an equally disproportionate
> share of aggregate compensable losses."[20]

I will address the last issue in chapter 21. In the meantime, however, it is fair to conclude that there is little data to support the general claim that jury verdicts are spiraling or that increases in jury awards are not based upon real, justifiable economic losses.

Empirical Evidence on the Deep Pockets Effect

Supporting Data

Many of the sources asserting that the deep pockets phenomenon exists have cited empirical studies based on jury verdict statistics that appear to support their position. These studies have typically compared the amounts awarded in damages in malpractice cases with the amounts awarded in automobile negligence cases. The most commonly cited studies were conducted by researchers at the Rand Corporation's Institute for Civil Justice (ICJ).

In one of the first ICJ studies Chin and Peterson compared the outcomes of over 1,000 civil trials that took place in Cook County, Illinois, between 1959 and 1979.[21] In making the comparisons, Chin and Peterson attempted to statistically control for severity of the plaintiff's injury, that is, compare awards across cases that had similar injuries. Their data showed that in cases in which the plaintiff was not severely injured health care provider defendants (doctors and hospitals) and corporation defendants paid approximately 30 percent more than other defendants, such as negligent automobile drivers, paid for similar injuries. When the plaintiffs were severely injured, however, health care providers had to pay up to four times the amounts assessed against other types of defendants. Using some of the same data, Hammit, Carroll, and Relles made other comparisons and concluded that "medical malpractice awards against doctors are almost 2.5 times as great as awards against other individuals in average type cases, and awards against hospitals are 85 percent larger."[22] Another Rand study compared jury verdicts in both Cook County and San Francisco, California, over the period 1960 to 1984. Consistent with the other studies malpractice awards were larger than awards in automobile negligence cases. For example, in the period 1980–84 the median malpractice award in Cook County was $121,000, but for automobile accidents the median award was only $7,000. In San Francisco, the figures were, respectively, $156,000 and $29,000.[23] The discrepancies between the mean, or average, awards were even more pronounced. In Cook County the average award for malpractice cases was $1,179,000 versus $88,000 for automobile negligence cases. In San Francisco, the figures were $1,162,000 versus $131,000.[24]

Several studies conducted by other researchers showed patterns similar to those found in the Rand studies. Stephen Daniels and Joanne Martin at the American Bar Foundation examined over 23,000 jury verdicts in 43 counties scattered over 10 states.[25] They found that awards in medical malpractice and product liability cases were generally "much higher" than in other types of cases. Randall Bovbjerg and his colleagues found similar results in another study, as did Patricia Danzon in a study that predated the Rand study.[26]

Problems with the Data: Alternative Explanations

On the surface the studies just referred to appear to lend support for proponents of the deep pockets hypothesis, but there is a major problem with the studies: there are plausible alternative explanations for the results that prevent a conclusion that juries treat malpractice defendants differently than defendants in automobile negligence cases. Juries may instead be deciding different cases, even when severity of injury is taken into consideration.

The first issue associated with the problem was acknowledged by some of the Rand researchers and emphasized by Bovbjerg, Daniels and Martin, and Danzon, namely, that the litigation processes for the two types of cases may be very different, resulting in the fact that juries are deciding very different cases.[27] This, of course, is the tip-of-the-iceberg problem discussed in chapter 2. Recall that in chapter 2 I documented the fact that while between 7 and 10 percent of malpractice suits go to trial only between 1 and 2 percent of automobile negligence suits do so and that whereas the plaintiff win rate in malpractice trials is about 30 percent, the rate for automobile injuries is between 60 and 70 percent.[28] Bovbjerg et al. speculated that plaintiff attorneys in malpractice cases select their cases for litigation on the basis of their possible appeal to jury sympathies, something presumably absent in automobile negligence cases.[29] Regardless of whether plaintiff sympathy, differential selection of cases for litigation, differential settlement rates, or a host of other unknown factors are involved, there appears to be an emerging consensus among researchers that litigation dynamics raise serious possibilities that very different kinds of cases may be going to trial.

However, assume that there were no selection differences and that a random sample of each type of case was selected for trial. There would still be a problem with comparing the jury awards to draw conclusions about deep pocket effects because of many other differences that distinguish medical and auto negligence cases. It is a classic case of attempting to compare apples and oranges. Consider a partial listing of the differences.[30]

Auto injury cases typically involve a single defendant, the driver of the car, but sometimes they involve multiple plaintiffs, for example, several persons riding in the car that was hit. In contrast, malpractice cases typically involve a single plaintiff, the injured patient, and, as I have already shown earlier, multiple defendants. Most auto injuries arise between persons with no prior relationship whereas malpractice cases arise out of a professional relationship between patient and physicians. Auto injuries often involve a single theory of liability but malpractice cases frequently involve multiple theories of causation and liability. The concept of negligence, as described earlier, involves a "reasonable man" standard in automobile cases but a standard of "professional practice" in medical negligence.

The trial itself may also be different. Research by Samuel Gross and Kent Syverud indicated that a high proportion of California malpractice trials appeared to be contested solely on the issue of liability, but in automobile injury trials the contested issue was frequently the amount of damages.[31] In chapter 8 I reported data indicating that in North Carolina malpractice defendants who went to trial most often were also contesting liability. In my interviews with defense lawyers they indicated that they were reluctant to dispute the amount of damages or to present expert evidence on damages on the theory that to do so would cause the jury to assume that the doctors were liable.[32] These interview responses are supported by a survey of the 25 cases in our second sample that went to trial between July 1987 and December 1989. In 16 cases, the plaintiff called one or more experts to testify about damages, but the defendants called no experts. In five cases both plaintiff and defense called experts to testify about damages, and in the remaining four cases neither side called experts. The consequence of this tendency for the defense to avoid contesting the amount of damages is that when the jury does find liability it often has only the plaintiff's evidence on damages to guide it. Moreover, the plaintiff's evidence is often compelling and presents the "Cadillac" version of past and future economic costs. Additionally, the plaintiff may supplement this evidence with "day-in-the-life" videos that vividly dramatize the pain and tribulations of a handicapped person.[33] In automobile negligence trials fought around damages the jury is likely to receive evidence about damages from two sides.

Another difference that may distinguish medical and automobile negligence cases is the degree of responsibility for the injury that can be apportioned between the plaintiff and defendant. Some states, North Carolina, for example, retain the common law rule of "contributory negligence" under which a plaintiff who is judged not to have taken reasonable precautions to avoid injury can be prevented from receiving anything. Many states, however, have adopted a "comparative negligence" standard in which the damage award is reduced according to the percentage of blame that the plaintiff is judged to bear in relation to the percentage ascribed to the defendant. However, long before comparative negligence rules were adopted, research indicated that juries might be applying some rough equities similar to comparative negligence and reducing awards in proportion to the plaintiff's degree of negligence.[34] The point of this observation is that whether by law or by the jurors' sense of justice, medical and automobile cases often differ in the extent to which the plaintiff may be judged partially negligent. In automobile accidents the driver of the car that was hit may be seen by the jurors to have failed to exercise reasonable care by not driving defensively. In malpractice cases, by contrast, the patient may be under anesthesia when the injury occurs or may otherwise be totally dependent on the doctor's skill, judgment, and treatment. There are, of course, exceptions in both types of cases. The automobile injury plaintiff may have been sitting on a park bench when the driver's car jumped the curb. The malpractice plaintiff may have had preexisting injuries or illness that jurors feel should not be paid in the award; there may be evidence that the patient undertook treatment after being informed of its risks; or the patient may have failed to follow the doctor's instructions prior to, during, or following treatment. Nevertheless, it seems plausible to hypothesize that when all cases are considered in total the likelihood of jurors perceiving plaintiff responsibility and reducing awards is higher in automobile negligence cases.

The hypothesis that the discrepancy in mean damage awards between medical and automobile negligence cases is due to jurors' attitudes that the rich can pay has a lot of competing hypotheses, some or all of which may combine to offer plausible explanations of why there is a difference in magnitude between auto and medical negligence damages.

Missing Evidence

The deep pockets hypothesis is predicated on assertions about juror attitudes and motives. Weiler's recitation of the hypothesis, for example, claimed that jurors worry about the size of auto negligence awards because they perceive them as affecting car insurance rates, but presumably they do not see the connection to the costs of health care.[35] Peter Huber made a similar assertion and, along with former Surgeon General Koop, additionally claimed that jurors ignore the question of negligence and render awards out of sympathy for the plaintiff and the belief that wealthy defendants can and should pay.[36] The Bovbjerg group's notion that malpractice cases were selected on the basis of their appeal to jury sympathies is a slight variation on this same theme.[37]

The problem with these assertions is that the verdict statistics sources provide no information whatever on what jurors thought or believed when they decided the cases. Moreover, none of the authors just discussed provided any other data to support their claims. The fact is, then, that the evidence on jurors' psychological motives and dispositions is totally absent. This part of the deep pockets hypothesis is based on pure conjecture.

Contrary Evidence

Several different kinds of findings from various studies, moreover, appear inconsistent with the deep pockets hypothesis. The first of these is that, as documented in chapters 3 and 4, plaintiff win rates seldom exceed 30 percent and are frequently much lower whereas the win rates in auto negligence cases frequently approach 70 percent or more.[38] Though this can probably be ascribed to case selection or other factors I have discussed earlier, the consistent low win ratios clearly suggest that juries do not automatically favor plaintiffs over doctors. Otherwise, plaintiff win ratios would be much higher.

Second, recall that the Taragin et al. New Jersey study concluded that the probability of the plaintiff winning on the issue of liability was not correlated with the severity of the injury.[39] If juror sympathy for plaintiffs was a significant factor, we should expect some positive correlation in which more severely injured plaintiffs would win more cases.

Perhaps, however, the deep pockets effect applies only after liability has been determined. None of the proponents of the hypothesis has articulated such a two-stage hypothesis, but we should be willing to entertain one and ask whether the phenomenon occurs only in the post-liability phase of deliberations.

Even considering this modified version, however, existing data still present a third problem. The Chin and Peterson study discussed earlier concluded that doctors and hospitals paid substantially lower awards when they were found liable as defendants in nonmalpractice cases, such as slip-and-fall or automobile negligence, than when they were found liable in malpractice cases.[40] This finding has been overlooked by people who have cited the other parts of their findings, but it raises a question of whether jurors are responding to deep pockets or some other factor because the depth of doctors' and hospitals' pockets remains the same in both types of cases.

The fourth piece of contrary evidence is more indirect. Various studies have compared the size of awards with the seriousness of the plaintiff's injuries and other variables.[41] These studies have consistently concluded that the best predictor of award size is injury seriousness. If the deep pockets effect is real, as these latter findings suggest, it must have an effect over and above injury severity, or at least an effect that combines with severity in some unspecified way.

Empirical Data on Pain and Suffering

The claims about noneconomic damages constituting the largest portions of awards are also subject to the criticism that they are without adequate empirical foundation. Weiler's claim that pain and suffering accounts for over 50 percent of malpractice awards and the AMA's claim that the figure is 80 percent cannot be found in the empirical studies that they cite.[42]

There are in fact several studies that attempted to estimate pain and suffering from jury verdict statistics.[43] The technique of these researchers was to take the total verdict and subtract from it estimates of economic costs such as past and future loss of income and medical expenses. The remainder was labeled "pain and suffering." The results have tended to show that the amount awarded for pain and suffering varies according to the severity of the injury but that there is much variability within the categories of severity. The authors of the studies have suggested that while jury verdicts do show some general rationality that is inconsistent with the extreme claims of jury critics, there is nevertheless evidence that juries are highly variable from case to case with the consequence that pain and suffering awards are random and inequitable.[44]

I have critiqued these studies in great detail elsewhere and concluded that they are seriously flawed on a number of methodological grounds.[45] The specifics of my critique involve some esoterica that will be of interest only to a few persons, and because they can consult the articles, I need only summarize the main points here. There is so much missing data about economic costs in the studies' databases that we have to suspect that they are unreliable and unrepresentative. Some findings indicate that the amount of awards ascribed to pain and suffering exceeds the total award, a logical impossibility. One researcher mixed disparate data sources that were unrepresentative and, further, included settlements and awards by judges as well as jury awards. In many instances, the portion of jury awards ascribed to economic damages was underestimated, and as a result, the pain and suffering component was inflated.

The bottom line is that the empirical studies that have attempted to make estimates of pain and suffering from verdict statistics are so flawed that they are not capable of reliably telling us anything about jury behavior.

Our Knowledge about Damages: Conclusions

The claims about spiraling awards, deep pockets tendencies, and juror sympathies in rendering pain and suffering awards are among the most serious charges against malpractice juries. My discussion in this chapter, however, raises serious questions about the ability of verdict statistics to demonstrate these alleged proclivities because there are plausible alternative explanations of the findings. This *does not* disprove the allegations; it only raises doubts about the merits of the evidence that has been interpreted as supporting them.

In the following chapters of part 4 I will address the claims in the light of evidence that I and other researchers have gathered. A good place to begin is with the deep pockets allegation.

18

Two Tests of the "Deep
Pockets" Hypothesis

Because verdict statistics studies are so confounded by variables that can offer plausible alternative explanations for the award differences between medical and automobile negligence cases, we must find alternative ways of examining the validity of the deep pockets hypothesis. One approach is to conduct simulation experiments in which confounding variables are controlled and another is to gather data about juror attitudes and behaviors in real trials. This chapter begins my examination using the first approach. It describes the results of two experiments that I and some of my students conducted.

Experiment 1

Overview and Rationale

Our research strategy was to vary two factors most central to the deep pockets hypothesis while keeping all other factors constant.[1] A sample of 147 jurors was asked to award damages for pain and suffering in the case of a young woman who suffered a broken leg and resultant complications. For some of the jurors the cause of negligence was ascribed to health care providers: either one doctor, two doctors, or a hospital corporation. For other jurors the cause of the injury was ascribed to negligence involving operation of a motor vehicle and, in parallel fashion to the medical negligence cases, either involved one defendant, two defendants, or a business corporation.

The automobile injury was chosen as the comparison case since it is typically used as the baseline against which malpractice cases are judged.[2] We varied the number and type of defendants because we believed that a crucial distinction between automobile and malpractice cases may be that the former frequently have a single defendant whereas the latter often involve multiple defendants, and research in other contexts suggests jurors may respond differently to negligence caused by individual versus corporate actors.[3] To control for any confounds due to differing assessments of responsibility, we stipulated to the jurors that the defendant had been found liable in a prior judicial proceeding and that the task of the juror was only to award damages. Because most of the speculation about jury largess has focused on pain and suffering, we also instructed the jurors that the medical and income losses were not in dispute, that their task was to simply give an award for pain and suffering.

As I discussed in the last chapter (and in chaps. 1 and 2), assertions about the deep pockets effect are accompanied by speculation about the attitudes of jurors who produce those awards, for instance, that they believe rich doctors and hospitals ought to pay. However, there have been no data at all to verify this claim. The experiment asked the jurors about their attitudes and thus provides us with a first look at what jurors think.

The Research Procedure

The sample of jurors consisted of 147 persons waiting to be called for jury selection in the Wake County (Raleigh, North Carolina) Superior Court who volunteered to take part in a study of juror decision making. Equal numbers of men and women participated, and they approximately mirrored the demographic characteristics of the jury pool. They were randomly assigned to one of the six conditions in the experiment.

Each juror was given a packet of materials consisting of background facts, results of a prior judicial proceeding establishing defendant liability, excerpts of the plaintiff's testimony about her pain and suffering, three xeroxed photographs of the plaintiff demonstrating the injury, and legal arguments from lawyers from each side. Instructions from the judge specified that the medical expenses and lost income amounted to $34,268 and were not in dispute. The judge's instructions also provided standard legal guidance on pain and suffering. Following the rendering of their award the jurors were asked to indicate their reasoning and their perceptions in an open format and on a series of rating scales.

The following are summaries of the case that the jurors decided in each of the six conditions.

Medical Negligence, One Defendant. The plaintiff was described as a 17-year-old female who elected surgery under general anesthesia to have a benign cyst removed from her back. She was given a sedative prior to general anesthesia and brought into the operating room. When the anesthesiologist negligently moved away from the disoriented patient, she fell off the operating table. She was placed back on the table and the operation was completed, but when she awoke in the recovery room with excruciating pain in her leg, doctors discovered that she had a broken femur. The leg was set in a plaster cast and the patient was discharged the next day. However, she required pain medication for two weeks, and when the cast was removed in two months, it was discovered that the fracture had not healed properly, resulting in a two-inch shortening of her leg. The result was determined not to be the fault of the doctor who set the leg. During the next six months, the plaintiff was unable to attend school or participate in normal physical activities and had to undergo four separate corrective surgeries: an osteotomy to lengthen the leg bone; osteosynthesis to attach a metal plate to the leg; surgery to remove the metal plate; and plastic surgery to cosmetically disguise the scars. During part of this time the evidence (illustrated by a photograph) showed that she was on crutches with an exterior metal plate on her leg. Testimony indicated that she also underwent intense and painful physical therapy.

The ultimate result was a good one: she recovered fully, and plastic surgery successfully corrected the surgical scars. However, she sued the anesthesiologist for medical expenses and her pain and suffering over the lengthy period of her recovery. The lawyer for the defendant did not dispute liability and conceded the economic damages of $34,268 but argued that the amount for past pain and suffering should be $30,000. The lawyer for the plaintiff argued that compensation for pain and suffering should be between $180,000 and $220,000.

Medical Negligence, Two Defendants. The facts of the case were identical except that in this instance the surgeon began the operation before the patient was fully anesthetized, causing her to kick and fall off the table. Prior judicial proceedings ascertained that both doctors were liable for the injury because the anesthesiologist is required to ensure that the patient is anesthetized and the surgeon is required to check with the anesthesiologist before beginning surgery.

Medical Negligence, Hospital Defendant. The facts of this case were identical except that hospital orderlies negligently dropped the patient when transferring her from the operating table, causing the broken femur. Under the legal doctrine of *respondeat superior* the hospital was legally liable for the acts of its employees.

Auto Injury Negligence, One Defendant. In contrast to the medical negligence conditions, the broken femur resulted from a driver who negligently caused his vehicle to swerve into an oncoming lane of traffic and struck the plaintiff's vehicle. All of the other facts about the plaintiff and her recovery remained identical.

Auto Injury Negligence, Two Defendants. In this condition, two drivers were responsible for the plaintiff's broken leg. One driver was distracted while talking on his cellular phone, and the other impatiently attempted to pass him near a curve. The startled first driver swerved, forcing the second into the path of the plaintiff's vehicle.

Auto Injury Negligence, Corporate Defendant. This version was similar to the single-driver version except that the driver was an employee of the Allied Products Company; under the doctrine of *respondeat superior* the corporation was held liable for the accident.

Regardless of condition, each juror was instructed to award $34,268 for medical bills and affix a sum for past pain and suffering under the following instructions:

> Damages should include such amount as you find, by the greater weight of the evidence, is fair compensation for the actual physical pain and mental suffering which were the immediate necessary consequences of the accident. There is no fixed formula for pain and suffering. You will determine what is fair compensation by applying logic and common sense to the evidence.

Following their verdicts, jurors were asked to explain the reasons behind the amount of their award and then they answered a series of rating scale questions bearing on the case.

The Results

The mean (average) pain and suffering award and the standard deviation, a measure of the variability of awards, for each of the six conditions, plus aggregate statistics, are presented in table 18.1. Consider the aggregate statistics first. The bottom right-hand figure, $89,908, is the mean award summed over all conditions. The two figures immediately above it report the mean awards for all jurors for whom the cause of the accident was medical negligence ($93,999) and for auto negligence ($87,783). Overall, the mean malpractice award was $6,216 more than the mean auto negligence award. The bottom row of three figures ($102,506, $75,682, and $94,484) is the mean awards, summed across the causes of injury for one defendant, two defendants, and hospital-corporation defendants, respectively.

Before I attempt to apply any substantive meaning to these figures, consider the results of a statistical test, called analysis of variance, that was applied to the data. The purpose of the test was to ascertain whether these differences were meaningful in a statistical sense or, alternatively, whether they could be ascribed to chance variation. The analysis of variance indicated that neither the $6,216 difference between the medical and auto negligence causes of the injury nor the differences between the defendant conditions was statistically significant. Put in layperson's terms, the test indicates several things. First, there is no support for the hypothesis that jurors would be prejudiced against medical providers in comparison to motor vehicle operators or to corporations who are legally responsible for them. Second, there was no general support for the hypothesis that the number or type of defendants makes a difference, despite the fact that the mean for the two-defendant conditions ($75,682) *appears* to be

TABLE 18.1.   Means and Standard Deviations of "Pain and Suffering" Awards by Condition and Number and Type of Defendants

	One Defendant ($)	Two Defendants ($)	Hospital-Corporation ($)	Mean Award ($)
Medical negligence	99,950[a] (60,482)	67,709[b] (43,278)	114,339[a] (61,243)	93,999
Motor vehicle negligence	105,063[a] (69,471)	83,655[a] (63,546)	74,630[a] (46,923)	87,783
Mean award	102,506	75,682	94,484	89,908

Notes: Standard deviations in parentheses. Comparisons between individual conditions: means with similar superscripts are not statistically different from one another.

substantially lower than the means for the one-defendant ($102,506) and corporation conditions ($94,484).[4]

These findings may be better understood by first examining the standard deviations, which are reported in parentheses for each condition in table 18.1. The standard deviation is a statistical measure of how much awards varied from the average. The table shows that in each condition there was considerable variability. Consider the one-defendant conditions. The standard deviation of $60,482 in the medical negligence condition indicates that two-thirds of the awards ranged between $39,468 and $160,432 (i.e., the mean of $99,950 ± $60,482). In the motor vehicle condition two-thirds of awards ranged between $35,592 and $174,534 (i.e., $105,063 ± $69,471). With this kind of variability in awards, it is not surprising that although the mean award in the motor vehicle negligence condition was $5,113 larger than the medical negligence condition, the difference was possibly due to chance fluctuation.[5] The same reasoning can be applied to comparisons between the other conditions.

To avoid any misinterpretation let me repeat the conclusion to be drawn from these findings about the pain and suffering awards. The fact that mean and median awards were actually slightly larger for single defendants when liability for the injury was ascribed to automobile as opposed to medical negligence and that the overall mean award was slightly larger for medical negligence can as easily be ascribed to chance fluctuations in the data with respect to any actual difference in the way that the medical and automobile cases were treated.

The jurors' responses to the rating scales yielded only a couple of statistically significant effects. The most interesting of these was that jurors perceived the plaintiff as bearing more responsibility for the accident when it resulted from motor vehicle negligence than when it resulted from medical malpractice. Concern with responsibility was also expressed by some of the jurors as they wrote explanations for their awards.

A juror in the single-physician condition wrote, "I think a 46 year old Dr. should have the expertise not to make careless mistakes on human life. That his job is to see that people are helped and treated with care" (awarded $220,000). Another juror in the same condition stated, "The doctor had major responsibility for the care and safety of his patient. Undue stress placed on the patient for an incident not even related to her original condition warrants such an amount" (awarded $127,000). A juror in the two-physician condition wrote, "The doctors allowing her to fall off the operating table is unpardonable. She suffered 20 times the pain which her cyst removal should have caused" (awarded $30,000). Another, also in the condition with two physician defendants, commented, "We depend on doctors not to be careless. We are leaving our lives in their hands. Basically, I feel that doctors should not make these kinds of mistakes" (awarded $100,000). Still another said, "It is my belief that in a job situation such as surgery or any medical area that each step should be double check [sic] to prevent unnecessary or previous incorrect performance of that job" (awarded $100,000).

These examples indicate that some jurors did focus on the role and responsibilities of physicians. However, jurors expressed parallel attitudes about responsibility in the motor vehicle negligence conditions as well: "The man's total carelessness should be thoroughly punished" (awarded $200,000); "Accident was avoidable. . . . Terrible ordeal because of carelessness with his car" (awarded $165,732); "[The driver] should pay attention to the highway because you have to drive for yourself and other people too" (awarded $10,000).

In both medical and vehicle negligence conditions, some jurors commented on what they perceived to be the defendant's acceptance of responsibility: "The doctors' attitudes about accepting responsibility was [sic] important" (awarded $50,000); "The fact that the hospital accepted responsibility was also important although I thought that the amount they were willing to pay for pain and suffering was not adequate" (awarded $80,000); "The willingness of [the negligent corporate vehicle defendant] to accept responsibility limited amount of 'pain and suffering' award" (awarded $100,000); "Important: Defendant [motor vehicle negligence] admitted his negligence—honesty" (awarded $30,000); "Time—it is now 5 years later and the hospital is stalling" (awarded $75,000).

These examples indicate that despite the fact that the jurors' task was defined solely as assessing the amount of damages, their attitudes about defendant responsibility were of concern as they made their decisions. It is noteworthy, however, that in both the hospital and the parallel corporate responsibility conditions, there were many fewer comments about responsibility than in the conditions in which defendants were individuals.

The responses commenting on the plaintiff's pain and suffering varied widely. Some jurors made much of the fact that a 17-year-old girl had a very traumatic experience: "[T]ime lost early [in life] may never be regained" (awarded $50,000); "She trusted the doctors and now she will always be afraid of hospitals and doctors" (awarded $100,000); "[eight] months of life taken from her. . . . The Dr. was distracted from his job. One second is all it took to destroy her" (awarded $200,000). Several jurors mused about future events, contrary to judicial instructions and the evidence that was presented: "[Alluding to potential problems with] early arthritis or with child-bearing" (awarded $150,000); "[T]his situation could trigger psychological problems later" (awarded $125,000); "I think events at that age will be carried into adulthood" (awarded $220,000). Others, however, minimized the trauma or took the position that sometimes pain must just be borne: "She had pain and suffering. But these things don't last long and you can learn how to get around the way you are" (awarded $220,000); "[She] lost a year. However, it is quite possible to carry on in a cast—personal experience" (awarded $30,000); "Pain is a part of life and money will not remove the pain. Mistakes occur daily by all people no matter what their occupation. We are all human, this action [mistake by doctors] was not negligence, it was an oversight (mistake). . . . Life goes on" (awarded $30,000); "We all go through hardships in life. . . . I do not feel anyone is deserving of massive amounts for an incident in her life that she has totally recovered from except for memory" (awarded $30,000). Concerns about getting something for nothing and the impacts of awards on society were also prominent in some jurors' responses: "The legal system has gotten out of hand in its pursuit of financial rewards due to damages through litigation that apparently does not apply in this case, but an award should be what is fair and right for both sides" (awarded $150,000); "I have a hard time giving enormous amounts of $ [sic] to victims even though I acknowledge her right to receive something" (awarded $50,000); "Accidents happen; no perm[anent] damage. I can't believe in lawsuits for excessive amounts" (awarded nothing); "Personally, I think financial judgments in general are too high and accordingly went with the lowest figure mentioned" (awarded $30,000); "I do not think she should get rich because of this accident, and accidents do happen and both doctors admitted that it did happen" (awarded $50,000); "I tried to balance award. . . .

keeping in mind very large awards may encourage other lawsuits for the sake of potential large settlements" (awarded $75,000).

It is also clear that jurors uniformly commented on the difficulty of putting a price on pain and suffering and used different methods of calculating the awards. Some roughly split the difference between the defendant's and the plaintiff's suggested figures. One juror doubled what the defendant said was fair, and another said it should be three times medical expenses. One juror said, "[Eight] months of pain and suffering missing out of her teen years. She should receive no more than what most people make in a year" (awarded $50,000). A number of jurors assessed pain and suffering on a per-month basis, such as $4,000 or $5,000, and multiplied by the eight months that the plaintiff was incapacitated. Other jurors indicated that they just came up with a figure that they thought was fair.

Of the 147 jurors only one mentioned that the ability of the defendants to pay was a consideration, and that juror was in the two-defendant vehicle negligence condition: "Not knowing the ability of the defendants to pay an exorbitant amount and considering an average salary to be $35,000 [per year] I feel both men could pay $70,000 together."

These explanations in the jurors' own words show highly varied responses to the case. Some expressed punitiveness and a desire to blame, but these responses were offset by those of the majority of jurors who attempted to come up with what they thought was a fair award. Further, it appears that punitiveness and blame were not disproportionately applied to cases of medical negligence; motor vehicle negligence evoked similar responses in jurors.

One additional interesting finding was that jurors who made strong statements about the irresponsibility of the defendant(s) and those who expressed sympathies for the plaintiff did not necessarily give the highest awards. This lack of correlation between juror reactions and size of awards leads to the hypothesis that even if the juror was inclined to punish the defendant or give the plaintiff a windfall, the actual amount judged appropriate to accomplish the goal differed. Thus, one juror might deem a $40,000 award to be big punishment of the defendant, whereas another juror who does not wish to punish might consider $100,000 fair compensation for the pain and suffering. The data do not allow further exploration of this hypothesis.

A Summary of the Findings

The experiment yielded no support for the deep pockets hypothesis or the psychological dynamics that are posited to be behind it. Whether medical or automobile negligence caused the accident made no statistically significant difference in the amounts of awards. There were some differences in juror perceptions consistent with the view that plaintiff responsibility was perceived to be greater in automobile negligence accidents, although these differences were not reflected in overall awards. Jurors' explanations of their reasoning demonstrated widely varying approaches to whether and under what conditions awards for pain and suffering were appropriate.

Experiment 2

Overview and Rationale

The second experiment was undertaken with the primary goal of determining whether malpractice versus automobile differences might be found in a case involving more severe and permanent injuries than the injuries described in the first experiment.[6] Secondarily, my students and I wanted to explore further the hints in the first experiment that jurors might be responsive to any perceived responsibility for the injury.

In the first experiment jurors tended to ascribe more responsibility to the plaintiff in the motor vehicle negligence conditions than in the malpractice conditions. Although this difference in responsibility ascription was not reflected in the awards, other research on juries has suggested that it is often important. Thus, in the second experiment four fact patterns were created. In the first scenario the injury arose in the course of elective surgery. In the second scenario the identical injury resulted from mandatory surgery. In a third scenario the injury resulted from an automobile accident in which the plaintiff was the driver of an automobile hit by the defendant. In the fourth scenario the plaintiff was sitting in the front passenger seat of a parked automobile that was hit by the defendant. Thus, two of the four fact patterns (elective surgery and plaintiff as driver) involved conditions in which the jurors might be able to ascribe some responsibility to the plaintiff. The other two fact patterns (mandatory surgery and plaintiff as passenger) involved conditions that were intended to eliminate or reduce the likelihood of jurors ascribing responsibility to the plaintiff.

Finally, to control for characteristics of the defendants, the drivers in the automobile negligence conditions were described as doctors. Recall from my discussion in chapter 17 that Chin and Peterson found that doctors and other health care providers who were defendants in automobile negligence cases paid lower awards than when they were defendants in malpractice cases.[7]

The Research Procedure

The sample of jurors involved 72 persons waiting to be called for jury duty in the Wake County (Raleigh, North Carolina) Superior Court who volunteered to take part in an experiment on jury decision making. The participants' demographic characteristics generally approximated the characteristics of the jury pool.

Each juror received a packet of material containing background facts, excerpts of testimony, two xeroxed photographs of the plaintiff's face demonstrating the extent of the injury, legal arguments from both sides, and instructions from the judge. The jurors were also told that the defendant's liability had been determined in a prior judicial proceeding and that their sole responsibility was to award damages. The individual jurors were assigned to one of four fact conditions.

Medical Negligence, Mandatory Surgery. The plaintiff was a 38-year-old female who required surgery to remove a cyst that had developed behind her ear. If this cyst were not removed surgically, it could cause permanent hearing loss. Surgery was, therefore, necessary. Upon injection of a local anesthetic into the upper portion of plaintiff's neck and cheek area, defendant mistakenly damaged the facial nerve by improperly implanting the needle.

Although the cyst surgery was performed successfully, the plaintiff suffered irreversible nerve damage that resulted in a permanent, severe facial distortion. Her facial paralysis was particularly accentuated when she smiled. When she was not smiling, the right side of her face appeared to be noticeably lower than the left side of her face, in a drooping manner. (The injury was clearly evident in the xeroxed photographs accompanying the jurors' materials.) However, she suffered no physical pain. Several medical experts testifying for the plaintiff all agreed that her facial paralysis was permanent.

The jurors learned that after the accident the plaintiff took a three-month leave of absence from her job. She is now working, although she is constantly aware of and embarrassed about her disfigurement. Her husband has felt compelled to seek professional counseling to deal with the trauma. In consequence, the plaintiff sued the physician for medical expenses, employment disadvantage, and mental anguish and disfigurement. The lawyer for the defendant did not dispute liability since it had already been determined, and he conceded the economic damages of $30,000. However, the defense lawyer did argue that the amount of the award should be $100,000. In contrast, the lawyer for the plaintiff argued that compensation should be $300,000.

Medical Negligence, Elective Surgery. The facts of the case were identical except that in this instance the plaintiff did not undergo mandatory surgery. Rather, she elected to have cosmetic surgery to enlarge her lips. She suffered the same facial injury as in the first condition when the defendant improperly implanted the anesthesia needle.

Auto Negligence, Plaintiff as Driver. The plaintiff was driving north on a two-lane road, and the defendant, a physician, was traveling northbound directly behind the plaintiff's car. The defendant pulled into the oncoming traffic lane, passing the plaintiff's car, and abruptly cut in front of her. Startled, the plaintiff hit her brakes but was unable to avoid the ensuing collision. At impact, her face hit the dashboard, compressing and permanently damaging her facial nerve. Her injuries were identical to the two medical negligence conditions.

Auto Negligence, Plaintiff as Passenger. The plaintiff was seated in the passenger seat of a legally parked car. The defendant pulled out of an adjacent parking lot and accidentally rammed into the rear right side of the car. All other facts are identical to the above conditions, including the injury suffered, stipulated liability and medical damages, and the amount in controversy.

The jurors were first asked to award the amount for pain and suffering that was to be added to the stipulated medical costs of $30,000. Next, they were asked to explain in their own words what factors they considered important or unimportant to their decision and why. Then they were asked to respond to three questions bearing on allocation of responsibility to the plaintiff. One question was as follows: "In your opinion, what percent of [plaintiff's] behavior contributed to the accident?" Another question asked whether they considered the defendant's ability to pay when they determined their awards. Then jurors were asked to explain their responses.

The Results

The mean, or average, awards and their standard deviations for each of the four conditions, plus aggregate means, are reported in table 18.2. The two award figures in the far right-hand column, $242,297 and $224,428, are the averages for the aggregated malpractice and both auto accident conditions, respectively, while the two figures in the bottom row, $233,472 and $233,750, report the aggregated conditions in which plaintiff responsibility was absent or negligible (mandatory surgery and auto passenger conditions) versus the conditions in which jurors might be able to psychologically ascribe responsibility to the plaintiff (elective surgery and plaintiff as driver).

An analysis of variance indicated that the $17,868 difference between the aggregated medical and automobile negligence conditions was not statistically significant nor was the $278 difference between the two aggregated responsibility conditions. In short, whether the cause of the injury was ascribed to medical or automobile negligence the jurors in the experiment did not give statistically different awards nor did the awards differ as a function of the responsibility conditions. Nevertheless, it must be noted that the somewhat higher award in the aggregated malpractice conditions repeats the pattern found in the first experiment.

TABLE 18.2.   Mean Damage Awards and Standard Deviations by Conditions

	Possible Plaintiff Responsibility		
Case Type	Absent ($)	Present ($)	Row Mean ($)
Medical negligence			
Mean	252,263	228,611	242,297
Standard deviation	92,638	65,165	
Automobile negligence			
Mean	209,000	238,888	224,428
Standard deviation	86,823	69,780	
Column mean	233,472	233,750	

The jurors did allocate responsibility differently between conditions. More responsibility for the injury was allocated to the plaintiff in the medical negligence conditions (13.4 percent) than in the automobile negligence conditions (3.9 percent). It appears that much of this difference is due to the fact that, on average, relatively high responsibility was allocated to the plaintiff in the elective surgery condition (21.1 percent) and very low responsibility was allocated in the passenger auto negligence condition (1.5 percent). However, even though the conditions did evoke differing perceptions of responsibility, these differences were not reflected directly in the amounts of damages that were awarded.

To further explore the relationship, or lack of it, between awards and perceived responsibility, correlations between these two variables were conducted *within* each of the four conditions. Both of the conditions involving possible plaintiff responsibility yielded significant correlations. In both the elective surgery and the plaintiff as driver conditions there were statistically significant correlations of, respectively, −.70, and −.51. In simple words, the more individual jurors in these conditions ascribed some responsibility to the plaintiff the lower were their awards. However, in the other two conditions there was no association between perceived plaintiff responsibility and amount of the award.

The jurors' written comments were content analyzed and yielded additional insights about responsibility ascriptions and awards. In the elective surgery condition 56 percent of jurors focused on the elective nature of the operation and were of the view that the plaintiff had assumed some risk in undertaking it: for example, "no one forced her to have the operation"; "it was voluntary and her vanity was involved—she should have investigated [the risks] more thoroughly." In contrast, only 20 percent of the jurors in the mandatory surgery condition made comments about risks assumed by the plaintiff, and these involved statements that the plaintiff should have gotten a second opinion before undergoing an operation. In the driver accident condition 39 percent of jurors specifically mentioned that the plaintiff should have been more alert: for example, "she could have put on her brakes to slow down"; "why didn't she see him passing her?"; "driver may have been speeding." Only one juror in the passenger condition wrote a comment bearing on plaintiff responsibility.

The question asking jurors whether the defendant's ability to pay was considered in making the award yielded a couple of interesting findings. Thirty percent of jurors said that they did consider the defendant's ability to pay, but this tendency did not significantly differ across conditions. Furthermore, none of these jurors mentioned that the award was made higher because of assumed deep pockets. Rather, more than half (55 percent) specifically indicated that they would have adjusted the award downward to avoid financially hurting the defendant if they had believed there was no insurance or the defendant did not have the capacity to pay. The other jurors simply noted that they had thought about insurance or how the defendant would pay. While this latter finding is open to different interpretations, it is important to note that no juror mentioned raising the award because of perceived ability to pay, and 70 percent of jurors said they did not consider the defendant's ability to pay.

An additional finding from analysis of the jurors' written comments is that, even though 62 percent expressly mentioned sympathy for the plaintiff, 27 percent also expressed the sentiment that injured people should not unduly profit from a misfortune. Taking two examples, one juror in a malpractice condition wrote, "As uncompassionate as it may seem, I don't feel Dr. Hall should pay anything for mental anguish because no amount can change her disfigurement"; and a juror in an automobile negligence condition wrote, "there is no amount of money that can give her back normalcy; It was a tragic accident but unfortunately accidents happen, and I don't feel destroying Dr. Hall's life will make Mrs. Wilson's ordeal any more bearable; I feel monetary awards granted in many cases are obscene and a result of our greedy society."

A Summary of the Findings

As in the first experiment, jurors did not give statistically different awards as a function of whether the injury was caused by medical or automobile negligence. However, as in the first experiment, the award was slightly higher for the aggregated malpractice conditions. The conditions varying potential plaintiff responsibility did result in differing responsibility ascriptions, but across conditions there was no association with amount of awards. However, in the two conditions allowing jurors to perceive the plaintiff as sharing some blame, the more the blame, the lower was the award. This latter finding is particularly interesting in light of the fact that the jurors were told that the defendant had been found legally liable. It is interesting to consider whether similar plaintiff blaming would occur in malpractice cases where informed consent is an issue or where the patient did not follow the pre- or posttreatment regimen prescribed by the doctor. The most important point, however, is that the results suggest that the jurors were attentive to possible plaintiff responsibility and that a substantial number of them expressed concerns that plaintiffs should not unduly profit from a misfortune, whether it be caused by medical or automobile negligence. An intriguing finding from analysis of jurors' explanations of their awards suggested that they would have adjusted the award downward if they believed there was no insurance or the defendant did not have the ability to pay.

Other Experiments

The findings of our two experiments are generally consistent with two other experiments. Goodman, Greene, and Loftus had jurors in King County, Washington, read a brief summary of a wrongful death case in which the defendant's liability had already been established.[8] For some jurors the cause of the death was described as due to medical negligence while for others it was described as due to automobile negligence or to product liability. The type of case had no significant effect on the amount of damages awarded. Martin Bourgeois and Irwin Horowitz conducted another study in which half of the jurors were told that the cause of a death was a surgical error and half were told it was due to an automobile accident.[9] In half of the surgical error cases the defendant was a physician and in the other half the defendant was described as a hospital. In parallel fashion the automobile negligence defendant was either a doctor or a hospital. The physician defendant in the malpractice condition was awarded almost three times more than the physician defendant in the automobile defendant condition. However, the data showed that the jurors ascribed significantly greater responsibility to the defendant in the former condition than the latter. Thus, differences in perceived responsibility appear to have been a mediating factor that affected the size of awards.

Cautious Conclusions and Unanswered Questions

Proponents of the deep pockets hypothesis assert that jurors treat medical malpractice and automobile cases differently. The two experiments reported in this chapter controlled for the variables that have contaminated comparisons of jury verdicts. Neither yielded statistically significant support for the hypothesis, and the data in some conditions were in an opposite direction to what the hypothesis would predict. For example, in the first experiment the jurors awarded more in the automobile negligence conditions when there were one or two defendants than they did in the malpractice conditions. Even though these differences were not *statistically* significant, they are contrary to the view that jurors award more when a doctor is the defendant. It also seems likely that jurors' ascriptions of responsibility to plaintiffs and defendant influenced the awards in some complex ways. This finding is consistent with other recent studies indicating that differences in perceived responsibility rather than perceived ability to pay is a more likely explanation of differential awards.[10] The jurors' written comments in the two experiments also yield no support for a deep pockets explanation.

The experiments leave some important questions. One is whether the pain and suffering award was exaggerated in some way—either inflated or deflated—as a result of the artificiality of the experiment. In most real trial cases jurors have to consider economic and noneconomic damages. The experiments provided no information about how these components of damages might interact with each other. A closely related, more general question is the extent to which any simulation mirrors the way actual jurors behave, given that a trial is a more complex environment. The purpose of a simulation is to tease out other variables in order to test relations between specified variables, but this strategy always raises the question of generalizability. A substantive question arises from suggestions in the data that in rendering awards jurors are sensitive to issues of relative perceived responsibility between defendant and plaintiff even when they are instructed that legal liability has already been determined. This question in turn raises questions about what effect responsibility ascriptions might have on judgments of medical versus automobile negligence and the degree to which they might explain differences in real-life medical and automobile negligence awards.

Two additional issues are of particular interest. The first is whether these data about the amount and the variability of awards and about ascriptions of responsibility are unique to jurors. Put another way, would judges or other people with legal training and experience react differently to the case and make different awards than jurors? The second issue arises out of the fact that the data in the two experiments involved individual juror decisions whereas jury decisions are a result of the pooled wisdom of 12 persons. What would jury decisions look like? How would they compare with those that a judge might render? Chapter 19 attempts to address these last questions. Subsequent chapters will address what jurors do in real cases and the correspondence between those findings and the experiments.

19

Jurors versus Legal Professionals: Two Studies (*with Jeffrey Rice and David Landau*)

In his well-known treatise on damages, Professor Dan Dobbs observed that monetary compensation for "pain and suffering" has been recognized for centuries as a legitimate element in American and English law.[1] In this century courts of appeal, responding to changes in societal thinking about such matters, have actually expanded the grounds under which injured persons may be compensated for noneconomic damages.[2] Yet the determination of noneconomic damages—"pain and suffering"—is a subjective and difficult task. Legal scholars and judges alike have continually acknowledged the unquantifiable nature of the jury's task and the fact that the jury has virtually unbridled discretion in determining the amount of compensation.[3] Usually the jury is simply told that the amount should reflect "fair compensation" or a "reasonable amount" without anything else to guide it. The studies I discussed in chapter 18 showed that there was considerable variability between jurors as to what was considered an appropriate award for pain and suffering and that the jurors struggled with the task.

The weakness of the jury system for determining pain and suffering awards is said to be that the jurors have no prior training in this matter and, in particular that they have no experience with prior awards in other cases involving similar injuries.[4] In contrast, an experienced judge or other legal professional will know about other cases and the approximate "going rate" for pain and suffering with respect to a class of injury that can be adjusted for the particular case at hand.

Implicitly or explicitly, then, the jury's performance with respect to its award of pain and suffering is compared to how a judge would award the damages if he or she had made the decision instead. One presumption is that juries will give larger awards than judges because of their sympathies for the plaintiff. Another is that their awards will be more erratic or unreliable than those of seasoned legal professionals, such as judges. A good example of this reasoning is contained in the AMA's proposed alternatives to the present tort system. While the AMA's proposal would place much of the responsibility for deciding liability in the hands of doctors the decision on damages would be left to a specialist administrative law judge.[5]

As I have attempted to do throughout this book, I decided to put these assumptions into the form of two hypotheses: (1) experienced legal professionals should produce awards that are, on average, lower than those that would be given by juries; (2) on average, legal professionals' awards for pain and suffering will be less variable than those that are given by juries. These hypotheses were put to a test, in fact to two tests.

Study 1: The Heart-Shaped Scar

The Case and the Subjects

The first test of whether juries award damages more excessively and less reliably than legal professionals was based on an actual case that was decided by a panel of arbitrators composed of three experienced lawyers (two males and one female).[6] A 32-year-old married woman underwent elective surgery to have a bunion removed from her foot. The operation required general anesthesia. During the surgery someone in the operating room accidentally placed an extremely hot, just sterilized surgical instrument on the operating table. The busy surgical team only discovered something was amiss when they smelled burning flesh. The instrument had been placed on the anesthetized patient's knee, causing second- and third-degree burns. A specialist was called immediately to treat the burn. The surgeon promptly told the patient's husband of the accident and informed her when she awoke in the recovery room. Despite heavy doses of pain pills, the woman experienced severe pain in the knee for over three weeks. The burn did not heal properly and, consequently, after five weeks a plastic surgeon had to perform graft surgery using skin taken from the woman's thigh. The woman experienced great anxiety about under-taking this second operation, which required general anesthesia, be-cause of the traumatic result of the first surgery. The second operation was successful in getting the burn to heal, but she has been left with a large, very unsightly scar in the shape of an upside-down heart that covers an area about two inches wide by four inches long; in addition she has a scar on her thigh from the skin graft.

Other evidence introduced at the arbitration hearing included testimony by a plastic surgeon that the scar cannot be improved by additional plastic surgery: its location on the knee, where the skin is subject to constant flexion and stress in walking and other activities, precludes the use of surgical interventions that might be appropriate if the scar were located elsewhere on her body. The plaintiff did not contest medical opinion that she was unrestricted in her physical movements or that it was unlikely that there will be any future deterio-ration in her condition. However, she did give convincing testimony about the extreme pain she had suffered following the injury. She also testified about her continuing embarrassment over the scar. She de-scribed her unsuccessful attempts to hide the scar with cosmetics, her need to wear clothes to hide the scar, and the stares of strangers when she goes to the beach, a favorite recreational activity.

The doctor never contested his liability for the accident nor the economic costs of $7,000 resulting from the plastic surgery and lost wages. However, the doctor (actually his medical liability insurer) argued that the amount that the woman should be awarded for her pain and suffering and her permanent disfigurement should be be-tween $15,000 and $23,000, or a total award for medical expenses and pain and suffering not to exceed $30,000. In contrast her lawyer ar-gued that she should receive an award between $75,000 and $100,000.

From the facts of this case Dr. Jeffrey Rice and I created a summary that included the basic facts of how the accident occurred, descriptions of the scar and its permanency (including actual color photographs of the woman's knee and her thigh), and portions of a transcript of the woman's testimony about her pain and suffering after the injury and her continuing embarrassment over the disfigurement. We included the doctor's admission of liability for $7,000 in medical expenses and lost wages. We also reproduced a summary of the plaintiff's argument that compensation for expenses, pain and suffering, and disfigurement should be between $75,000 and $100,000 and the defense lawyer's submission that the total award should be $22,000 ($7,000 for expenses and $15,000 for the noneconomic damages).

These materials were followed by a summary of judges' instructions that the plaintiff should receive $7,000 in economic damages and instructions on the law regarding the plaintiff's past "pain and suffering" and her "scars and disfigurement." The instructions were standard judicial instructions including the admonitions that "There is no fixed formula for pain and suffering" and that "You will determine what is fair compensation by applying logic and common sense to the evidence."

To test whether jurors would award damages differently than legal professionals we gave these materials to groups of jurors and to legal professionals and asked them to indicate the award that the woman should receive. For the juror sample we recruited 47 persons awaiting jury duty in Durham, North Carolina, and 42 persons awaiting similar service in Greensboro, North Carolina. The legal professionals were recruited from a list of screened and qualified senior North Carolina lawyers held by Duke Law School's Private Adjudication Center. These lawyers serve as arbitrators for personal injury, contract, and labor disputes. Of the 21 arbitrators, 5 had previously been judges in North Carolina superior courts; all but two were male and only one indicated that his law practice was predominantly plaintiff-oriented.

The jurors and arbitrators were given the identical case summary and instructions and asked to render a damage award for the case. Then they were asked to explain, in their own words, the reason for their award and to fill out a brief series of rating scales about their reactions to the case.

Awards of Jurors Compared to Legal Professionals

In the actual case from which our experiment was devised the arbitration panel gave a total award of $58,300. It can be used as one comparison point for the awards rendered by the subjects in our study.

The basic data from the experiment are reported in table 19.1. The table shows that the median award of the 21 lawyers acting as arbitrators was $57,000, a figure very close to what the actual panel had given. The table also shows that the median award for the 89 jurors was $47,850. Despite the fact that this figure is $9,150 lower than the arbitrators', the difference was not statistically significant.

The remaining rows of table 19.1 help us to understand more about the awards. The mean, or average, awards for the arbitrators and jurors were, respectively, $50,433 and $51,852. These differences from the median award indicate that in both samples of decision makers a number of individuals gave awards that were at the lower end of the distribution. The most important lesson to be learned from the mean and median awards is that they yield no support for the hypothesis that jurors are more generous in awarding noneconomic damages. There was no statistically significant difference between the laypersons and the legal professionals.

However, the last two rows of the table do show that the jurors' awards were much more variable than those given by the professionals, thus appearing to support the hypothesis that lawyers are more reliable judges of noneconomic damages. Jurors' awards ranged from $11,000 to $197,000 while the arbitrators' awards ranged from $22,000 to $82,000. Thus, the difference between the highest and lowest award for jurors was $186,000 while for arbitrators the difference was only $60,000. The standard deviation is another way of summarizing variability. It is a statistical measure of the extent of dispersion of scores around the mean. The larger the standard deviation, the greater the dispersion or variability. One standard deviation above and below the mean captures two-thirds of an award distribution. The bottom row of the table thus shows that the jurors were much more variable in their awards (the standard deviation was $28,981) than the lawyers (their standard deviation was $16,730). Put in concrete terms, two-thirds of the lawyers' awards fell between $33,703

TABLE 19.1. Total Damage Awards for Lawyers and Jurors in the Scarred-Knee Case: Medians, Means, Ranges, and Standard Deviations

	Lawyers ($)	All Jurors ($)	Jurors: Group 1 ($)	Jurors: Group 2 ($)
Median	57,000	47,850	47,000	48,500
Mean	50,433	51,852	47,674	56,429
Range	22,000–	11,000–	11,000–	14,000–
	82,000	197,000	107,000	197,000
Standard deviation	16,730	28,981	24,358	33,017

and $67,730, a range of $33,460. In contrast, two-thirds of jurors' awards fell between $22,871 and $80,981, a range of $58,110.

Three things need to be said about these measures of variability in awards that bear on the competence of jurors versus legal professionals. First, we should perhaps not be surprised that legal professionals have a narrower range of awards than the lay jurors. After all, as critics of the jury system have pointed out, while jurors typically have no experience in awarding damages the professionals do have both training bearing on the calculation of damages and, equally important, a perspective on what appropriate awards are, based on their knowledge of other cases. If the data went no further than this, the conclusion would have to be that jurors are less reliable—or more capricious—than professionals. Second, however, the picture is not so good even for the experienced lawyers. Their awards ranged from $22,000 to $82,000. These data demonstrate, if any demonstration is needed, that the awarding of noneconomic damages is a pretty subjective process even for trained, experienced legal professionals. There is a lot of variability in the decision-making process; how much will be awarded depends on which professional decides the case. The third point is that the data, as presented so far, do not give a fair test to the jury system because juries are composed of a group of 12 jurors. We conducted a further analysis.

Awards of Juries versus Legal Professionals

The alleged strength of the jury is that it combines the experience and judgment of 12 persons from different walks of life. Their collective wisdom is asserted to be superior to that of a judge deciding a case alone. In regard to damages, verdicts are produced by the process of pooling their individual judgments.

To approximate this pooling process, consider a "jury" formed by randomly choosing 12 persons from the pool of the 89 jurors who participated in the study. We can make an estimate of the damage award that this "jury" would render by assigning it the value of the median award of its 12 individual members. The verdict will vary, of course, depending on which 12 jurors are chosen. Our interest, however, is not with any single jury but with the typical, or average, jury and how variable the awards of randomly selected juries would be in comparison to the awards rendered by randomly chosen judges.

Now, while most medical malpractice cases probably are tried before 12-person juries, in most federal courts and in some state courts they are tried before 6-person juries. The 6-person jury has gained popularity over the last quarter century, largely on the grounds, asserted by its advocates, that it is cheaper and more efficient and does not sacrifice much to the quality of decision making.[7] Critics of jury size reduction, however, have argued that the quality of decision making is impaired and—particularly when it comes to awarding damages—precisely because the number of persons making judgments about the appropriate award is halved. Their reasoning is supported by a statistical theorem indicating that a larger jury should produce more reliable estimates of damages. The reader may want to pursue the logic of this debate further, but for our present purposes we need only get to the bottom line.[8] It is that this debate permits us to hypothesize that, lawyer training and experience notwithstanding, 12-person juries may yield more reliable (i.e., less variable) estimates of noneconomic damages than individual lawyers. Moreover, we can further hypothesize that 6-person juries will yield estimates of damages whose reliability is greater than individual lawyers but less reliable than 12-person juries.

Following this reasoning we constructed a "jury." From the pool of 98 jurors we randomly drew 100 12-person and 100 6-person juries, returning the selected jurors to the pool for each draw. For each jury we assigned a damage award based on the median award given by each of its 12 (or 6) members. The results of this exercise are summarized in table 19.2 along with (for comparative purposes) the individual lawyer awards data (from table 19.1).

The new table shows that for 12-person juries, the average award for the heart-shaped scar injury was $48,900 and for 6-person juries it was $51,390. The means of these juries were not significantly different than the mean award of $50,433 given by the legal professionals.

However, when we compare the standard deviations a very striking difference appears. Observe that the standard deviation for the 12-person juries was $10,970 and for 6-person juries it was $12,290. Both of these standard deviations are statistically different from the $16,730 standard deviation of the legal professionals. Recall that the larger the standard deviation, the larger is the variability. This leads to the conclusion that our juries yielded more reliable estimates of noneconomic damages than the legal professionals and the awards of 12-person juries were more reliable than those of 6-person juries.

This is a very important and controversial finding so let me restate it in somewhat more concrete terms. The standard deviation statistic allows us to estimate the parameters of the likely award distribution: two-thirds of all awards should fall between one standard deviation above and below the mean award. From table 19.2, therefore, we can estimate that if we randomly drew a series of 12 persons to decide the damages in the heart-shaped scar case, two-thirds of the awards would fall between $37,930 and $59,870, a range of $21,940. If, instead, 6-person juries were drawn, two-thirds of the awards would fall between $39,100 and $63,680, a range of $24,580. If, however, we ran a series of trials of the case using randomly picked senior legal professionals to serve as the judge, we would expect two-thirds of the awards to fall between $33,703 and $67,163, a range of $33,460. While these data could also be calculated for two, or even three, standard deviations, the basic relationship between the types of decision makers would remain the same: the judges' range of awards would be expected to be larger. The conclusion from this important exercise, then, is that jury awards for noneconomic damages would be more reliable (i.e., less variable) than if the decision were left to individual judges.

Before proceeding on to other data, let me briefly address a limitation of the study. The "juries" in our exercise were statistical creations whereas real juries deliberate to reach a verdict. While very little is understood about how jurors combine their individual judgments during deliberation, one study by Professors Shari Diamond and Jonathan Casper found that deliberation inflated the jurors' median awards by about 25 percent.[9] Although the Diamond and Casper study obtained this effect in a different context and it has not yet been replicated, if the finding were generalized to the present study the mean award for 12-person juries would be over $60,000 and for 6-person juries over $64,000. However, other than the one study by

TABLE 19.2.   Mean Awards and Standard Deviations of Lawyers and Twelve- and Six-Person "Juries" in the Scarred-Knee Case

	Lawyers ($)	12-Person "Juries" ($)	6-Person "Juries" ($)
Mean	50,433	48,900	51,390
Standard deviation	16,730	10,970	12,290

Diamond and Casper there is no other evidence to suggest that the process of deliberation does indeed inflate awards by 25 percent or any other amount. Furthermore, in an actual trial the range of juror awards might be expected to be more truncated than it was in our experiment. Through pretrial questioning prospective jurors are questioned about biases toward plaintiffs or doctors, resulting in the elimination of persons likely to have strong biases toward one side or the other. This winnowing process should have the effect of reducing the range of noneconomic awards, making the advantage of the jury over individual judges with respect to reliability of awards even greater than it was in the present study.

Other Comparisons between Jurors and Lawyers

Although I have been reporting the data in terms of total awards, in fact both groups of subjects were asked to distinguish between the amount for past pain and suffering and the amount for the woman's disfigurement. Jurors and lawyers did not differ in the way that they awarded the separate components.

Both groups of subjects also responded to a series of rating scales about their perceptions of the seriousness of injury and the amount of physical pain and suffering the woman experienced and about their belief in the doctor's negligence. These variables were modestly related to the amount of the award in both groups. By and large there were no differences between lawyers and jurors in how they perceived the case. Similarly, when we analyzed the comments in which the subjects were asked to explain in their own words the reasoning behind their awards there were no substantial differences between the lawyers and the jurors.

Study 2: The Injured Teenager

Our confidence in research findings and their generalizability is increased when similar results are found in another study, particularly when the other study differs substantially from the first.[10] Consequently, David Landau and I attempted a replication of my experiment with Jeffrey Rice by determining if legal professionals would give different awards than the jurors gave in the first deep pockets study described in chapter 18.

The Case and the Subjects

Recall that in that experiment, a 17-year-old female suffered a broken femur requiring an osteotomy to lengthen the leg bone. This accident required four separate operations, the implantation and removal of an external metal plate, much pain and suffering, and a healing process that extended over the better part of a year. In the experiment the cause of the injury was ascribed either to medical or to driving negligence, and the defendants were either one or two doctors or drivers or a corporation (hospital or delivery business). The amount of damages requested for pain and suffering by the plaintiff was between $180,000 and $220,000 whereas the defendant contended that the amount should only be $30,000.

We recruited an entirely different group of lawyers than participated in the heart-shaped scar study. They were 56 experienced attorneys who had been certified by the state of North Carolina to act as mediators. Most had represented both plaintiffs and defendants in personal injury cases; 27 percent of these lawyers were women.

For reasons of economy, we limited our comparisons to four of the original conditions: medical negligence with either a doctor defendant or a hospital (corporate) defendant and automobile negligence with either an individual or a corporate defendant. The lawyers were randomly assigned to one of the conditions. With some slight changes the comparison data with jurors were taken from the original study.[11]

Results

The mean awards and the standard deviations for the jurors and lawyers for each condition are presented in table 19.3. These data were analyzed in substantial detail in a separate article that addresses some small anomalies in the data, but for my present purposes I will summarize only the primary findings.[12] When the awards were aggregated over all conditions the mean for the jurors was $100,183 and for the lawyers $100,363, a statistically nonsignificant difference between the two groups. Thus, as in the heart-shaped scar study there was no support for the hypothesis that juries are more generous than lawyers in awarding noneconomic damages. When the mean awards were compared separately for medical and automobile negligence both ju-

rors and lawyers gave higher awards in the medical negligence case
(jurors = $112,430; lawyers = $110,325) than in the automobile negligence case (jurors = $89,213; lawyers = $92,607). The lower awards
for automobile negligence can be primarily attributed to some differences in the way that jurors and lawyers responded to the individual
versus corporate defendants in the automobile negligence condition.
In this condition jurors tended to give somewhat lower awards in the
corporate defendant condition while, in contrast, the lawyers tended
to give lower awards in the individual defendant condition. While
neither of these differences was statistically significant, when the data
were compared only for jurors or lawyers their combined effect resulted in an overall lower mean for the automobile as contrasted to
the medical negligence condition. However, we do not need to give
more attention to this effect for the purposes of my discussion here.
The more important findings are that when a comparison is made
over all cases or by considering just medical or automobile negligence
there are no statistically significant differences in the average awards
of jurors and lawyers.

Table 19.3 also shows that, like the results in the scarred-knee
study, the standard deviations of the juror awards were larger than
those of the lawyer sample. Combined over all four conditions the
standard deviation of juror awards was $61,744 while the standard
deviation of the lawyer awards was $46,902. This was a statistically
significant difference. Individual jurors awards were, once again, more
variable. Recall, however, that we need to recognize that this is not the
appropriate comparison: juries, not jurors, render damage awards.

TABLE 19.3.   Mean and Standard Deviations of Awards by Lawyers and
Jurors in the Injured Teenager Case

Cause of Injury	Individual Defendant		Corporate Defendant	
	Jurors ($)	Lawyers ($)	Jurors ($)	Lawyers ($)
Medical negligence	108,450	111,687	115,890	108,146
	(64,878)	(45,865)	(60,295)	(36,073)
Automobile negligence	105,065	80,431	74,631	104,782
	(69,470)	(48,075)	(46,923)	(51,256)

Note: Standard deviations contained in parentheses.

Juries versus Legal Professionals

We thus conducted the same modeling exercise as in the previous study. From the sample of 91 jurors we randomly drew the awards of 12 jurors 100 times; for each of these juries the median award of its members was designated as the jury award. We also created 100 6-person juries by the same procedure.

Table 19.4 presents the mean awards and standard deviations of our juries and of the legal professionals. The astute observer will quickly note that the average award for the juries is substantially below the mean award of the individual jurors, which was $100,183. This is not a fluke. A number of the individual jurors gave high awards, but the process of aggregating 12 (or 6) awards into a median award moderates extreme awards. Also, do not forget that we are addressing the question of what the average jury would do.

Table 19.4, then, shows that the mean award of the 12-person juries was $83,270, and for the 6-person juries it was $91,950. The mean award of the legal professionals was $102,204. The $18,934 difference between the 12-person juries and the lawyers was statistically significant. The $10,254 difference between the 6-person juries and the lawyers fell short of being statistically significant.

Table 19.4 also shows that the standard deviation of our 12-person juries was less than half ($22,893 versus $46,452) that of the lawyers. These differences are statistically significant. While the difference between the standard deviations of the awards for 6-person juries and lawyers ($29,890 versus $46,452) was less pronounced it too was a statistically significant result.

Finally, even if we were to increase the mean of our jury awards upward by 25 percent to account for any possible deliberation effects suggested by Diamond and Casper's research the adjusted awards for the 12-person juries would be $104,087 and for the 6-person juries $114,937. Neither of these adjusted mean awards would be statistically different from the lawyer awards. And even with the adjustment the "juries" are still advantaged over the lawyers because they produce more reliable estimates of damages.

A Comparison of Perceptions and Reactions

In a manner similar to the first study, we attempted to discover if there were differences in the way that jurors and lawyers perceived the

TABLE 19.4. Comparison of Awards for Pain and Suffering between Lawyers and Six-and Twelve-Person "Juries" in the Injured Teenager Case

	Lawyers ($)	12-Person "Juries" ($)	6-Person "Juries" ($)	Adjusted 12-Person "Juries" ($)	Adjusted 6-Person "Juries" ($)
Mean	102,204	83,270	91,950	104,087	114,937
Standard deviation	46,452	22,893	29,890	22,893	29,890

case. Both jurors and lawyers saw the injury as causing the teenage girl more pain when it was ascribed to malpractice than when it was ascribed to an automobile accident, but they did not differ from one another in making the evaluation. They also perceived it as more avoidable when it was ascribed to malpractice. Jurors, in comparison to lawyers, did indicate that car drivers should ordinarily assume some responsibility for an accident, but the two types of respondents tended about equally to disagree with the view that patients should assume some responsibility for medical accidents during surgery. Thus, while the data showed that in this experiment there were some differences in the way that malpractice and automobile negligence cases were evaluated there were only minor differences between jurors and lawyers in these perceptions.

Concluding Perspective

Neither of the studies lends support to the hypothesis that juries will be significantly more generous than experienced lawyers in rendering noneconomic damage awards. Additionally, while the first study found no differences in the average awards of lawyers and juries the second study found that the mean unadjusted award of 12-person juries was actually lower than the average awards of the lawyers. With respect to the second hypothesis, both studies strongly suggest that juries are likely to yield more reliable estimates of pain and suffering than a judge. These data are clearly in the opposite direction of that predicted by the hypothesis.

In retrospect, should we be surprised? Professor Dobbs pointed to the very nature of the problem, namely, that while noneconomic loss is real in terms of the quality of an injured person's life there is no metric for translating the loss into monetary terms.[13] One has to consider the circumstance of the individual person, estimate the severity of their suffering, and arrive at a "fair" amount. It seems almost elementary that the combined judgment of 12, or 6, persons should be more reliable than that of a single individual.

The considerable variability of the awards given by the experienced lawyers in this study is consistent with a study undertaken some years ago by Professor Gerald Williams.[14] Professor Williams persuaded 40 seasoned Iowa lawyers to evaluate the worth of the same personal injury case and attempt to negotiate a settlement. The lawyers were divided into pairs and randomly assigned to represent the plaintiff or the defendant. Each lawyer was given the identical case files on the cause and extent of the injuries. The files also contained information on comparable jury awards that had been given by juries in Des Moines, Iowa. This latter information, of course, supplemented the knowledge that these experienced lawyers had about previous cases.

While the negotiations between the lawyer pairs involved considerations of probable liability as well as damages and also involved different negotiating skills between lawyers the important findings for my purposes here involve the wide variability in the negotiated outcomes. They ranged from $15,000 to $95,000, and the mean was $47,318. This high variability should be viewed in light of the fact that the award included claims for economic damages, presumably more easily and objectively determined than noneconomic damages.

The high variability in lawyer awards in our two experiments does not seem surprising viewed from the perspective of Williams's study. Determining damages is a difficult task, but the evidence seems to lead to the conclusion that, everything else being equal, a jury, on average, can do the task better—that is, perform more reliably—than a randomly selected lawyer wearing a judicial robe.

Final support for the conclusions of our two experiments comes from a study reported by Michael Brady and Peter Cubanske.[15] They examined the actual awards rendered by arbitrators in a state-mandated arbitration program for personal injury cases. Under the program, if a case involves under $50,000 in damages it must first be tried by an arbitrator, normally a lawyer in private practice. If one or both parties are not satisfied with the result they can then have the case tried anew by a jury. Brady and Cubanske studied 45 automobile injury cases that were tried first by an arbitrator but then tried again by a jury. In 73 percent of these cases the jury award was lower than that given by the arbitrator. While these findings involve automobile negligence cases I have been told that in both California and Oregon health maintenance organizations dropped a clause in their contracts with patients that called for mandatory arbitration by lawyers when there was an allegation of medical negligence.[16] The companies' confidential assessments were that juries' awards were less generous than arbitrator awards. While I want to forthrightly acknowledge that this latter evidence is only "hearsay" it seems highly consistent with our experimental findings.

20

Voices from the Jury Room

I should now address the question concerning the extent to which jurors who decided real cases have the same concerns as those expressed by the jurors in the experiments discussed in the last two chapters. Let us revisit some of the trials discussed earlier and introduce a few new cases.

The Permanent Blindness Case

Chapter 13 described the case of Ms. C., a 26-year-old unmarried mother of a small child, who, the jury decided, became blind as a result of the negligence of her neurologist. Her son was a co-plaintiff in the case who asked damages for emotional distress and costs of his education. It was not an easy case for the jury, and several of them agreed to a finding of negligence only with great reluctance. On the other hand, several jurors had wanted to find the co-defendant radiologist negligent as well but were persuaded that the evidence was not sufficient to find liability.

At trial the defendants fought the case solely on the theory that they were not negligent and, as a consequence, produced no evidence or arguments about damages. Strikingly, however, the plaintiff's lawyer also did not call expert evidence with respect to damages although he had promised to do so in his opening arguments. Instead, in his closing arguments he asked the jurors to consider the plaintiff's medical costs, the economic consequences of her blindness, and pain and suffering. He further asked the jury to award a sum to her co-plaintiff son for his education, for psychological help due to the trauma resulting from having to live with his aunt rather than his mother, and for his emotional distress. The lawyer then asked the jurors to come up with a reasonable sum for both parties. He suggested that a sum of slightly over $5 million was a fair and reasonable amount. (It may be that the lawyer decided not to call experts on the grounds that the plaintiff was not well educated and that her pre-injury earning capacity was low; by not having a precise figure these negative facts might be obscured during the jury's deliberations.)

The trial judge's instructions on damages stressed that the jury's decision should be a fair and reasonable amount based on the evidence at trial. Moreover, any amount awarded should be reduced to present value.

In their deliberations the jurors did not turn to the issue of damages until they finally reached consensus on the neurologist's liability. The first damage issue that they discussed was the co-plaintiff's damages. The jurors uniformly expressed sympathy for the child, but they quickly concluded that he should not receive a damage award. Their reasoning was that the judge had instructed them to decide damages on the basis of trial evidence, but no evidence on the child's damages had been produced at trial. There was no testimony about his need for professional counseling or educational assistance, and his aunt had testified at trial that he was reasonably adjusted and happy living with her and that he saw his mother on a regular basis.

The jurors then turned to the mother's damages but immediately felt frustrated because of the lack of evidence and legal guidance. As a consequence, they decided to have everyone write a "suggested" figure on a slip of paper, and these suggestions were then collected and read aloud. The initial figures ranged from $800,000 to $8 million. A vigorous debate ensued. Perhaps not surprisingly those jurors who had initially expressed inclinations to find neither of the doctors negligent offered the lowest figures. The jurors next attempted to adopt the plaintiff attorney's vague equation of "things to consider" as a framework for their discussion, but the only concrete expenses available to them were medical bills. The jurors also speculated about the fees that the lawyer would charge, and these were considered in their negotiations over what was a fair amount.

Only one of the jurors had understood the judge's instruction to reduce the award to "present value." He subsequently explained it and used it to argue that the jurors with the higher awards should move downward. Eventually, the jurors reduced their range of disagreement from a low figure of slightly under $2 million to a high of slightly over $3 million. After further heated discussion that included threats to compromise no further, and thus deadlock, the jurors agreed on a verdict of $2.4 million.

The Brain-Damaged Baby

This case was described in chapter 12. An eight-person jury in a special two-day trial concluded that the obstetrician was negligent in his treatment of a mother resulting in a severely brain-damaged baby, who at the time of trial was just under three years old. The child is retarded, blind, deaf, unable to use his arms or legs, unable to sit in a chair without support, and will require constant medical attention for the rest of his life. By statutory law, in North Carolina the jury is told that unless contradicted by other evidence, they are to assume that the plaintiff will live to be 72 years of age.

In advance of the special trial the two sides had entered into a high-low agreement whereby the plaintiff would receive a settlement of several hundred thousand dollars even if the jury found no liability, and the defendant would pay no more than $1.5 million even if the verdict exceeded that amount. However, the jurors had no knowledge of this agreement before or after the trial. Thus, they deliberated under the belief that their award could be any amount and was the final verdict. The defendant fought the case on the grounds that he was not negligent.

For the damages part of the trial the plaintiff first presented a short video portraying a day in the life of the child that vividly showed not only the injuries but also the enormous amount of care that he required. The video was bolstered by the testimony of his parents who testified at different points in the trial. Next, the plaintiff's lawyer presented a video deposition of a pediatric psychiatrist who testified about the long-term health care needs of the child. These needs were extensive, and the witness described them in detail. They included modification of the parents' house and relief for the parents in the form of substitute care of the child. The latter expenses, the psychiatrist testified, were necessary to relieve the enormous psychological and emotional pressures on the parents and their other two children by allowing them to take breaks and vacations like normal families. The plaintiff then presented a video deposition by an economist who calculated the cost of the health care plan in present-day dollars to be $5.3 million. He also gave testimony on the child's projected lost wages as an adult and other costs. The expert's estimate of total economic losses was $8 million. The defendant attorneys called no experts to testify about damages, and their final arguments to the jury were devoted solely to arguing that there was no liability. (I later learned that while the defense team characterized the plaintiff's first expert as presenting a "Cadillac" plan of health care they had actually obtained their own estimates of economic damages from three different experts; the estimates ranged from $2.1 million to $4.3 million.)

After one hour and 45 minutes of deliberation, the jurors returned a verdict for $8 million. They were interviewed as a group immediately after their decision, and follow-up interviews were conducted with individual jurors within the next two weeks.

The initial vote on negligence was seven to one, but after a brief discussion of the evidence the jurors voted unanimously to find the doctor was liable. The difficult part of the deliberations involved the amount for damages because not all of the jurors felt confident about the evidence, and they were concerned about the "huge" dollar amount involved. In the subsequent interviews the jurors variously characterized the figures as "unbelievable," "exorbitant," and "running wild." Nevertheless, their first vote on damages ranged from $5 million to $10 million. In the ensuing discussion at least two jurors raised concerns about the consequences of the award for the doctor. The issue of whether the doctor had liability insurance was raised, and some of the jurors were puzzled as to why it had not been mentioned during the trial. Questions were raised as to whether his insurance rates would go up and if he could even get insurance in the future. The jurors also expressed concerns about the rising costs of medical care and the stories of doctors being forced from practicing medicine because of malpractice insurance rates. All of the jurors believed that the doctor had insurance primarily because they believed that *all* doctors have insurance, but they were not sure about how much coverage he had. Many felt strong sympathy for the doctor, who they perceived as trying hard to be a good doctor; and they worried about the consequences of the lawsuit for his reputation and practice.

Despite their concerns for the doctor and their reluctance to award millions of dollars they felt bound by the judge's instruction to decide the award solely on the evidence, and the only evidence before them was from the plaintiff's experts. Consequently, they calculated from those figures because they believed they had no other choice. They voted again, and several jurors had settled on $8 million. The rest then agreed to this sum. However, in post-trial interviews the jurors continued to express their reluctance to give such a large award. One juror stated that he felt $1 million would have been enough. Most of the jurors voiced frustration at the defense lawyers for not addressing the damage issue. They also expressed frustration toward the judge and were puzzled as to why he had not given them more guidance.

The Brain-Damaged Mother

The case of Mrs. B. was discussed briefly at the end of chapter 13. As a result of cesarean surgery, Mrs. B. suffered a severe peritoneal infection that, at age 28, left her with a permanent brain injury that impairs her hearing, vision, speech, and memory. Her balance is also affected, requiring her to use a cane or a walker, and many activities undertaken by ordinary adults are restricted.

Much like the brain-damaged baby case, the trial lasted two and a half days under an abbreviated trial procedure that the parties had agreed to. The jury consisted of six persons.

At the trial the jury was shown a day-in-the life video of the difficulties Mrs. B. encounters in her daily existence. Mrs. B. was also called to testify, and her difficulty in walking to and from the witness stand was given rapt attention by the jurors. She described her inability to do such things as carry her child or give it prompt attention when it needed it and about the extra household burdens that were placed on her husband, including cooking, grocery shopping, and driving. She also told of her embarrassment and frustration at being "treated like a cripple" or sometimes perceived in a restaurant as a "drunk" or "retarded" because of her walk and slurred speech.

No experts were called on the issue of damages, though the jury was provided with evidence of medical bills resulting from her injury that amounted to several thousands of dollars. Under the rules of trial procedure, the defense counsel made his final argument to the jury first, with the plaintiff getting the last word. The defense counsel asked the jurors to consider whether the doctors did anything improper that caused her problem and the degree to which her injury may have resulted from other factors beyond the defendants' control. However, he then said that if the jury did decide she was entitled to an award, he wanted it to consider that Mrs. B. had few medical expenses because they had been paid by the hospital and doctors. The evidence also indicated that at the time Mrs. B. became pregnant, she had quit her relatively low-paying job and had expressed no intention to work after the child was born. Moreover, if she wanted to work in the future, she could undergo rehabilitative therapy. Finally, he suggested that while her injuries are real their effect is to slow her down not to prohibit her from engaging in them entirely.

In his summation arguments the plaintiff's lawyer focused on Mrs. B.'s injuries and the evidence. He further pointed out that the defendants had not called their own evidence on damages nor, he argued, did they contradict anything said by the plaintiff or her husband. He also observed that while Mr. and Mrs. B. loved each other and were attempting to cope with her disability, if something happened to the marriage, as occurs in even normal marriages, Mrs. B. would potentially be left in severe financial straits because she would never be in a position to support herself. He concluded with the following plea:

> I'm not going to ask you for $10 million or $6 million for her injury. But, I suggest to you that for the 40 to 50 years that she will have to live with this injury, you have to be in the $1 million to $1.5 million category. In fact, $1 million to $2.5 million would be absolutely fair.

In his instructions on damages the judge told the jury that they should consider the amount of compensation Mrs. B. should have and what Mr. B. should receive for loss of consortium but that the two issues should be treated as one in reaching a verdict. He further instructed the jury that damages must be reduced to their present worth, considering that Mrs. and Mr. B. would each be expected to live about 44 more years. He further cautioned the jurors that they were not to be governed by the amount of damages suggested by the plaintiff's lawyer but only by the evidence. The amount must be fair, just, and reasonable and not determined by sympathy.

The jurors deliberated for three and a half hours and returned a verdict of $850,000. Although it was delivered in a lump sum for the two plaintiffs, as the judge had instructed them to do, the subsequent interview with the jurors indicated that all of the award was for Mrs. B.'s injuries. No money was awarded to Mr. B. for loss of consortium. The jurors felt that, first, he was not the physically injured party and, second, taking the marriage vow to be loyal "in sickness and in health" meant just that, and he should not receive money for her injury.

As to the basis of the award for Mrs. B., the jurors indicated that they thoroughly discussed the liability issue before turning to damages. The foreperson stated, "In our minds we had to come to the decision of liability before we could give damages . . . we could have come back with zero dollars." However, they strongly complained about the ambiguity involved in determining Mrs. B.'s award. One female juror said, "I was under the impression we'd have guidelines; I feel we were thrown in a box and had to come out with a number." Another juror commented that while the plaintiff's lawyer "did throw in a figure, I'm surprised the other guy [the defense lawyer] didn't say anything." Several jurors were of the opinion that if the defense lawyer had put forth a "reasonable" lower figure, they might have been persuaded to move their award downward. However, one of them said, with a wry smile, that if the figure had been too low it would have turned him against the defense.

These jurors, in contrast to the jurors in the brain-damaged baby case, appeared to be indifferent about the financial consequences for the defendants and said they did not discuss either insurance or legal fees. They attempted to keep their focus on the plaintiff and her injuries and pain and suffering but had difficulty in remembering the technical elements of the judge's legal instructions. The plaintiff lawyer's comment about the potential consequences of the injury on her marriage and its financial implications also received consideration. The jurors did not take written ballots regarding the amount of the award but through the process of discussion decided that the $850,000 figure was "about right." Several expressed their feeling that doing their duty "was difficult for all of us."

Comparison: Wrongful Death due to Driving Negligence

Since so many comparisons have been made between malpractice and automobile negligence cases, we should make a brief foray into the deliberations of a jury that decided the damages in a wrongful death suit. The basic facts of the case are the following. In 1989 a 21-year-old female college student from a rural North Carolina town was killed instantly when a tow truck driver swerved in front of her car. There was no dispute about the liability of the driver and the small towing company that owned the truck. However, the amount of damages was disputed, with defendant's insurer initially offering $80,000 and the plaintiff demanding up to $1 million (but probably willing to settle for three-quarters of that figure). The parties agreed to put the dispute before an eight-person jury.

At trial the parents testified about their grief and its impact on their family, including their only other child, a 10-year-old son. Family friends and teachers also testified in videotaped depositions about the qualities of the deceased daughter who, in addition to attending bible college, played the piano in church, was a constant companion to her mother, and helped elderly ladies on weekends. The jury also learned that the father, a bricklayer, earned between $10,000 to $12,000 per year and that the mother earned $16,000 working in a radiology clinic. The plaintiff also presented a one-and-a-half-hour videotaped deposition by an economist who made detailed estimates about the deceased's potential earnings as a teacher, her intended vocation, and about the financial contributions she would have made toward her parents' welfare in their old age. The expert's testimony covered such topics as an expected present-day salary of $18,000 per year, the mother's life expectancy, wage inflation, estimates of reductions to present value, tax rates, fringe benefits, self-maintenance, expectancy of unemployment, morbidity rates, and "bank rate" assumptions. From these factors he calculated residual income that could have been applied to assist the mother in the expected 29 remaining years of her life and, with reductions to present value, gave an estimate of her economic worth to the mother of $188,663.

The defense case consisted of testimony by the tow truck driver and the owner of the company, both of whom admitted negligence and their sorrow. The defendants did not present any evidence by an economic expert. However, in closing arguments the defense attorney challenged the assumptions of the plaintiff's economist, including the crucial fact that he had made no assumptions about the deceased being married and having her own children even though trial testimony by her mother indicated that she planned to marry and have four children. This latter fact, of course, would have a substantial bearing on any residual income that might have been available to give to her mother.

In summation arguments, the plaintiff's attorney asked for an award of $1 million. The defense attorney argued, however, that an award of $5,866 for funeral expenses and $100,000 for pain and suffering was the most fair and reasonable award. The judge instructed the jurors that under North Carolina law they were to consider "services, protection, care, and assistance" (the matters covered by the economist) but also reasonable funeral expenses, the loss of "society, companionship, guidance, and friendly office" and the "pain and suffering" of the deceased's family.

The jury deliberated one hour and 40 minutes and returned with a verdict of $205,866. An 80-minute interview with the jurors immediately after the trial indicated that they had engaged in detailed recalculation of the economist's figures and took issue with many of his assumptions, particularly his failure to take into account the deceased's probable marriage and children in estimating residual income. As a group, the jurors were not highly educated, but two members were in businesses that required knowledge of inflation rates and other variables. They also understood the concept of reduction to "present value." As a consequence the jury calculated economic losses at approximately $64,866 (including funeral expenses).

The "pain and suffering" and "loss of companionship" components of the award presented the difficult part of the deliberations. As in the malpractice cases just described and the two experiments discussed in the last chapter the jurors expressed concerns that plaintiffs should not be unjustly enriched as a result of a misfortune. One juror soliloquized that while the parents were experiencing great grief now, the pain would diminish with time; that we all lose loved ones, and sometimes they are our children; that we learn to adapt; that while the pain will dull, no amount of money would compensate for the ache. One juror mentioned $100,000 as an appropriate award for the emotional pain, and two others liked this figure. Then someone raised the matter of whether the defendants' insurance would pay such a large award or whether they even carried insurance. Other jurors were sympathetic to this line of argument but concluded that "If he's not smart enough to carry insurance—or enough of it—then too bad." The jurors did agree that they "didn't want to punish the defendant." In this context the jurors discussed the fact that the defendant's admission of liability was important. If the defendants had "drug their feet" and fought the case several jurors said that they would have been more sympathetic to the plaintiff and perhaps raised the award by some unspecified amount. Another factor that the jurors considered in arriving at a "fair" award was the amount of money in comparison to the parents' annual combined income. For instance, one juror expressed the opinion that $100,000 would mean much more to the parents than it would mean to parents who had a yearly income of $250,000.

After this extended discussion, the jurors settled on $100,000 for pain and suffering. However, after they tallied the economic figures with this sum and found that it was $164,866 they reconsidered whether it was enough. For the first time someone raised the question of lawyer fees. After more discussion the jurors concluded that he would charge between $25,000 to $40,000 (in the interview following their verdict none were very aware of contingency fees as a percentage of plaintiff recovery, though one mentioned that lawyer fees may be about one-third). Someone then suggested "rounding" the total figure to $200,000 to take lawyer costs into consideration and another suggested adding the funeral expenses on top for a total award of $205,866.

The deliberations in this case were similar to those of a jury in still another North Carolina malpractice case. The jury there gave an award approaching $1 million to the estate of a woman who died of cancer, leaving a husband and young children. After deciding that the defendant was liable, the jurors scrutinized the economic figures provided through expert testimony as well as documents bearing on loss of services and income. In calculating noneconomic damages they balanced figures bearing on loss of "good offices and counsel," loss of "consortium," and "pain and suffering." They then raised questions bearing on legal fees but decided this factor should be ignored. The jurors also worried about the impact of the award on the defendant. The loss of consortium and pain and suffering components of the final award constituted approximately 23 percent of the total.

The Melis Case Revisited—Briefly

The juror voices on damages in the Melis case were described and analyzed in chapters 9 and 10. Two significant parts of that case are

worth recalling to complete this chapter. The first is that, like some of
the North Carolina juries, the *Melis* jury carefully analyzed the economic evidence. (Recall also that the trial judge, who also heard the
evidence, agreed that the jury's verdict on these points was reasonable.) The second is that the jurors' verdict on pain and suffering was
not independent of their perceptions of responsibility for the injury.
In fact, Steve Cohen's narrative of their deliberations in chapter 9
virtually admits that the $19 million award for pain and suffering was
a reaction to what the jurors perceived as egregious behavior on the
part of the defendants. This latter example indicates that juries do
have the capacity, and in *Melis* the inclination, to incorporate what in
effect are punitive damages into compensatory damages.

A Résumé of What the Voices Say

Individual jurors do not speak with a single voice; some tilt toward
plaintiffs and some tilt toward defendants, but it is the emergent
consensus that produces the damage award. Different juries approach damages in a variety of ways, and while some of the variability
may be due to the unique composition of the jurors comprising each
jury, the case studies make it abundantly clear that much of the variability may reside in the evidence that is presented, or not presented,
at trial. Juries were frequently puzzled and frustrated at defense lawyers for not addressing the damages issue, leaving them solely dependent on the plaintiff's evidence and the judge's strong admonition to
decide the damages only according to the trial evidence.

All of the juries that I and my students interviewed decided the
issue of liability before turning to damages, but there was evidence
that damage awards are not independent of judgments about responsibility. In the case of the blind woman the jurors who had reserva-
tions about liability showed a preference for lower awards. There was
evidence in two cases that when defendants admitted liability, the
jurors took note of it during their discussion of damages. This tendency was also noted in some of the comments of jurors in our simulation experiments. Finally, as we observed, the *Melis* jury apparently
let its negative reaction to the doctor's behavior greatly inflate its pain
and suffering award.

Many jurors expressed concerns about plaintiffs getting too much
compensation for an unfortunate injury. As a group, the jurors did

not express attitudes that could reasonably cause one to conclude that they were prejudiced in favor of plaintiffs or that they distinguished between defendants in automobile and malpractice cases. Lawyer fees, taxes, and liability insurance were raised in deliberations about the amounts of awards and appear to have had some influence on awards in some cases but not in others. Many individual jurors had difficulty with the concept of reducing awards to "present value," in large part because it was so poorly explained to them.

Interviews conducted with individual jurors yielded comments that some of their fellow jurors were ignorant, lazy, or prejudiced. Yet their overall feeling was that, as a group, the jurors approached their task with gravity and diligence. A final finding from the interviews is that juries were uniformly frustrated over the task of determining monetary compensation for noneconomic damages. It was described as an "impossible job." Most jurors said that they wished the judge would have given more guidance. Some of the jurors expressed the view that the award for pain and suffering should be decided by the judge because he "has more experience." Of course, the studies discussed in chapter 19 raise serious doubts about whether judges can do it better.

Economic Loss and
Punitive Awards

In bringing the analysis of damage awards to a close, we need to consider two additional matters not covered by the experimental or case studies. The first involves the comparison of jury awards with external estimates of economic damages. The second involves the matter of punitive damages.

To What Extent Do Verdicts Deviate from
Economic Losses?

Plaintiffs who prevail in medical malpractice cases do indeed often receive sizable amounts of money, and these awards attract the attention of journalists, health care professionals, legal commentators, and legislators. The direct implication that many draw from these awards is that most jury verdicts are substantially out of line with actual economic losses. This in turn helps lead to the assertion that a high percentage of the awards is for pain and suffering and that verdicts are driven by jury sympathies for severely injured plaintiffs.[1] Systematic research evidence, however, tends to contradict these assertions.

Injury Severity and Size of Award

The study by Taragin et al. of New Jersey malpractice cases, discussed in chapter 14, found that while severity of the plaintiff's injury was not related to the likelihood of the jury finding defendants liable, the amount of the award for prevailing plaintiffs was correlated with the severity of injury.[2] This finding is consistent with the findings of Randall Bovbjerg, Frank Sloan, and James Blumstein who studied jury awards in 898 personal injury lawsuits and compared them to a scale of injury severity.[3] Bovbjerg and his colleagues concluded that the "best available single predictor of award amount is the severity of the injury."[4] Similarly, after reviewing the literature on jury verdicts in tort cases, Michael Saks concluded that,

> In the aggregate, jury awards are remarkably predictable. Over half the variation can be accounted for merely by knowing the severity of the plaintiff's injuries.[5]

Nevertheless, the data also suggest that within categories of injury severity there is wide variation in amounts that are awarded to plaintiffs. Bovbjerg et al. found that the highest awards were frequently many times larger than the lowest awards, causing those researchers to characterize the variation as "enormous."[6] Nevertheless, they recognized that because of the limitations of their data it was quite possible that the variation "may legitimately reflect claimants' precise individual circumstances" rather than jury caprice.[7] For instance, their data sources provided no information on the age of the claimant, the amount of the patient's preinjury earnings, or the amount of medical care that had been received or would be required in the future. The qualification by Bovbjerg et al. leads to this question: to what extent is the variation in awards due to the unreliability or capriciousness of the jury and to what extent is it due to differences in actual economic losses associated with widely varying incomes of claimants or differences in their life expectancies or their medical care needs?

The Florida Study

The recently completed research of Professor Frank Sloan and his colleagues goes a very long way toward answering the assertions about both the tendency of juries to overcompensate plaintiffs and the variability of awards at least with respect to the birth and emergency room injury malpractice cases that they studied in Florida.[8] For each of the 186 cases in their study (37 of which were decided by juries) an attempt was made to estimate the claimants' precise economic losses resulting from the injury.

Utilizing extensive interviews with the claimants, medical records, and liability insurer reports, the research team attempted to determine both past and future costs of health care, including surgical operations, hospitalization, long-term care facilities, and private duty nursing. They also estimated past and future income losses and "nonmarket" losses, which include the loss of household production such as cooking and child care for dependents and survivors. Also included were family members' loss of earnings resulting from the need to care for the injured person, alterations to homes, special transport vehicles, and special schools. The figures were adjusted to take into account government benefits and services that would ordinarily be provided at no cost to the patient or family. The calculations also took life expectancy into consideration; older persons and severely injured persons normally have shorter life expectancies. The economic value of all losses was based on estimates derived from government and other standard sources. The estimates included no figures for noneconomic losses like pain and suffering or loss of enjoyment of life.[9] Sloan and his co-researchers cautioned that even with their careful attention to details, their figures were based on a lot of assumptions. However, in my opinion, their assumptions are generally conservative, and there is little question that the study provides some of the best data ever collected on the costs of injuries in malpractice cases.

The Magnitude and Variability of Losses. While all of the Sloan et al. findings cannot be reported here, a number of them have direct relevance for understanding jury verdicts. One finding is that economic loss can be substantial. Sloan and his colleagues divided the cases into five categories of increasing injury severity, including death. Among birth injury cases, the average first-year economic loss for families with the least severely injured children was $15,500 whereas for the most severely injured children that had died by the time of the study, the loss was $118,900. The average total economic loss, that is, past and future costs projected over the injured person's life expectancy, was $123,500 for the least severely injured children. For the remaining categories of injury estimates of lifetime losses exceeded $1.5 million.[10] However, the data also showed considerable variability of economic losses within the categories of injury severity. For instance, among the most seriously injured children about 40 percent of the cases yielded estimates of losses in the range of $1.2 to $1.4 million, but about 10 percent had losses in the range of $2.4 to over $3.0 million.[11]

The data on emergency room injuries showed that claimants who survived the injury incurred first-year losses that averaged $38,000. If they died, their families' or estate losses averaged $20,800. The total average loss for past and future expenses was $111,000 for the least severely injured survivors. For the other categories of survivors the average loss was $1.3 million, mostly due to high medical and custodial expenses. Even for patients who died immediately or shortly after the injury the average economic loss was estimated at $0.5 million. However, as in the birth injury data, there was considerable variability within categories of severity. For instance, excluding the least injured persons about 28 percent of the claimants incurred losses ranging between zero and $200,000, but about 14 percent had losses exceeding $3 million. For patients who died, the economic losses ranged from near zero to about $1.2 million.[12]

One important conclusion from the findings is that the economic consequences of medical injuries can be very substantial. Moreover, Sloan et al. argue, persuasively I think, that they may have seriously underestimated future medical and related expenses of the emergency room injuries because considerable information bearing on these costs was missing from their data.

The second important conclusion is that while economic costs were related to seriousness of injury—more seriously injured persons tended to incur greater losses—there was great variability within categories. This should not be surprising to anyone who gives the matter even cursory thought. For instance, a business executive with an annual income of $200,000 and four dependents will ordinarily incur a much greater calculable income loss than a similarly injured laborer with a $20,000 annual income and no dependents. A 70-year-old woman would be expected to incur fewer future medical expenses than a 7-year-old girl with an identical injury because she will be expected to live a much shorter period of time.

These last findings provide grounds for a very plausible alternative hypothesis to the theory that high variability in jury awards is due to incompetence, sympathy, or capriciousness. The awards may instead be reflecting the economic realities as they are portrayed to the jury in trial evidence.

Jury Awards Compared to Economic Loss. The Florida study also provided an opportunity to more directly assess the reasonableness of jury awards and settlements by comparing in each case the amounts received by the claimants in relation to economic losses.[13] The results of these comparisons were, in many respects, startling. Overall, the claimants in birth injury cases who obtained some compensation received, on average, only 57 percent of their economic losses. Claimants for emergency room injuries received, on average, approximately 80 percent of their economic losses.[14]

In additional analyses Sloan et al. combined the birth and emergency room cases in order to increase the size of the sample. Then they disaggregated the data for cases that were won at trial. They caution that their jury award figures probably contain some posttrial downward adjustments of awards resulting from judicial *remittitur* or an agreement by the parties. However, while we must keep this qualification in mind the figures are quite revealing, particularly if we keep another fact in mind. The state of Florida places no cap on the amount that can be awarded for pain and suffering, and thus, in theory, there was no limit to the damages that the juries could have awarded in these cases. The average award in the jury trial cases was $1,283,000 compared to an average economic loss of $1,051,639.[15] In short, plaintiffs who won at trial received 22 percent more than their economic loss. I am willing to classify this percentage as the amount for pain and suffering. Taking into consideration the fact that Sloan and his colleagues likely underestimated economic losses by some unknown amount the 22 percent figure could be too high. Nevertheless, accepting it at face value the data in this careful study strongly contradict the claims, reviewed in chapter 17, that 50 or even 80 percent of jury awards in malpractice cases are for pain and suffering!

Additional Thoughts about the Florida Study. Sloan and his colleagues observed that despite the overall findings about compensation a few cases (including settled as well as jury cases) resulted in payments that were much larger than economic losses. Most often this occurred for less serious injuries. Consider that while the average compensation for birth injury cases overall was 57 percent of economic loss claimants with the least serious injuries received compensation that was 330 percent of their losses.[16] For emergency room injuries the least seriously injured claimants received 238 percent of economic losses versus an overall case average of 80 percent. This finding that minor injuries are overcompensated while more serious injuries are undercompensated has been documented in previous studies.[17]

Apparently, jurors—and legal professionals such as those in my experiments reported in chapter 18—have a low threshold for awarding relatively generous amounts for pain and suffering when the injury is minor. However, the Florida data suggest that ordinarily jurors have an upper limit in the amounts that they will give—22 percent in the Florida cases—even when the patient is seriously injured. I have no more data about this phenomenon, if it exists, but it certainly deserves future research attention.

Punitive Damages

The contentious topic of punitive damages extends far beyond the malpractice debate to include lawsuits about products liability and breaches of contract.[18] Punitive damages are said to be frequent, unjustified, and given in amounts far in excess of the harms caused or needed to deter negligent conduct. In recent decisions, however, the U.S. Supreme Court has reaffirmed the principle of punitive damages and its place in American law, albeit with some vigorous dissent by some of the justices who would place severe limits on such damages and on the role of the jury in deciding them.[19] I will, however, continue to limit discussion to malpractice cases.

The Incidence and Magnitude of Punitive Awards

Recall from chapter 5 that 13 percent of the malpractice suits in the samples of North Carolina cases initially asked for punitive damages but that most of these claims were dropped or dismissed early in the life of the lawsuit. Only two jury verdicts in the total sample of about 1,300 cases eventually resulted in punitive awards. One was in the amount of $6,000 and the other was for $7,000.[20] Professor Sloan and his colleagues did not find a single instance of a punitive award in their 186 cases.[21] Mark Peterson, Syam Sarma, and Michael Shanley of the Rand Corporation's Institute for Civil Justice undertook a study of punitive damage awards in Cook County, Illinois, and San Francisco, California, during the years of 1960 to 1984.[22] They did not specifically separate malpractice from other types of personal injury cases. However, they did note that several of the largest punitive awards were against hospitals and doctors.[23] Nevertheless, their data also led them to the conclusion that "[m]ost defendants were held liable for punitive damages because juries found that they had intentionally harmed plaintiffs."[24] I will return to this subject in a moment in the discussion of a study by Koenig and Rustad.

Stephen Daniels and Joanne Martin of the American Bar Foundation have conducted the most extensive empirical study of the incidence and amount of punitive damages.[25] Their data set involved 25,627 civil jury trials occurring between 1981 and 1985 and represented 47 jurisdictions around the country. There were 1,917 medical malpractice cases. The juries found the defendant liable in 621 cases or 32.4 percent of the time. Of the 621 cases punitive damages were awarded only 18 times. Put in terms of percentages, punitive damages were awarded in only 0.9 percent (18 ÷ 1,917) of malpractice cases; they were awarded in 2.9 percent (18 ÷ 621) of the cases in which the defendant was found liable. The study also revealed that juries were least likely to award punitive damages when the injury involved physical harm but most likely if the injury resulted in emotional or reputational harm.[26] Daniels and Martin did not report separate figures for the amounts of the awards in malpractice cases, but their data indicated that, for the most part, the median punitive damages could be characterized as "low to modest."[27] Of 20 jurisdictions with 10 or more punitive awards, three-quarters of them had medians of $40,000 or less. A further analysis of a subset of cases revealed that when the awards were ranked according to magnitude only one malpractice case was in the top 25 percent.[28]

The Nature of the Claims for Punitive Awards

While the Daniels and Martin study indicates that the incidence of punitive awards in malpractice cases is quite low and that awards are likely to be modest in size it gives little insight into the nature of the claims made to justify the damages when they are given. A recent study by Professors Thomas Koenig and Michael Rustad helps to fill this gap in our knowledge.[29]

Koenig and Rustad conducted an extensive nationwide search of reports of punitive damage awards. They identified 265 malpractice cases occurring between 1963 and 1993 that involved punitive damages. (Some of the cases were decided by judges or arbitrators.) They found that 68 percent of the awards involved female plaintiffs and that there were four major recurring patterns, or categories, of alleged wrongdoing: sexual assault or abuse of transference during psycho-therapy; intentional injuries, including fraud and false imprisonment, arising out of medical treatment; extreme violations of medical standards of care; and, lastly, abandonment, neglect, or failure to treat a patient when there was a medical duty to provide treatment.

Koenig and Rustad provide some examples of each of the case types that were gleaned from the court records or interviews with one or more lawyers involved in the case. The sexual transference and sexual assault cases typically involved instances in which a psychiatrist or other mental health professional engaged in sexual intercourse with a patient, violating professional ethical standards proscribing such behavior. For example, in a case called *Hinkle v. Petroske* a psychiatrist engaged in sex with a female patient every week for over 12 years and continued to prescribe drugs to which she had become addicted. The trial evidence indicated that the psychiatrist's behavior aggravated her psychiatric disturbance and caused her to attempt suicide.[30] The jury awarded the plaintiff $900,000 in compensatory and $1 million in punitive damages. Other cases identified by Koenig and Rustad involved nonconsensual sexual contact or intercourse with a patient.

The second category, intentional injuries, often involved claims of failure to obtain informed consent for medical procedures, such as sterilization. In a case called *Crandall-Miller,* a 31-year-old female plaintiff was admitted to a hospital for a hysterectomy.[31] She was unaware that her 65-year-old estranged husband, an obstetrician and gynecologist, assisted in the operation. During the surgery her bladder was perforated and, later, her vaginal opening was so filled with scar tissue that it was nearly obliterated. She sued the primary surgeon, her husband, and the hospital. At trial the woman claimed that her husband had intentionally injured her as punishment for a suspected extramarital affair. Trial evidence indicated that the hospital knew that her husband was assisting and also that his privileges had been revoked at another hospital. The jury award included $5 million in punitive damages.

The category of cases involving claims of extreme violation of medical standards of care often involved injury to a woman's reproductive system, bungled cosmetic surgery, or failure to provide services to patients who were in obvious medical danger. The final category, failure to treat or abandonment, most frequently involved poor or elderly patients. In *Jones v. Hospital for Joint Diseases*, for example, a 41-year-old black woman with an infected knee remained in a hospital for seven days but was never treated and then was discharged because she did not have a medical treatment card.[32] Eventually, her leg had to be amputated at mid-thigh.

Assuming that the allegations in the cases studied by Koenig and Rustad were supported by evidence and testimony at trial it is difficult to argue that the juries' punitive damage awards were unreasonable. Their findings should also be viewed in the context that after an extensive search of many different types of records nationwide these researchers uncovered only 265 such awards in three decades. Daniels and Martin's research similarly documented the very low incidence of punitive awards. Like other claims about malpractice juries the assertions about the proclivities of juries to award punitive damages are not supported by empirical evidence.

A Summary Perspective on Damage Awards

The research described in the preceding chapters does not support the widely made claims that jury damage awards are based on the depth of defendants' pockets, sympathies for plaintiffs, caprice, or excessive generosity. It also yields no support for the assertions about the proclivities of juries in handing out punitive damages. Nor are the findings consistent with claims that pain and suffering account for 50 or even 80 percent of malpractice awards or that judges can make these awards more reliably than juries. I have only a few additional observations to make about our state of knowledge on these matters.

The Florida study by Professor Sloan and his colleagues provides, in my judgment, the best available evidence on the reasonableness of jury awards because it provides a well-defined economic yardstick, and a conservative one at that, by which to measure jury verdicts. Scientifically, its findings must be given much greater weight than reports based on anecdotes or unrepresentative cases or on studies that have made highly questionable assumptions about economic losses. On the other hand, the Florida study is based on a small sample of jury decisions and is confined to two types of malpractice cases. Replication of research is always desirable, and our confidence in the Florida findings should be qualified until that replication takes place.

Yet I suspect the results will be confirmed. After all, the cases studied by Sloan et al.—birth injuries and emergency room injuries—are among the types of cases often used in anecdotes and stories about the negative effects of malpractice suits on the practice of medicine. I also note that the Florida findings are consistent with the generally conservative awards in North Carolina, with my case studies based on juror interviews, and with Taragin's New Jersey study.

They are also consistent with the findings of Valerie Hans and her colleagues in their research on civil cases in Delaware. Recall that her interviews with jurors and her survey research found the public from which jurors are drawn to be deeply concerned about plaintiffs getting rich on undeserved awards. These basic attitudes have been documented by other researchers such as David Engle and Edith Greene and her colleagues, as I reported in chapter 14.

The Florida data showing high variability in claimants' economic losses, even when injury severity is taken into account, provide a plausible alternative explanation to the hypothesis that the variability in jury awards is due to jurors' incompetence, caprice, or sympathies for some injured plaintiffs. Perhaps some of the differences are due to the economic losses. Perhaps some are due to the unique combination of jurors and their individual differences over what they deem to be appropriate compensation. Some of it may also be due to variability in the evidence presented to the jury. Recall that my research reported in chapter 20 showed that in most cases only the plaintiff presented expert evidence on economic losses, in others both sides presented experts, and in still others neither side used experts, leaving the jury to find its own figures. If evidence on damages differs from trial to trial, differences in awards should be ascribed to the fault of the trial process or the parties involved, not the jurors.

I do not want to suggest that there is never variability that can be ascribed to juror sympathies, prejudices, or misjudgments. The Florida study documented some "outlier" awards that appear to have substantially exceeded economic losses. Even though my own experiments indicated that juries would, on average, be more reliable than judges, there was still considerable range in the estimated amounts of the juries' pain and suffering awards. There are hints that some of the award variability in my experiments and in the case studies that I reported may be due to how the jury ascribes responsibility to the doctor. Steve Cohen's report on the *Melis* jury deliberations (chapter 9) even suggests to me that sometimes jurors may be so offended by their perceptions of doctor misconduct that they incorporate a punitive component in the pain and suffering award.

However, I also need to draw attention to the fact, often ignored in discussions about awards, that the jury's verdict is not the final word. As I discussed in chapters 10 and 21 before the award becomes a legal judgment it is reviewed by the trial judge. The judge may adjust the award upward or downward through the legal devices of *addititur* and *remittitur*. Regardless of what the judge does, the parties may appeal the judgment to a higher court for additional review of the reasonableness of the award. The trial judge or appeal court may even order a new trial. Also, when they are faced with the lengthy and costly process of appeal the two sides not infrequently engage in post-verdict negotiations that result in the defendant paying an immediate but discounted award.

Professor Ivy Broeder undertook a study of jury awards of $1 million or more that occurred in 1984 and 1985.[1] Broeder found that, on average, medical malpractice verdicts were reduced by 27 percent as a result of various posttrial review or settlement mechanisms. In another study Michael Shanley and Mark Peterson of the Rand Corporation obtained a random sample of 880 jury verdicts occurring between 1982 and 1984 in Cook County, Illinois, and San Francisco, California.[2] Seventy-six of them were malpractice cases and the average award was $528,000. However, posttrial adjustment processes resulted in the defendant paying, on average, only 67 percent of what the jury had decided was appropriate. In other words, the awards were reduced by almost one-third, a figure slightly higher than that found in Broeder's study but in the same general range.

Finally, a number of state legislatures have placed caps or limits on the amounts that can be awarded for pain and suffering. Many have a limit of $250,000, though some have raised the limit to $1 million.[3]

In short, there are quite a number of formal and informal mechanisms that control excesses in jury verdicts when they do occur. It should be clear from this postmortem summary of damage awards that there are still questions that cry out for more investigation. On the other hand, the accumulated body of knowledge is substantial and, in my personal judgment, it not only exonerates the jury system from claims about its excesses but in fact gives it a pretty decent report card.

5. Conclusion

23

Diagnosis of Misdiagnosis:
The Tort Reform Debate—
A Concluding Essay

Claims versus Evidence

"Runaway juries," "the jury lottery," "the pernicious effects of the jury system," the "defective" jury system, jury "irrationality," "exorbitant pain and suffering awards," the "deep pockets" effect, jurors' "gullibility," "junk science," awards that "wreak havoc on the health care system," "unbridled juror sympathies," and "spiraling damage awards"—all of these terms, and more, have been used by doctors, insurers, the mass media, defense lawyers, and legal scholars to describe the behavior and effects of juries with respect to medical malpractice cases.

The purpose of this book has been to empirically examine the merits of the claims that malpractice juries deviate extensively from medical standards and that they are a primary culprit behind the ills that plague the American health care system. Almost amazingly, given the extent of the charges about jury incompetence and malfeasance, the evidence indicates a major misdiagnosis. Multiple sources of data strongly indicate that, on the whole, juries do not favor claimants over doctors and do not make negligence judgments based on the depth of defendants' pockets or the severity of patients' injuries. In fact, their verdicts are remarkably consistent with doctors' ratings of negligence. There is even some evidence to suggest that far from holding prejudice against doctors and health care providers juries display a tilt slightly in favor of them.

On the issue of damages the story is much the same. There is no reliable evidence to support the deep pockets hypothesis or the claim that pain and suffering makes up the vast proportion of jury awards.

To the contrary, awards are generally proportional to seriousness of injury and are not unreasonably above independent estimates of economic loss. A good case can be made that variability in jury awards may reflect the fact that the jury is responding to trial evidence about actual economic losses rather than acting out of whim or incompetence. A credible case can be made that, everything else being equal, juries will yield more stable estimates of pain and suffering than the trial judge. Punitive awards are rare in malpractice cases and may be justified when they are given. Finally, when the occasional jury does go astray with respect to its verdict on liability or on damages a number of post-verdict legal mechanisms operate to correct and adjust the error.

The Roots of Myth and Misdiagnosis

A critical question must now be addressed: why are the widespread claims of jury errancy so out of line with empirical reality? Before attempting to answer this question I do need to point out that such negative opinions of the jury are not held by the majority of the professionals who observe the jury system more frequently and intimately than anyone else. Various surveys of both state and federal court judges indicate that the overwhelming majority of them hold the civil jury system in high regard. They believe that juries typically are competent and conscientious in carrying out the tasks that are assigned to them.[1]

The roots of the beliefs about juries can be understood by considering the mass media, legal scholars, doctors, the "tort reform" movement, and the research community. Although, in reality, these entities are not independent of one another, as I will show, a separate discussion of each is helpful.

The mass media play a major role in affecting the perceptions of the general public, legislators, legal scholars, and doctors. Unfortunately, the reporting of malpractice verdicts and other civil jury verdicts tends to be one-sided. The media are in the business of reporting stories that will get the attention of and provoke interest in their audiences. A multimillion-dollar award in a malpractice case is interesting and receives major coverage, sometimes nationwide coverage. A defense victory or a small award receives either no coverage in the newspaper or brief mention on the inside pages. A further problem is that the reporters assigned to cover trials often report the story inaccurately. In my own experience as an observer of trials for this book and for other research projects I have sometimes wondered if the reporter and I were in the same courtroom when I read about the trial in the newspaper the next morning. Reporters are often assigned to cover a number of trials at once and typically spend only brief periods in each courtroom. Facing an editorial deadline they attempt to get a synopsis of the case from a bailiff, clerk, or one of the attorneys. Further, the pressing need to write interesting stories results in emphasis on the sensational testimony or claims that may later be contradicted by other evidence or have little bearing on the ultimate verdict. Post-verdict adjustments of awards also seldom get reported because they are not easily available, are conducted privately, or are "stale" news. The consequence of all of these factors is a portrait of overly generous and irresponsible juries based upon selective and inaccurate reporting.

The views of legal scholars who are critical of the jury system are usually based upon anecdotes, appeals to "common sense," and uncritical acceptance of scientifically flawed empirical research. Judge Richard Posner and Professor Marc Galanter, both noted legal scholars, have each written about major inadequacies in legal teaching and scholarship that promote reliance on anecdote over reasoned empirical analysis.[2] In essence, training in law encourages reliance on "intuition" and "causal assertions" about the state of the law rather than concern for data that reflect the actual workings of the legal system.[3] Professor Galanter charges that:

> The derelict state of the discourse about legal policy is surprising because lawyers, in their roles as adversaries, are dogged in challenging and dissecting evidence. But adversarial contention is not the same as delighting in employment of the most severe critical standards. And acuteness in dealing with evidence and inference in specific cases does not necessarily carry over to analysis of large social aggregates.[4]

Throughout this book and elsewhere I have repeatedly documented the tendency of some legal scholars to make unwarranted or misleading assertions, particularly their proclivity to accept empirical data without questioning its reliability or validity as long as the data are congruent with their ideology about the tort system.[5] Of course, if it needs pointing out, many legal scholars do support the jury system. It may be that many of them have views that are no more founded on empirical evidence than those of jury critics. It just turns out that in this instance the empirical evidence supports their position.

Doctors' views about the jury are, of course, colored by the fact that they are the targets of malpractice actions. In chapter 7 I reviewed research from the New York Medical Malpractice Project suggesting that at least some doctors, while admitting that negligent mistakes are made, are reluctant to classify them as due to legal negligence. I also suspect that Galanter's statement about lawyers having the ability to analyze individual cases but not the ability or inclination to examine aggregate data sets also probably applies to doctors, particularly because they are out of their field of expertise when they make generalizations about juries and the legal system. When I have presented some of my findings to medical groups, a common response, at least initially, has been incredulity supported by the telling of anecdotes about doctors who have been sued. In another instance the findings that I presented at a conference on medical malpractice were reported in several newspapers. This provoked an angry letter from the leader of a North Carolina medical group who said that even if my findings were true they should not be publicized because they would hamper doctors' efforts to achieve tort reform in North Carolina. This latter incident raises an interesting question about other factors possibly underlying doctors' attitudes toward the jury.

In an insightful article, F. Patrick Hubbard, a law professor, argues that a sociological analysis of the medical community's behavior makes it clear that:

> "tort reform" functions as a symbol used by physicians to register their protest against a broad range of changes in the American health care system. Physicians are seeking social support for a symbolic reaffirmation of their role and importance in society. Consequently, from their point of view, opposition to the fairness or efficacy of the reform proposals is tantamount to opposition to the medical profession.[6]

Hubbard's lengthy article argues that doctors' arguments about liability insurance being unavailable or unaffordable today are not borne out by statistics.

Furthermore, even in 1976 when there was an insurance availability crisis medical groups ignored other very plausible major contributors to the crisis, such as increases in legitimate malpractice claims or bad economic forecasting by liability insurers that forced them to raise insurance rates. I do not want to explore Hubbard's thesis further here, but I would add a small caveat to his article. If he is correct in his general point, doctors' complaints about malpractice suits are, nevertheless, not a new phenomenon. In chapter 1 I reported that Kenneth Deville's book on the origins of medical malpractice litigation in America shows doctors protesting about juries and suits in the 1800s.[7] Other parts of his study document a medical journal editorialist complaining in 1847 that, "Legal prosecutions for malpractice occur so often that even a respectable surgeon may well fear the results of his surgical practice" and another in 1851 was outraged by "mischievous" prosecutions.[8] Like today, assertions were made that, as a result, many doctors had "abandoned the practice of surgery."[9] Hubbard seems to be on to something in drawing our attention to the importance of symbolic issues in the "tort reform" debate, including claims about the jury.

For more than two decades two categories of competing groups have clashed over the American tort system.[10] A "tort reform" group consists of a loose alliance of the insurance industry, various corporate and professional organizations, including the AMA, and political groups with conservative business agendas. Its goal has been to seek a solution to a broad "crisis" that it claims has raised insurance rates or made insurance unavailable altogether, has stifled creativity and product innovation, and has reduced American business competitiveness. The group asserts that the "crisis" has been brought about by enormous business costs of the American tort system, the primary legal mechanism through which injured parties seek redress. Tort reformers claim that anti-business changes in legal rules governing liability, massive social engineering schemes, litigiousness prompted by undeserving plaintiffs and rapacious lawyers, inefficiency in the settlement of disputes, and large jury awards are the primary sources of an economic decline both within the United States and in relation to other countries.[11] On the other side of this issue is an alliance of consumer interest groups and trial lawyer associations, the latter primarily composed of plaintiff lawyers. This group claims that there is no "crisis" or that, if there is one, it is due to other causes such as inefficient business practices. Indeed, this group argues that, due to the obduracy and economic clout of corporate interests, many negligently injured persons do not receive the compensation that they deserve.[12]

The tort reform debate deserves a book-length discussion rather than treatment in a couple of paragraphs, but its essence is this: "tort reform" is a political struggle in which both sides engage in lobbying and propaganda that contains some element of real problems, half-truths, and outright distortions. The tort reform group has the burden of attacking the existing system. The other side defends the status quo by arguing that the tort reformers are attempting to dismantle protections built into the U.S. Constitution and refined through decades of progressive social enlightenment. Both sides cloak themselves in appeals to American values and claim that the other poses a threat to the American way of life.

Stephen Daniels and Joanne Martin of the American Bar Foundation have written extensively about the role of the jury in the tort reform debate.[13] Their writings discuss how the jury has been singled out by the tort reformers as a primary symbol of the legal system's "problems." The jury is the most visible part of the legal system. Jury verdicts do influence how other cases are negotiated and settled. Absent the context and economic facts in which awards are made, large jury awards can seem too high, even outrageous. The fact that the jury is composed of laypersons rather than professionals makes it vulnerable to appeals to "common sense" that it cannot be competent. Lastly, compilations of verdicts statistics produced by research organizations can be used in ways that create misleading impressions about what juries actually do.[14] In one study Daniels has carefully documented how tort reformers have attempted to create a negative image of the jury in order to influence public opinion.[15] He shows how the jury has been the subject of insurance company advertisements in major magazines and newspapers, testimony before Congress, and speeches to business groups. Attempts have even been made to influence scientists through inflammatory and misleading articles in SCIENCE, the leading journal of the American scientific community.[16] This propaganda effort has had a considerable measure of success and is a major source of misimpressions about the civil jury.

Another source of misleading information about the jury system comes from empirical studies on jury verdicts that have been conducted by social scientists. As I have discussed throughout this book, some researchers have not been cognizant of—or have ignored—the serious methodological shortcomings of their data sets. Recall that these problems include differential selection of cases for trial, unrepresentative or missing data, uncontrolled variables that could provide alternative explanations of the verdicts, and emphasis on averages to the exclusion of median summary statistics. In articles published prior to this book I have pointed out that these types of methodological problems are common and widely recognized in the social sciences.[17] In an attempt to explain why they were overlooked in the particular instance of jury verdict research I speculated about a number of possible reasons. One is that some researchers have been seduced by large data sets that involve hundreds or even thousands of real verdicts. On their face these data promise to tell judges, policy makers, and social scientists about the behavior of juries in the legal system— at least if the underlying assumptions are ignored. Another reason is that the data are expensive to collect. Once they have been collected it is perhaps not surprising that researchers are inclined to rationalize and minimize methodological problems that jeopardize the validity of their substantive conclusions. I also offered the speculation that some researchers focused on the elegance of their econometric and statistical regression models by which the data were analyzed and consequently ignored or gave cursory attention to the major limitations of the data to which the models were applied. My own insights into these problems of the data sets emerged only after I had been thoroughly immersed in first-hand collection and coding of data in court records, insurer files, jury trials, and interviews with lawyers and judges. Many of the verdict researchers have not been forced to engage in these activities and have, therefore, never understood the problems attending the data.[18] A final reason may accrue from the fact that at least some of the most highly cited studies were published in sources that did not subject them to independent peer review by other social scientists. The peer review process of science is not perfect in its ability to screen out questionable scientific conclusions, but it certainly tends to eliminate a lot of flawed research. I believe that neutral peer review would likely have resulted in some of the studies being relegated to dusty shelves and storage closets rather than being cited before legislative committees.

The entities discussed above are interrelated. Legal scholars and tort reformers draw upon the verdict studies to support their conclusions that juries are misfits and the source of aberrations in the rational, fair resolution of disputes. Newspaper and magazine reporters present the research uncritically, accompanied by vivid and persuasive, but misleading, anecdotes. High-profile personages like former Surgeon General Koop and Walter Cronkite (who introduced and moderated the videotape that featured Dr. Koop's claim that juries decide cases on the basis of sympathy) draw conclusions and make public statements about juries and the tort crisis. In turn, their public statements are cited by the mass media and tort reform groups as sources of authority on the tort "crisis." Doctors read newspapers and the journals of their professional organizations. In short, myth prevails over empirical reality. It blocks questions about alternative visions of jury behavior and leads to a misdiagnosis.

Randall Bovbjerg of The Urban Institute has also written about the role of myth in the medical malpractice debate. He has put his finger squarely on a final source of the problem: "Folklore, anecdote, and stereotypes predominate partly because solid information was scarce for many years."[19] Bovbjerg observes that a better information base is emerging to counter the myths. The research reported in this book adds to that information base and, I hope, will be used as an antidote to anecdote.

Implications for the Tort Reform Debate

Malpractice Juries in Context

The focus of this book has been limited to the study of jury performance in malpractice cases. The larger debate about tort reform involves many other issues.[20] Among them is how the civil jury performs in other types of tort cases, such as products liability. Additional issues include the effectiveness of the tort system in providing compensation to negligently injured persons and its effect on litigation rates and settlements. In addition to the goal of compensation to injured persons, the debate also involves major differences of opinion about whether the tort system actually serves to deter people and organizations from acting negligently.[21]

Taking first the issue of jury performance in other areas, such as products liability, I would urge caution in generalizing the findings about malpractice juries. Apparent jury restraint when defendants are physicians or hospitals could be lessened or absent when the defendant is a large corporation charged with negligence in the development or promotion of a product. Research by Professor Valerie Hans and by Professor Robb MacCoun has indicated that jurors do use different standards for ascribing responsibility when corporate actors are involved.[22] We must also keep in mind that the selection that determines which cases go to trial may follow different paths in products liability and malpractice cases. The evidence at trial may be different with respect to both liability and damages. Even the substantive laws on products liability are different and may have an impact on how juries decide cases.

It is true, however, that popular writers like Peter Huber and Walter Olson and many legal scholars, like Professors David Sugarman and Gary Schwartz, usually lump malpractice juries and products liability juries together in discourses about the present tort system.[23] I believe that the findings in this book raise very serious questions about their basic assumptions about jury behavior. This should further lead us to ask whether their broad indictments of products liability juries deserve close scrutiny. My caution, however, is to avoid the logical error of *falsus in uno, falsus in omnibus*. We sorely need more empirical research on the behavior of juries in products liability and other types of cases. And yet, it seems to me, the findings discussed in this book raise very serious problems for critics of the tort system. They have identified the malpractice jury as a central villain in the tort system. Many of their arguments about other ills of the tort system emanate directly from this premise. In fine, if one of their major premises is wrong we need to look very critically at the rest of their arguments.

More Modest Jury Reforms

In place of abolishing the jury, a number of scholars, such as Judge William Schwartzer, director of the Federal Judicial Center and an experienced trial judge, and Professor Peter Schuck of Yale University, have discussed more modest reforms to aid or constrain the jury in its decision making.[24] A reading of their writings shows that their proposals are based on the premise that the jury has some major performance difficulties. While the present research suggests that the premise should at least be questioned with regard to malpractice trials, the reforms that they discuss still deserve consideration.

Recall that in the present research the jurors themselves complained about complexity of evidence and difficulty in understanding jury instructions. Despite the fact that my experiments indicate that juries will, on balance, yield more reliable estimates of pain and suffering than judges it is also true that there was still a substantial range of variability between juries in these awards. I also identified the problem of occasional "outlier" verdicts, where the jury does deviate from legal norms and standards. This book has shown that the jury is a good decision maker, at least in malpractice cases, but we should be open to the possibility that it could be made better.

Judge Schwartzer offers a lengthy list of possible modifications to trial procedure. These include clearer identification of issues in pretrial proceedings and limitations on the scope and length of trial. He also suggests that consideration be given in some cases to selection of jurors according to education and experience bearing on the issues in the case. This form of jury is often called a "blue ribbon" jury. He advocates improvements in jury instructions and also argues that more consideration should be given to forms of the verdict. For instance, special verdicts that require the jury to answer individual issues about liability and damages (exemplified in the *Melis* case discussed in chaps. 9 and 10) could be superior to general verdicts because they offer structured guidance to the jury and allow a more precise review of the reasonableness of the verdict by trial and appeal court judges. Judge Schwartzer also proposes consideration of bifurcated trials that proceed in two phases: first, the jury considers only the liability issues; then, if it finds liability, it turns to damages. Other possible trial modifications include interim summations by the opposing lawyers at various points throughout the trial in order to help the jurors see just covered issues more clearly before the trial proceeds to new topics and evidence.

Professor Schuck discusses measures that would constrain jury discretion through changes in substantive laws.[25] One set of reforms would limit the kinds of issues put to the jury. Another would require juries to defer to the decisions of experts on certain matters that bear on their verdict. He also suggests consideration of special verdicts and limitations on the jury's discretion in awarding damages. Limitations on damages might include schedules that classify injuries and the range of awards that should be allowed for each type of injury. Another possibility is to inform juries of the range of previous awards in similar cases in order to provide the jury with some standards for their own verdict.[26] Professor David Baldus and his colleagues have been conducting research intended to improve judicial review of jury awards through the legal mechanisms of *additur* and *remittitur*.[27]

Although many of these proposed ideas to improve jury functioning may be vigorously fought by plaintiff lawyers and consumer groups they deserve consideration. There is little in the research in this book that would argue against experimentation. My view is supported by others. In a study of jury trials in the Bendectin tort litigation Professor Joseph Sanders identified problems in the trial process and proposed mechanisms that could improve jury performance.[28] Professors Shari Diamond and Jonathan Casper have studied a number of problem areas that result when juries are "blindfolded," that is, prevented from hearing certain types of evidence, which then may result in their making erroneous assumptions.[29] I also have little doubt that some of the jurors that I interviewed would heartily agree with a number of the proposed modifications because they speak directly to those jurors' own complaints.

My plea, and that of other jury researchers, is that experimentation with jury reforms be undertaken on a limited scale and subjected to empirical study. Too often legal reforms are implemented without careful thought or evaluation, and they produce unwanted results. For instance, a widespread movement in federal and state courts has allowed juries to be reduced from 12 to 6 members. There is evidence that reduction in size may have reduced the reliability of jury decisions.[30] Some states introduced mandatory screening panels or mediation for medical malpractice cases before they were allowed to proceed to trial. These reforms, too, were often not only ineffective but frequently produced results opposite to those intended.[31] Several colleagues and I showed that a North Carolina reform intended to expedite the processing of malpractice cases probably resulted in slower processing in some courts.[32] Professors Joseph Sanders and Craig Joyce have identified similar problems in their analysis of tort reform in Texas.[33]

Let me conclude this plea for the need for evaluation and limited experimentation with a single example. The idea of special verdicts that require the jury to identify each element of the damage claim and indicate the amount given for that element is intuitively appealing. It provides structure to the jury and may prevent the members from coming up with a simple ballpark figure that may inflate the award over what a more considered evaluation of damages would warrant. As a first response to this idea I want to point out that interviews with North Carolina jurors indicated that when the trial evidence involved specific claims for damages and there was trial evidence to support it the jurors attempted to construct their general award in this way. More importantly, however, a number of authors have pointed out that there are reasonable grounds to hypothesize that special verdicts could have an opposite effect from that intended.[34] Drawing the jury's attention to each element of damages and requiring them to calculate each element may overcome any inherent conservatism the jurors have about the size of the overall award! Surely, any thought about wholesale adoption of special verdicts to aid the jury should be tempered until empirical research has been conducted.

Alternative Dispute Resolution

The jury is a last resort. Trials occur when the opposing parties cannot agree on how the dispute should be resolved. Yet malpractice trials are painful and expensive—for plaintiffs and physicians alike. A main goal of the medical malpractice research project that gave rise to this book on juries was to investigate means of alternative dispute resolution. We achieved some success in referring some cases to arbitration. In other instances, which Jeffrey Rice and I described in an article in the FLORIDA STATE LAW REVIEW, we experimented with what we called a "jury-determined settlement."[35] This hybrid procedure had some of the elements of a jury trial and some elements of binding arbitration, with a group of jurors serving as the ultimate decision maker. It was private rather than public, the contesting parties determined the broad outlines of how the case would proceed, and there were frequently high-low agreements that guaranteed the plaintiff a minimum amount of recovery but placed a limit on the upper end of the award. In our limited experience with this novel procedure the opposing parties were generally happy with the result. Even though I believe this book generally supports the competence of the malpractice jury, nothing in the findings argues against mediation, arbitration, jury-determined settlements, or other forms of alternative dispute resolution.

Conclusion

This book is not going to be the last word on civil juries and medical negligence. That is as it should be. There are still unanswered questions about aspects of jury performance and about modifications that could improve the way the jury functions. On the other hand, the word "vindication" surely seems appropriate in light of the contumely that has been thrown at the malpractice jury.

Throughout this book I have concentrated single-mindedly on the issue of jury performance because that is where the debate has centered. In concluding I should also draw attention to the fact that civil juries serve other societal functions.[36] They provide a check against elitism and arbitrariness by the professionals in the legal system. They help inject a measure of community values into the legal process. They help impart a sense of legitimacy to the legal process for the parties and the community as a whole. And, as Alexis de Tocqueville observed in his often quoted essay in DEMOCRACY IN AMERICA, the civil jury institution also provides those who serve on it with some important civics lessons about rights and responsibilities.[37] But those are topics for another book.

Notes

Chapter 1

1. For reviews of this debate see Michael J. Saks, *Do We Really Know Anything about the Behavior of the Tort Litigation System—and Why Not?* 140 U. PA. L. REV 1147 (1992); Marc Galanter, *Reading the Landscape of Disputes: What We Know and Don't Know (and Think We Know) about Our Allegedly Contentious and Litigious Society,* 31 UCLA L. REV. 4 (1983); Peter H. Schuck, *Mapping the Debate on Jury Reform, in* VERDICT: ASSESSING THE CIVIL JURY SYSTEM (Robert E. Litan ed., Washington, D.C., Brookings Institution, 1993).

2. *See* Saks, *supra* note 1; Galanter, *supra* note 1; *The Role of the Jury in Civil Dispute Resolution,* U. CHI. LEGAL F. entire issue (1990); Vidmar (ed.), *Is the Jury Competent?* 52 LAW & CONTEMP. PROBS. 4, entire issue (1989).

3. *See, e.g.,* Kirk Johnson, Carter Phillips, David Orentlicher & Martin Hatlie, *A Fault-Based Administrative Alternative for Resolving Medical Malpractice Claims,* 42 VAND. L. REV. 1365 (1989).

4. Reported in United States General Accounting Office (U.S. GAO), *Report to Congressional Requesters, Medical Malpractice: Case Study in North Carolina* (Dec. 1986).

5. *Id.* at 21, 22.

6. American Medical Association (AMA) Specialty Society Medical Liability Project, *A Proposed Alternative to the Civil Justice System for Resolving Medical Liability Disputes: A Fault-Based Administrative System,* 7–8 (1988); see Johnson et al., *supra* note 3, for a revised version of this report.

7. James Griffith, *What Will It Take to Solve the Malpractice Crisis,* MED. ECON. 195 (Sept. 27, 1982).

8. *See* Stephen Daniels, *The Question of Jury Competence and the Politics of Civil Justice Reform: Symbols, Rhetoric, and Agenda-Building,* 52 LAW & CONTEMP. PROBS. 269–310.

9. For discussion and references, *see* A. Russell Localio, *Variations on $962,258: The Misuse of Data on Medical Malpractice,* L., MED. & HEALTH CARE 126–27 (June 1985).

10. Peter Huber, LIABILITY: THE LEGAL REVOLUTION AND ITS CONSEQUENCES (1988).

11. *Id.* at 12.

12. *Id.* at 185.

13. Walter Olson, THE LITIGATION EXPLOSION (1991).

14. *See* Stephen Daniels, *supra* note 8, chap. 1; Sharon Begley, *The Meaning of Junk*, NEWSWEEK, March 22, 1993, at 62; Rowland Evans & Robert Novak, *America's Most Powerful Lobby*, READER'S DIGEST, Apr. 1994, at 131–35; Monica Langley, *Generous Juries*, WALL ST. J., May 29, 1986.

15. Philip Hilts, *Bush Enters Malpractice Debate with Plan to Limit Court Awards*, N.Y. TIMES, May 13, 1991, at A1.

16. Pete Domenici & C. Everett Koop, *Sue the Doctor? There's a Better Way*, N.Y. TIMES, June 6, 1991, at A25.

17. Paul Weiler, MEDICAL MALPRACTICE ON TRIAL (1991), at 48.

18. *Id*. at 54.

19. *Id*. at 72.

20. William Blackstone, COMMENTARIES, St. George Tucker's ed. (1803), at 122–23. The history is discussed in Kenneth Allen DeVille, MEDICAL MALPRACTICE IN NINETEENTH-CENTURY AMERICA: ORIGINS AND LEGACY (1990).

21. DeVille, *supra* note 20, at 7.

22. *Id*. at 54.

23. *Id*. at 54.

24. *Id*. at 59.

25. For a brief review, see Valerie Hans & Neil Vidmar, JUDGING THE JURY (New York, Plenum Press, 1986).

26. *See* Valerie Hans, *Attitude toward the Civil Jury: A Crisis of Confidence?* in Litan, *supra* note 1, ch. 1.

27. For discussion of the history of jury criticism, *see* Hans & Vidmar, *supra* note 25, chap. 1, and Stephan Landsman, *The Civil Jury in America: Scenes from an Unappreciated History*, 44 HASTINGS L. REV. 579 (1993).

Chapter 2

1. *See* Stephen Daniels, *supra* note 8, chap. 1; Michael J. Saks, *supra* note 1, chap. 1, at 1225–50; Robert Hayden, *Neocontract Polemics and Unconscionable Scholarship*, 24 L. & SOC. REV. 863–74 (1990).

2. CAT stands for computer axial tomographic scanning: a diagnostic technique in which X rays are passed through tissues. Patients are usually given an intravenous injection of a contrast dye to distinguish various tissues. A test dye is given to ensure that the patient is not allergic to the chemicals. For the original story of the psychic and the CAT scan, see Robert Malott, *America's Liability Explosion: Can We Afford the Cost?* 52 VITAL SPEECHES OF THE DAY (1986), at 180.

3. *See* Frederic N. Tulsky (1986) *Did Jury's Award Consider Psychic's Loss of 'Powers'?* NATIONAL L. J., April 14, 1986, at 9; Fred Strasser, *Tort Tales: Old Stories Never Die*, NATIONAL L. J., Feb. 16, 1987, at 39; see also Saks *supra* note 1, at 1160. The jury did decide for the plaintiff, but the trial judge subsequently set the verdict aside on grounds unrelated to the psychic issue and ordered a new trial.

4. *Id*. Tulsky; *id*. Strasser.

5. President's Council on Competitiveness, A REPORT FROM THE PRESI-
DENT'S COUNCIL ON COMPETITIVENESS: AGENDA FOR CIVIL JUSTICE REFORM IN
AMERICA (1991), at 5; Peter Huber, GALILEO'S REVENGE: JUNK SCIENCE IN THE
COURTROOM (1991), at 5; Walter Olson, *supra* note 13, chap. 1., at 152–53; W.
Kip Viscusi, REFORMING PRODUCTS LIABILITY (1991), at 1; Sharon Begley, *supra*
note 14, chap. 1, at 62.

6. *See* Saks, *supra* note 1, chap. 1, at 1160.

7. For more extended discussion of this point, see Saks, *supra* note 1,
chap. 1, at 1161.

8. Weiler, *supra* note 17, chap. 1, at 48, n.14, at 190.

9. Hayden, *supra* note 1. Research on public attitudes, which I discuss
later in this book, would seem to be supportive of Hayden's hypothesis.

10. *See* James Griffith, *What Will It Take to Solve the Malpractice Crisis*, MED.
ECON., Sept. 27, 1982.

11. *See* BUSINESS WIRE, March 25, 1991; NATIONAL L. J., Jan. 20, 1992, at 510.

12. Gail Cox, *Tort Tales Lash Back*, NATIONAL L. J., Aug. 3, 1992, at 1.

13. *See* Daniels, *supra* note 8, chap. 1; Saks, *supra* note 1, chap. 1; Localio,
supra note 9, chap. 1.

14. *See* Localio, *supra* note 9, chap. 1.

15. *See, e.g.,* Monica Langley, *Generous Juries*, WALL ST. J., May 29, 1986, at
1; *The Insurance Crisis: Now Everyone Is in a Risky Business*, BUSINESS WEEK,
March 10, 1986, at 88; *Sorry, Your Policy Is Cancelled*, TIME, March 24, 1986, at
16; *Stopping the Bloodbath in Medical Malpractice*, BUSINESS WEEK, April 22, 1985,
at 93; Nancy Gibbs, *Sick and Tired: Uneasy Patients May Be Surprised to Learn
Their Doctors Are Worried Too*, TIME, July 31, 1989, at 49; Nancy Gibbs, *Do You
Want to Die? The Crisis in Emergency Care Is Taking Its Toll on Doctors, Nurses, and
Patients*. TIME, May 28, 1990, at 59–65.

16. *See* Daniels, *supra* note 8, chap. 1.

17. *See* Localio, *supra* note 9, chap. 1.

18. *Id.*

19. John Guinther (1988), THE JURY IN AMERICA at, 177–78.

20. Daniels, *supra* note 8, chap. 1, at 301.

21. Michael J. Saks, *In Search of the "Lawsuit Crisis,"* 14 L., MED. & HEALTH
CARE, 77–82.

22. *See* Localio, *supra* note 9, chap. 1; Daniels, *supra* note 8, chap. 1.

23. *See* Localio, *supra* note 9, chap. 1; Daniels, *supra* note 8, chap. 1; Stephen Daniels & Joanne Martin, *Jury Verdicts and the "Crisis" in Civil Justice*, 11
JUSTICE SYSTEM J. 321–87 (1986).

24. Audrey Chin & Mark A. Peterson, *Deep Pockets, Empty Pockets: Who Wins
in Cook County Jury Trials* (Santa Monica, The Rand Corporation, 1985).

25. Mark A. Peterson, CIVIL JURIES IN THE 1980s: TRENDS IN JURY TRIALS
AND VERDICTS IN CALIFORNIA AND COOK COUNTY, ILLINOIS (The Rand Corporation, 1987).

26. *Id.* at 17.

27. *Id.* at 22.

28. *Id.* at 22.

29. Patricia A. Danzon, Medical Malpractice: Theory, Evidence and Public Policy, chap. 3, at 30–57 (1985a).

30. *Id.* at 31.

31. *Id.* at 51.

32. *See, e.g.,* Saks, *supra* note 1, chap. 1. Saks points out that the complications go deeper than just filed cases. Different types of cases may have different rates for injury incidence, for the numbers of claims arising out of those incidents, and for prelawsuit settlement. This further complicates attempts to compare jury verdicts across time, jurisdictions, and case types. This fact compounds the iceberg problem even more, but I do not need to pursue the matter here.

33. For more extensive discussion of this matter, *see* Saks, *supra* note 1, chap. 1, and Samuel A. Gross & Kent D. Syverud, Getting to No: A Study of Settlement Negotiations and the Selection of Cases for Trial, 90 Michigan L. Rev. 319 (1991).

34. *See, e.g.,* Robert E. Litan, Peter Swire & Clifford Winston, *The U.S. Liability System: Backgrounds and Trends in* Liability: Perspective and Policy (Robert Litan & Clifford Winston, eds., 1988, Washington, D.C.: The Brookings Institution). The authors, for example, cite the Rand data and conclude that "awards in medical malpractice and products liability cases . . . increased at a faster pace than those for personal injury cases generally," at 9; James K. Hammitt, Stephen J. Carroll & Daniel Relles, *Tort Standards and Jury Decisions,* 14 J. of Legal Stud. 751–62 (1985) conclude there is a "deep pocket" effect by comparing only jury verdicts. Peterson, *supra* note 25, chap. 2, stated that his data showed that "plaintiffs are increasingly advantaged in jury trials, at ix; "Cook County jury verdicts were increasingly favorable to plaintiffs," at vii.

35. For further elaboration of the problems with the statistical data, see Neil Vidmar, *Empirical Evidence on the "Deep Pockets" Hypothesis: Jury Awards for Pain and Suffering in Medical Malpractice Cases,* 43 Duke L. J. 217–66 (1993); Neil Vidmar, *Making Inferences about Jury Behavior from Jury Verdict Statistics: Cautions about the Lorelei's Lied,* 18 L. & Hum. Behav. 599 (1994).

36. *See* Vidmar, *Making Inferences, supra* note 35, chap. 2.

37. *See* Saks, *supra* note 1, chap. 1.

38. Peterson, *supra* note 25, chap. 2, at 11.

39. *Id.* at 11.

40. *Id.* at 13–14.

41. Stephen Daniels, *Tracing the Shadow of the Law: Jury Verdicts in Medical Malpractice Cases,* 14 Just. Sys. J. 4 (1990).

42. *See* Vidmar, *supra* note 35, chap. 2, for more extended discussion of data bearing on this problem.

43. *Id.*

44. *See* Peterson, *supra* note 25, chap. 2, at 15.

45. Weiler, *supra* note 17, chap. 2, at 48.

46. Manhattan Institute for Policy Research, Liability: Injustice for All, videotape (1992).

Chapter 3

1. *See* Neil Vidmar, *The Unfair Claims about Medical Malpractice Juries*, 76 JUDICATURE 118 (1992).

2. A copy of this questionnaire is reproduced in Neil Vidmar, Laura Donnelly, Thomas Metzloff & David Warren, *An Empirical Examination of a Legislated Procedural Reform: Court-Based Management of Medical Malpractice Litigation* (The Private Adjudication Center, Duke University School of Law, 1992).

3. The insurance file samples can be characterized as "convenience" samples. The insurers gave us access to whatever files were available at the time the research team visited. The insurers' filing systems did not allow for random or systematic selection of cases. The files were the raw files and sometimes contained very sensitive information. We have no reason to conclude that the sample was edited by the insurers or that it was unrepresentative.

4. The term "approximately" is used in a number of places in this chapter. It does not reflect a cavalier attitude toward numbers but rather the fact that different ways of counting may produce slightly varying results. For instance, as will be shown later in this chapter, some cases that went to trial and must be considered "trial cases" also involved settlements from some of the original defendants.

5. Insurers and others have indicated increased desires to settle meritorious cases without trial over the last several years, and this could be a first indication of its effects.

6. For further discussion of expected value and additional references, see Gross & Syverud, *supra* note 33, chap. 2.

7. This is possibly a very conservative figure. A number of plaintiff attorneys have given me estimates of at least $15,000, with the figure being substantially higher in some very big cases. In MEDICAL MALPRACTICE: LAW, TACTICS, AND ETHICS (1994), Professor Frank M. McClellan reports that assessing the merits of the case in 1991 costs at least $2,000 and often $5,000 to $10,000; if the case goes to trial, expenses may total $50,000 to $75,000, at 102.

8. The "set off" or "off set" principle is a Common Law rule that applies when a single injury is caused by joint tort-feasors. Under the rule, there can be but one recovery for the plaintiff, and therefore any amount paid in settlement by a codefendant is subtracted from the award. *See, e.g.,* Holland v. Southern Public Utilities Co., N.C. S.E. 2d 592 (1935).

9. Informing anyone of anything overheard about the jury deliberations at this stage in the trial is illegal, but any experienced courtroom observer knows that it occurs from time to time.

10. The complexities of developing the evidence include, e.g., missing or incomplete medical records; frightened, inarticulate, recalcitrant, or mendacious clients (both plaintiffs and physicians); and the search for qualified, favorable experts. Pretrial procedural maneuverings include, e.g., demands about failure to name experts; motions for continuances, venue change, summary judgment, motions in limine; or requests for sanctions against opposing counsel.

11. In the combined samples in our North Carolina data, 71 percent of malpractice suits occurred from incidents in hospitals, 15 percent from incidents in the physician's office or clinic, and 2 percent occurred in nursing homes. In the remaining 12 percent, the location of the incident occurred in some other setting or could not be ascertained from the court records.

12. In both samples there were a number of instances in which one or more defendants were added to the suit subsequent to the initial pleadings.

13. Defendants who settle are recorded as "Dismissed with Prejudice," meaning that the plaintiff cannot reopen the case against them. Most of the time this indicates a settlement but in a substantial number of instances it means that the plaintiff has dropped the claim against the defendant without receiving either an admission of liability or payment of money.

Chapter 4

1. United States General Accounting Office (U.S. GAO), *Medical Malpractice: Characteristics of Claims Closed in 1984*, Report to Congressional Requests GAO/HRD 87–55 (April 1987); Frank A. Sloan & Chee Rhuey Hsieh, *Variability in Medical Malpractice Payments: Is the Compensation Fair?* 24 L. & Soc. Rev. 997–1040 (1990).

2. Alvarado, *N.C. Trails Nation in Malpractice Claims*, RALEIGH NEWS AND OBSERVER, Aug. 15, 1987, at 24c.

3. For elaboration of this idea, *see* Saks, *supra* note 1, chap. 1.

4. Contributory negligence involves a legal doctrine that asserts that if the plaintiff contributed to the conditions that led to the injury, then he or she cannot recover damages from the defendant, even if the defendant was also negligent. Under the newer comparative negligence doctrine, negligence is measured in terms of percentages, and any damages allowed are reduced in proportion to the amount of the defendant's contribution. The jury's assessment of liability may be affected by whichever rule is operable.

5. U.S. GAO, *supra* note 1, chap. 4.

6. Patricia A. Danzon, *supra* note 29, chap. 2; Patricia Danzon, *Report on Awards for Noneconomic Loss, in* FLORIDA MEDICAL MALPRACTICE POLICY GUIDEBOOK (Henry G. Manne, ed., 1985b); National Association of Insurance Commissioners (NAIC), as reported in Danzon (1985b, at 133); Peterson, *supra* note 25, chap. 2; F. Patrick Hubbard, *"Patterns" in Civil Jury Verdicts in the State Circuit Courts of South Carolina: 1976–1985,* 38 S.C. L. REV. 699 (1987); Daniels, *supra* note 41, chap. 2; Gross & Syverud, *supra* note 31, chap. 2; Randall Bovbjerg, Frank Sloan, Avi Dor & Chee Hsieh, *Juries and Justice: Are Malpractice and Other Personal Injuries Created Equal?* 54 LAW & CONTEMP. PROBS. 5–42 (1991); Kevin M. Clermont & Theodore Eisenberg, *Trial by Jury or Judge: Transcending Empiricism* 77 CORNELL L. REV. 1124 (1991); Mark A. Taragin, Laura Willet, Adam Wilczek, Richard Trout & Jeffrey Carson, *The Influence of Standard of Care and Severity of Injury on the Resolution of Medical Malpractice Claims,* 117 ANNALS OF INTERNAL MED. 780 (1992); Frank A. Sloan, Penny Githens,

Ellen Clayton, Gerald Hickson, Douglas Gentile & David Partlett, SUING FOR MEDICAL MALPRACTICE (U. of Chicago Press, 1993).

7. Daniels, *id*. at 17.

8. Daniels & Andrews, *The Shadow of the Law: Jury Decisions in Obstetrics and Gynecology Cases in* MEDICAL PROFESSIONAL LIABILITY AND THE DELIVERY OF OBSTETRICAL CARE (Victoria Rostow & Roger J. Bulger, eds., Washington, D.C., 1989).

9. NAIC, *supra* note 6, chap. 4.

10. Daniels, *supra* note 8, chap. 1, at n. 4.

11. U.S. GAO study, *supra* note 1, chap. 4, at 2.

12. U.S. GAO, *supra* note 1, chap. 4.

13. Danzon (1985a), *supra* note 29, chap. 2.

14. *Id*. at 51.

15. *Id*. at 51.

16. Henry Farber & Michelle White, *Medical Malpractice: An Empirical Examination of the Litigation Process*, 22 RAND JOURNAL OF ECONOMICS 199–217 (1991). This study will be discussed further in chapter 14.

17. *Id*. at 217.

18. *Id*. at 216.

19. Roger Rosenblatt & Andy Hurst, *An Analysis of Closed Obstetric Malpractice Claims*, 74 OBSTETRICS & GYNECOLOGY 710–13 (1989).

20. *Id*. at 712.

21. Taragin et al., *supra* note 6, chap. 4, at 780–84.

22. *Id*. at 782.

23. Sloan et al., *supra* note 6, chap. 4, at 166–68.

24. *Id*. at 166–67.

25. *Id*. at 166.

26. Peterson, *supra* note 25, chap. 2.

27. Daniels & Andrews, *supra* note 8, chap. 4.

28. Bovbjerg et al., *supra* note 6, chap. 4.

29. Clermont & Eisenberg, *supra* note 6, chap. 4, at 1137.

Chapter 5

1. *See* National Association of Insurance Commissioners (NAIC), *Malpractice Claims: Final Compilation* (M. Sowka, ed., 1980), at 48–66; Randall Bovbjerg, Frank A. Sloan & James Blumstein, *Valuing Life and Limb in Tort: Scheduling "Pain and Suffering,"* 83 Nw. U. L. REV. 908 (1989).

2. Our original classification was based on one developed by the Risk Management Foundation of the Harvard Medical Institutions and subsequently used by the General Accounting Office, *see, e.g.,* U.S. GAO, *supra* note 1, chap. 4, at 74–76.

3. I need to caution that the lower settlement rates in these multiple defendant cases did not mean that plaintiffs received fewer settlements. For the purposes of this analysis we are treating any case that had some defendant's outcome decided by a jury as a jury trial case; as noted in chapter 3 a

significant portion of these jury trial cases resulted in a settlement with the plaintiff by some of the defendants.

4. Henry Farber & Michelle White, *supra* note 16, chap. 5, found in a study of one large hospital's malpractice suits that only 13 of 252, or 5 percent, of cases went to trial.

5. Our unit of analysis was actually the law firm rather than the lawyer since the lead lawyer was often assisted by other lawyers in the firm who shared their expertise with him or her.

6. Frank Sloan, Penny Githens, Ellen Clayton, Gerald Hickson, Douglas Gentile & David Partlett, SUING FOR MEDICAL MALPRACTICE (1993). The methodology and other findings of this research will be discussed in more detail in later chapters of the present book.

7. *See* chapter 21 for more discussion of punitive damages. *See also* Frank M. McClellan, *supra* note 7, chap. 3, at chap. 8.

Chapter 6

1. For more detailed descriptions of the discovery process, *see* Frank M. McClellan, *supra* note 7, chap 3; Kevin Clermont, CIVIL PROCEDURE (2d ed.) (1988); Mary Kay Kane, CIVIL PROCEDURE IN A NUTSHELL (1991).

2. For more information on disposition times, *see* Neil Vidmar, Laura Donnelly, Thomas Metzloff & David Warren, *An Empirical Examination of a Legislated Procedural Reform: Court-Based Management of Medical Malpractice Litigation* (The Private Adjudication Center, Duke University School of Law, 1992).

3. Thomas B. Metzloff, *Resolving Malpractice Disputes: Imaging the Jury's Shadow,* 54 LAW & CONTEMP. PROBS. 43–130 (1991), at 53.

4. *Id.* at 57. The dividing line between the end of discovery and trial preparation is very amorphous, which qualifies these data.

5. McClellan, *supra* note 7, chap. 3, at 102.

Chapter 7

1. McClellan, *supra* note 7, chap. 3.

2. For more details of disposition times, *see* Neil Vidmar, Laura Donnelly, Thomas Metzloff & David Warren, *supra* note 2, chap. 6.

3. Paul C. Weiler et al., A MEASURE OF MALPRACTICE: MEDICAL INJURY, MALPRACTICE LITIGATION AND PATIENT COMPENSATION (1993), at 48. For a review and critique of this and related findings in Weiler et al.'s research, see Michael J. Saks, *Medical Malpractice: Facing Real Problems and Finding Real Solutions,* 35 WM. & MARY L. REV. 693–726 (1994). For more discussion of this topic, *see* Sally Lloyd-Bostock, *Propensity to Sue in England and the United States of America: The Role of the Attribution Process,* 18 J. L. & SOC. 428 (1991); Tom Durkin, *Framing the Choice to Sue: Victim Cognitions and Claims,* American Bar Foundation Working Paper No. 9119 (1991); Herbert Kritzer, *Propensity to Sue in England and the United States of America: Blaming and Claiming in Tort Cases,* 18 J. L. & SOC. 428 (1991); Herbert Kritzer, William A. Bogart & Neil Vidmar, *The*

Aftermath of Injury: Cultural Factors in Compensation Seeking in Canada and the United States, 25 L. & Soc. Rev. 499 (1990).

4. Marlynn May & Daniel Stengel, *Who Sues Their Doctors? How Patients Handle Medical Grievances,* 24 L. & Soc. Rev. 105 (1990).

5. Sloan et al., *supra* note 6, chap. 5, at 50–71.

6. *See* Sloan et al., *supra* note 6, chap. 5, at 72–91, for discussion of difficulties that some patients had in finding a lawyer who would take their case.

7. Interviews with several lawyers who were not specialists in malpractice indicated that they had not subjected their cases to such a screening practice but filed suits and subsequently had difficulty in finding experts.

8. For more extensive discussion of the law pertaining to medical malpractice, *see* McClellan, *supra* note 7, chap. 3, at chaps. 3 and 4.

9. An exception may occur in cases where, say, a surgeon leaves a forceps in the patient. Under the common law doctrine of *res ipsa loquitur* (meaning "the thing speaks for itself") the fact that the forceps was left in the body cavity may be sufficient for the jury to infer that the standard of care was breached without expert testimony. For more discussion, *see* McClellan, *supra* note 7, chap. 3, at 35–36.

10. BLACK'S LAW DICTIONARY (5th ed., 1979). The terms "prudent" and "reasonable" are often substituted for "average." *See* McClellan, *supra* note 7, chap. 3, at chap. 3.

11. *See* McClellan, *supra* note 7, chap. 3, at chap. 3 to 5. Weiler, *supra* note 17, chap. 1, at 19–26; Elizabeth Rolf, HEALTH CARE DELIVERY AND TORT: SYSTEMS ON A COLLISION COURSE (1991); Eleanor Kinney & Marilyn Wilder, *Medical Standard Setting in the Current Malpractice Environment: Problems and Possibilities* 22 U. CAL. DAVIS L. REV. 421 (1989); Gerald Roberts, *Requirements for a Malpractice Suit,* 29 CONTEMP. OBSTETRICS & GYNECOLOGY 33 (1987).

12. Some examples are given in chapter 12.

13. For further discussion, *see* McClellan, *supra* note 7, chap. 3, at chap. 4.

14. Richards, *Doctors Seek Crackdown on Colleagues Paid for Testimony in Malpractice Suits,* WALL ST. J., Nov. 7, 1988. Sloan et al., *supra* note 6, chap. 5, at chaps. 4 and 6, argue that the "conspiracy of silence" has partially eroded in recent years.

15. The Harvard Medical Malpractice Study, *Patients, Doctors, and Lawyers: Medical Injury, Malpractice Litigation, and Patient Compensation in New York* (1990), at 10. This finding is also discussed in Weiler et al., *supra* note 3, chap. 7.

16. Sarah Avery, *The Avenging Angel of Plaintiffs,* RALEIGH NEWS AND OBSERVER, June 17, 1994, at 1c. Most malpractice lawyers in the state do not have the resources of this lawyer and his law firm. Also, his success rate has put him in the highly enviable position of choosing which cases to take among many that are referred to him.

17. Douglas Rosenthal, LAWYER AND CLIENT: WHO'S IN CHARGE? (1974); Herbert M. Kritzer, LET'S MAKE A DEAL: UNDERSTANDING THE NEGOTIATION PROCESS IN ORDINARY LITIGATION (1991).

18. Sloan et al., *supra* note 6, chap. 5, at 87–89.

19. *See* Galanter, *Why the Haves Come Out Ahead: Speculations on the Limits of*

Legal Change, 9 L. & Soc. Rev. 95–160 (1974). One-time players are much less sophisticated about the litigation process than repeat players such as insurance companies and other institutions that are involved in litigation.

20. *See* Sloan et al., *supra* note 6, chap. 5, at chap. 5, for additional discussion of plaintiff–lawyer relations.

21. *See* Hazel Genn, HARD BARGAINING: OUT OF COURT SETTLEMENT IN PERSONAL INJURY ACTIONS (1988).

22. *See* Gross & Syverud, *supra* note 33, chap. 2.

23. *See* McClellan, *supra* note 7, chap. 3, at chap. 4.

24. *See* J. Patrick Lavery, *The Physician's Reaction to a Malpractice Suit,* 71 OBSTETRICS & GYNECOLOGY 138 (1988); F. Patrick Hubbard, *The Physician's Point of View concerning Medical Malpractice: A Sociological Perspective on the Symbolic Importance of "Tort Reform,"* 23 GA. L. REV. 295 (1989).

25. Gross & Syverud, *supra* note 33, chap. 2.

26. *See* Lavery, *supra* note 24, chap. 7. The North Carolina liability insurer's closed claim files document a number of cases where a physician defendant insisted that his own personal attorney be called in to assist the malpractice attorney hired by the liability insurer. In some cases the personal attorney deferred to the more experienced malpractice attorney and merely served as a conduit to assure the physician that the case was being properly handled. In other files there was documentation that the physician used a personal attorney to "demand" that the insurer settle the case for the policy limit rather than proceed to trial.

27. *See* Galanter, *Why the Haves, supra* note 19, chap. 7.

28. Patricia A. Danzon (1985a), *supra* note 29, chap. 2; Sloan et al., *supra* note 6, chap. 5, at chap. 8.

29. *See* Stephen Sugarman, *The Need to Reform Personal Injury Law Leaving Scientific Disputes to Scientists,* 248 SCI. 823–27 (1990).

30. *See* John F. Vargo, *The American Rule on Attorney Fee Allocation: The Injured Person's Access to Justice,* 42 AM. U. L. REV. 1567–636 (1993), for discussion and references bearing on financial burdens of plaintiffs.

Chapter 8

1. Specifically, see the discussion of Patricia A. Danzon (1985a), *supra* note 29, chap. 2; Harvey Farber & Michelle White, *supra* note 16, chap. 4, at 217; Taragin et al., *supra* note 6, chap. 4; Frank Sloan, *supra* note 6, chap. 5.

2. Peter Huber, *Liability, supra* note 10, chap. 1; Peter Huber, *Junk Science and the Jury,* 1990 U. CHI. LEGAL F. 273 (1990); Olson, *supra* note 13, chap. 1, at 164–65; John C. Coffee Jr., *Understanding the Plaintiff's Attorney,* 86 COLUM. L. REV. 669 (1986).

3. Gross & Syverud, *supra* note 33, chap. 2, discuss this theory and cite additional sources.

4. *See* chapter 6.

5. For a discussion of economic costs for lawyers working on a contin-

gency fee basis, *see* David M. Trubek et al., *The Costs of Ordinary Litigation*, 31 UCLA L. REV. 72–127 (1983); and Herbert M. Kritzer, *supra* note 17, chap. 7.

6. George Priest & Benjamin Klein, *The Selection of Disputes for Litigation*, 13 J. LEGAL STUD. 1 (1984); George Priest, *Reexamining the Selection Hypothesis* 14 J. LEGAL STUD. 215 (1985); *see also*, Keith Hylton, *Asymmetric Information and the Selection of Disputes for Litigation*, American Bar Foundation Working Paper No. 9115 (1991).

7. Gross & Syverud, *supra* note 33, chap. 2; Theodore Eisenberg, *Test the Selection Effect: A New Theoretical Framework with Empirical Tests*, 19 J. LEGAL STUD. 337 (1990).

8. Gross & Syverud, *supra* note 33, chap. 2, at 360.

9. Farber & White, *supra* note 16, chap. 5.

10. Troyen Brennan, A. Russell Localio & Nan Laird, *Reliability and Validity of Judgments concerning Adverse Events Suffered by Hospitalized Patients*, 27 MED. CARE 1148–58 (1989); Robert Caplan, Karen Posner & Frederick Cheney, *Effect of Outcome on Physician Judgments of Appropriateness of Care*, 265 J. AM. MED. ASS'N. 1957–60 (1991); Neal Dawson et al., *Hindsight Bias: An Impediment to Accurate Probability Estimation in Clinicopathologic Conferences* 8 MED. DECISION MAKING 259–64 (1988); Samuel Weir, Peter Curtis & Robert McNutt, *Expert Testimony Based on Decision Analysis: A Malpractice Case Report*, 5 J. INTERNAL MED. 406–9 (1990).

11. There are exceptions such as the plaintiff lawyer, mentioned in chapter 7, who has developed the resources that put him on an equal or superior footing with respect to defense teams. *See* Sarah Avery, *The Avenging Angel of Plaintiffs*, RALEIGH NEWS AND OBSERVER, June 12, 1994, at 1C.

12. Hylton, *supra* note 6, chap. 8.

13. Gross & Syverud, *supra* note 33, chap. 2. Robert Mnookin & Lewis Kornhauser, *Bargaining in the Shadow of the Law: The Case of Divorce*, 88 YALE L. J. 950 (1979); Robert Cooter et al., *Bargaining in the Shadow of Law: A Testable Model of Strategic Behavior*, 11 J. LEGAL STUD. 225 (1982); and, generally, Herbert M. Kritzer, *supra* note 17, chap. 7.

14. *E.g.*, Barry Staw, *The Escalation of Commitment to a Course of Action*, 6 ACAD. MGMT. REV. 577 (1981); Alan Teger, TOO MUCH INVESTED TO QUIT (1980); Dean G. Pruitt & Jeffrey Z. Rubin, SOCIAL CONFLICT: ESCALATION, STALEMATE AND SETTLEMENT (1986); D. Ramona Bobocel & John P. Meyer, *Escalating Commitment to a Failing Course of Action*, 79 J. APPL. PSYCH. 360 (1994).

15. Margaret Neale & Max Bazerman, COGNITION AND REALITY IN NEGOTIATION (1991); Elizabeth Loftus & Willem Wagenaar, *Lawyers' Predictions of Success*, 28 JURIMETRICS J. 437 (1988); Jane Goodman & Elizabeth Loftus, *Lawyer Overconfidence in Dispute Resolution*, TECHNICAL REP. G2-8804 (Fund for Research on Dispute Resolution, 1991).

16. Gross & Syverud, *supra* note 33, chap. 2.

Chapter 10

1. *See* Mary Kay Kane, *supra* note 1, chap. 6; Kevin Clermont, *supra* note 1, chap. 6; Gene Shrene & Peter Raven-Hansay, Understanding Civil Procedure (1989).

2. Melis v. Kutin, No. 20105-80, 88 L03317 (Sup. Ct., trial division, Oct. 1990). Verdict for Pain, Suffering Cut to $1.7 Million from $19 Million, N.Y. L. J.; Melis v. Kutin, Sup. Ct., N.Y. L. J., Oct. 10, 1990; Cerisse Anderson, *Malpractice Award withstands Challenge*, N.Y. L. J., Dec. 27, 1990, at 1; Cerisse Anderson, *Big Awards that Time Made Small*, Nat'l. L. J., Jan. 21, 1991, at 56.

3. *See* chapter 16 for more discussion of damages.

4. Sastoque v. Maimonides Medical Center et al., 566 N.Y. Supp., 2d Series 108, 161 A.D.2d 754.

5. *See* chapter 16 for discussion on instructions for reducing award to "present value."

6. Anderson, *supra* note 2, chap. 10.

7. *See* Anderson, *supra* note 2, chap. 10.

8. *See* chapter 16.

9. *See* Hans & Vidmar, *supra* note 25, chap. 1, at chaps. 1 and 8.

10. Punitive damages will be discussed in chapter 22.

11. For a discussion of special versus general verdicts, *see* Elizabeth Wiggins & Steven Breckler, *Special Verdicts as Guides to Jury Decision Making*, 14 L. & Psychol. R. 1 (1990); William Schwartzer, *Reforming Jury Trials*, U. Chi. Legal F., 119–46 (1990); McClellan, *supra* note 6, chap. 3, at chap. 7.

12. *See* Weiler, *supra* note 17, chap. 1, at 32 and 54; Berkley Rice, *The Malpractice Shootout in Washington*, 71 Med. Econ. 106 (Feb. 7, 1994).

Chapter 11

1. Thomas M. Julian et al., *Investigation of Obstetric Malpractice Closed Claims: Profile of Event*, 2 Am. J. Perinatology 320–24 (1985).

2. *Id*. at 323.

3. H. L. Hirsh & E. R. White, *The Pathologic Anatomy of Malpractice Claims*, 6 J. Legal Med. 25–32 (1978); James Nocon & David Coolman, *Perinatal Malpractice: Risks and Prevention*, 32 J. Reprod. Med. 83–90 (1987); Rosenblatt & Hurst, *supra* note 19, chap. 4.

4. Paul Weiler, Howart Hiatt, Joseph Newhouse, Troyan Brennan & Lucian Leap, A Measure of Malpractice (1993).

5. AMA/Specialty Society Medical Liability Project, *supra* note 6, chap. 1, at 8.

6. Letter quoted in U.S. GAO, *supra* note 4, chap. 1.

7. Clark Havighurst, Health Care Law and Policy (1988).

8. Stephen Sugarman, *supra* note 29, chap. 7.

9. *Id*.

10. McClellan, *supra* note 6, chap. 3, at chaps. 3 and 4; *see also*, Paul C. Weiler et al., *supra* note 12, chap. 10, at 19–26; Robert C. Clark, *Why Does*

Health Care Regulation Fail? 41 MD. L. REV. 1 (1981); Page Keeton, *Medical Negligence: The Standard of Care*, 10 TEX. TECH. L. REV. 351 (1979).

11. *See* McClellan, *supra* note 6, chap. 3, at 33; Weiler et al., *supra* note 12, chap. 10, at 23–26; Marjorie Schultz, *From Informed Consent to Patient Choice: A New Protected Interest*, 95 YALE L. J. 219 (1985); Aaron Twerski & Neil Cohen, *Informed Decision Making and the Law of Torts: The Myth of Justiciable Causation*, U. ILL. L. REV. 607 (1988).

12. *See* McClellan, *supra* note 6, chap. 3, at 35; Weiler et al., *supra* note 12, chap. 10, at 19–26.

13. *See* McClellan, *supra* note 6, chap. 3, at chaps. 3 and 4 for more examples and discussion.

Chapter 12

1. The jurors did not realize that it is often difficult to get local doctors to testify against another doctor who practices in the same geographic area. This fact was reported in interviews with North Carolina plaintiff attorneys and appears to be a problem in other states as well; see David Seidelson, *Medical Malpractice Cases and the Reluctant Expert*, 76 CATH. U. L. REV. 158–85 (1966); Bill Richards, *Doctors Seek Crackdown on Colleagues Paid for Testimony in Malpractice Suits*, WALL ST. J., Nov. 7, 1988; McClellan, *supra* note 6, chap. 3, at chap. 10.

2. I subsequently learned that the defense had obtained three estimates of damages. They ranged from $2.1 million to $4.3 million. Since even the lowest of these estimates exceeded the high end of the high-low agreement for the abbreviated trial, no evidence or damages was tendered at the trial.

Chapter 13

1. Valerie Hans & Sanja Ivkovich, *Jurors and Experts*, 16 ADVOCATE: THE MAGAZINE FOR DELAWARE TRIAL LAWYERS 17–21 (1994).

2. *Id.* at 20.

3. A summary jury trial is an abbreviated trial using jurors to decide the case just as they would in a full trial. *See* Neil Vidmar & Jeffrey Rice, *Jury-Determined Settlements and Summary Jury Trials: Observations about Alternative Dispute Resolution in an Adversary Culture*, 19 FLA. ST. L. REV. 89 (1991).

Chapter 14

1. Literature from physicians and risk management experts and independent researchers would seem to refute the viability of assuming that doctors never make negligent errors. *See, e.g.*, Thomas Julian et al., *Investigation of Obstetric Malpractice Closed Claims: Profile of Event*, 2 AM. J. PERINATOLOGY 320 (1985); Nocon & Coolman, *supra* note 3, chap. 11; Lori B. Andrews, *Medical Error and Patient Claiming in a Hospital Setting*, paper presented at the annual meeting of the Law and Society Association, May 30, 1993; Harvard Medical Malpractice Practice Study Group, *Medical Care and Medical Injuries in the State*

of New York: A Pilot Study, 59 (1987); California Medical Association, *Medical Insurance Feasibility Study* (1977). *See also,* Sue Browder, *Deadly Doctors,* WOMAN'S DAY 100 (Sept. 12, 1993).

The alternative to having some individual or group determining whether the physician was negligent is to have a no-fault system in which injured parties are compensated without reference to blame or fault. Some states have enacted such legislation for birth-related neurological injuries (*see, e.g.,* AMA, *supra* note 6, chap. 1; this report was revised and published as Johnson, Phillips, Orentlicher & Hattie, *A Fault-Based Administrative Alternative for Resolving Medical Malpractice Claims,* 42 VAND. L. REV. 1365, at 1379 [1989]). For discussion and rationales of this approach, *see, e.g.,* Jeffrey O'Connell, *Neo-No-Fault Remedies for Medical Injuries: Coordinated Statutory and Contractual Alternatives,* 49 LAW & CONTEMP. PROBS. 125 (1986).

2. *See* Johnson et al., *supra* note 3, chap. 1.

3. *Id.* at 1367–73.

4. *Id.* at 1379. The early stages of the proposed resolution process would rely almost exclusively on physician review. Patients dissatisfied with the review could appeal to a panel of reviewers composed of doctors, attorneys, and administrators and appeal still further to begin litigation. However, patients would incur substantial cost in time and expenses in invoking the appeal process.

5. Physician Payment Review Commission, ANN. REP., 1992, at 186.

6. Taragin et al., *supra* note 4, chap. 6.

7. *Id.* at 780–81.

8. "Not discoverable" here means that it is a privileged work document of the hospital legal team and, therefore, cannot be subpoenaed by the plaintiff.

9. The level of statistical significance exceeded the .001 level of probability, *id.* at 781.

10. *Id.* at 782.

11. The insurance company's decision may not be the result of errors since a rational strategy would be to be conservative in deciding doctor liability so as to avoid paying nonmeritorious claims.

12. Henry Farber & Michelle White, *supra* note 16, chap. 4.

13. *Id.* at 204.

14. I calculated these percentages from the data of Farber and White, *id.,* presented in their table 1 at 205.

15. Robert Caplan, Karen Posner & Frederick Cheney, *supra* note 10, chap. 8.

16. *Id.* at 1959.

17. *See, e.g.,* Jonathan Casper, Kennette Benedict & Jo Perry, *Juror Decisionmaking, Attitudes, and the Hindsight Bias,* 13 LAW & HUM. BEHAV. 291 (1989).

18. On "hindsight bias" *see* Dawson et al., *supra* note 10, chap. 8. On subjective and biased expert testimony, *see* Samuel Weis, Peter Curtis & Robert McNutt, *Expert Testimony Based on Decision Analysis,* 5 J. GEN. INTERNAL MED. 406 (1990).

19. *See* Casper et al., *supra* note 17, chap. 14.

20. Harvard Medical Malpractice Study Group, *supra* note 1; this report was subsequently put into book form: Weiler et al., *supra* note 4, chap. 11.

21. *Id.* at 10.

22. The most biased persons toward either side will typically be not chosen for jury service as a result of the voir dire questioning and peremptory challenges.

23. Sloan et al., *supra* note 6, chap. 4; Henry Farber & Michelle White, *A Comparison of Formal and Informal Dispute Resolution in Medical Malpractice*, 23 J. Legal Studies 777 (1994).

24. *Id.* at 167 (calculated from table 8.2).

25. *Id.* at 168.

26. Daniels & Andrews, *supra* note 8, chap. 4.

27. *Id.* at 189.

28. *Id.* at 191.

29. See chapter 2.

30. Valerie Hans & William Lofquist, *Jurors' Judgments of Business Liability in Tort Cases: Implications for the Litigation Explosion Debate*, 26 L. & Soc. Rev. 85 (1992).

31. *Id.* at 94–95.

32. David Engle, *The Overbird's Song: Insiders, Outsiders, and Personal Injuries in an American Community*, 18 L. & Soc. Rev. 551 (1984).

33. For surveys of jurors, see Edith Greene, Jane Goodman & Elizabeth Loftus, *Jurors' Attitudes about Civil Litigation and the Size of Damage Awards*, 40 Am. U. L. Rev. 805 (1991). For surveys of the general public, see Valerie Hans & William Lofquist, *Perceptions of Civil Justice: The Litigation Crisis Attitudes of Civil Jurors*, 12 Behavioral Sci. & L. 181 (1994).

34. Hans & Lofquist, *Id.* at 96, also found some jurors to have proplaintiff sympathies.

35. Paul Rosen, *Nature of Jury Response to the Expert Witness*, 28 J. Forensic Sci. 528–31 (1983); *See also* E. J. Imwinkelreid, *A New Era in the Evaluation of Scientific Evidence* 23 Wm. & Mary L. Rev. 261–90 (1983).

36. *See, e.g,* Neil Vidmar & Regina Schuller, *Juries and Expert Evidence: Social Framework Testimony*, 52 Law & Contemp. Probs. 133 (1989); Jonathan D. Casper & Shari S. Diamond, *Estimating Damages and Predicting Violence: The Influence of Experts in the Courtroom*, paper presented at the annual meeting of the Law & Society Association, Chicago (May 1993).

37. For a partial review, see Richard Lempert, *Civil Juries and Complex Cases: Taking Stock after Twelve Years, in supra* note 1, chap. 1.

38. Samuel Gross, *Expert Evidence* 1991 Wis. L. Rev. 1114 (1991).

39. Quoted in Gross, *id.,* at 1121.

40. For studies of judges' decision making, see Saks, *supra* note 1, chap. 1; Richard Lempert, *supra* note 37, chap. 14. For the typicality of the reaction of the *Wells* judge, see Stephen Fienberg, The Evolving Role of Statistical Evidence in the Courts (1989).

41. Lempert, *supra* note 43, at 192–219.

Chapter 15

1. *See* discussion in chapter 8. *Also see* Galanter, *Jury Shadows: Reflections on the Civil Jury and the "Litigation Explosion" in* THE AMERICAN CIVIL JURY (Morris & Arnold et al., ed., 1987); Saks, *supra* note 1, chap. 1.

2. Taragin et al., *supra* note 6, chap. 4.

3. Shari S. Diamond & Jonathan D. Casper, *Blindfolding the Jury to Verdict Consequences: Damages, Experts, and the Civil Jury,* 26 L. & SOC. REV. 513 (1992).

4. *Id.* at 558, footnote omitted from quotation.

5. Harry Kalven, *The Dignity of the Civil Jury,* 50 VA. L. REV. 1055 (1964); *see also* Valerie Hans & Neil Vidmar, *supra* note 25, chap. 1.

6. R. Perry Sentell, *The Georgia Jury and Negligence: The View from the Bench, supra* note 27, chap. 1; R. Perry Sentell, *The Georgia Jury and Negligence: The View from the (Federal) Bench, supra* note 27, chap. 1.

7. Gordon Bermant, Joseph Cecil, Alan Lind & Patricia Lumbard, PROTRACTED CIVIL TRIALS: VIEW FROM THE BENCH AND BAR (1981).

8. Larry Heuer & Steven Penrod, *Trial Complexity: A Field Investigation of Its Meaning and Effects,* unpublished manuscript.

9. Richard Lempert, *supra* note 37, chap. 13.

10. *Id.* at 234.

11. *Id.* at 235.

12. See the review by Peter H. Schuck, *supra* note 1, chap. 1, 312: "The judge is usually the implicit or explicit standard of comparison."

13. *See* chapters 9 and 10.

14. Kevin Clermont & Theodore Eisenberg, *supra* note 6, chap. 4. Regarding the differences between verdicts for plaintiffs versus juries, see Samuel Gross, *Settling for a Judge: A Comment on Clermont and Eisenberg,* 77 CORNELL L. REV. 1178 (1992).

15. *See, e.g.,* Stephen Fienberg, *supra* note 40, chap. 14; Lempert, *supra* note 9; MacCoun, *Inside the Black Box: What Empirical Research Tells Us about Decisionmaking by Civil Juries,* in Robert Litan, *supra* note 1, chap. 1.

16. *See* Lempert, *supra* note 9, chap. 16, and Fienberg, *supra* note 16, chap. 16, for reviews and citations.

17. Gary Wells, *Naked Statistical Evidence on Liability: Is Subjective Probability Enough?* 62 J. OF PERSONALITY & SOC. PSYCHOL. 739 (1992).

18. Stephan Landsman & Richard Rakos, *A Preliminary Inquiry into the Effect of Potentially Biasing Information on Judges and Jurors in Civil Litigation,* 12 BEHAV. SCI. & L. 113 (1994).

Chapter 16

1. For a more extended discussion of damages, see Frank M. McClellan, *supra* note 6, chap. 3; Edward C. Martin, PERSONAL INJURY DAMAGES: LAW AND PRACTICE (1990).

2. McClellan, *supra* note 1, at 108.

3. For more discussion, see McClellan, *supra* note 1, at chap. 7.

4. *See* McClellan, *supra* note 1, at chap. 8 for a very informative discussion of punitive damages.

5. Thomas Koenig & Michael Rustad, *His and Her Tort Reform: Gender Injustice in Disguise,* paper presented at the annual meeting of the Law & Society Association, Phoenix, Ariz. (June 15–19, 1994).

Chapter 17

1. U.S. Department of Justice, *Report of the Tort Policy Working Group on the Causes, Extent and Policy Implications of the Current Crisis in Insurance Availability and Affordability* (1986), at 35–36.

2. AMA/Specialty Society Medical Liability Project, *supra* note 6, chap. 1.

3. Paul C. Weiler, *supra* note 12, chap. 10, at 48.

4. AMA Report, *supra* note 6, chap. 1.

5. Physician Payment Review Commission, Annual Report to Congress (1991).

6. Weiler, *supra* note 12, chap. 10, at 48.

7. *Id.* at 54.

8. *Id.* at 55.

9. George Priest, *The Current Insurance Crisis and Modern Tort Law,* 96 YALE L. J. 1521, at 1554 (1987).

10. AMA Report, *supra* note 6, chap. 1.

11. Johnson et al., *supra* note 3, chap. 1, at 1369.

12. *See* Gary Schwartz, *Product Liability and Medical Malpractice in Comparative Context in* THE LIABILITY MAZE: THE IMPACT OF LIABILITY LAW ON SAFETY AND INNOVATION (Peter Huber & Robert Litan, eds., Washington, D.C.: The Brookings Institute, 1991) at 73; Patricia A. Danzon, *The "Crisis" in Medical Malpractice: A Comparison of Trends in the United States, Canada, the United Kingdom, and Australia,* 18 L., MED. & HEALTH CARE 48–49 (1990).

13. *See, e.g.,* Leslie Spencer, *Troubling Days for Trial Lawyers,* FORBES, June 11, 1990; Susan Dentzer & Dorian Friedman, *America's Scandalous Health Care,* 108 U.S. NEWS & WORLD REPORT 14 (Mar. 12, 1990); For a thorough review of the punitive damages literature, *see* Stephen Daniels & Joanne Martin, *Myth and Reality in Punitive Damages,* 75 MINN. L. REV. 1 (1990).

14. Richard Mahoney & Stephen Littlejohn, *Innovation on Trial: Punitive Damages versus New Products,* 246 SCI. 1395 (1989); *also see* Daniels & Martin, *Myth and Reality,* note 13, chap. 17.

15. AMA Report, *supra* note 6, chap. 1, at 32.

16. Schwartz, *supra* note 12, chap. 16, at 73.

17. *See* AMA Report, *supra* note 6, chap. 1, at 7–11; Randall Bovbjerg, Frank Sloan & James Blumstein, *Valuing Life and Limb in Tort Scheduling "Pain and Suffering,"* 83 NW. L. REV., at 908, 928–30, 938–60 (1989); *see also* Peter H. Schuck, *Mapping the Debate in Jury Reform,* in *supra* note 1, chap. 1.

18. AMA Report, *supra* note 6, chap. 1; Schwartz, *supra* note 12, chap. 16, at 73; Bovbjerg et al., *supra* note 17, chap. 17.

19. Stephen Daniels & Joanne Martin, CIVIL JURIES AND THE POLITICS OF REFORM (1995).

20. Weiler, *supra* note 12, chap. 10, at 48.

21. Chin & Peterson, *supra* note 24, chap. 2.

22. James K. Hammit, Stephen J. Carroll & Daniel Relles, *supra* note 34, chap. 2.

23. Mark Peterson, *supra* note 25, chap. 2.

24. *Id.* Recall that averages can be inflated by a relatively small number of large awards. This apparently held true in both Cook County and San Francisco because there is such a large discrepancy between the median and average awards.

25. Stephen Daniels & Joanne Martin, *supra* note 23, chap. 2; *also* Stephen Daniels, *supra* note 41, chap. 2.

26. Randall Bovbjerg et al., *supra* note 6, chap. 4; Patricia A. Danzon, note 29, chap. 2.

27. Bovbjerg et al., *supra* note 6, chap. 4; Daniels & Martin, *supra* note 23, chap. 2; Danzon, *supra* note 29, chap. 2; Chin & Peterson, *supra* note 24, chap. 2; Peterson, *supra* note 25, chap. 2.

28. *See* chapter 2.

29. Bovbjerg et al., *supra* note 6, chap. 4, at 35–36.

30. Additional discussion is contained in Neil Vidmar, *Empirical Evidence, supra* note 35, chap. 2.

31. Gross & Syverud, *supra* note 33, chap. 2.

32. It is also that in some cases there is little dispute about the quality of damages, particularly if they are primarily economic damages.

33. *See, e.g.,* J. Ric Gass, *Defending against Day in the Life Videos,* 34 FOR THE DEFENSE 8 (July 1992).

34. Dale Broeder, The University of Chicago Jury Project, 38 NEB. L. REV. 744, at 756–60 (1959); Harry Kalven, *The Jury, the Law and the Personal Injury Damage Award* 19 OHIO ST. L. J. 158, at 167–68 (1958).

35. Weiler, *supra* note 12, chap. 10, at 48.

36. *See* Peter Huber, *Liability, supra* note 10, chap. 1, at 12; C. Everett Koop in *Liability: Injuries for All* (videotape) Manhattan Institute for Policy Research (1992).

37. Bovbjerg et al., *supra* note 6, chap. 4.

38. See chapter 3, at 25; chapter 4, at 38–39.

39. Taragin et al., note 6, chap. 4.

40. Chin & Peterson, *supra* note 24, chap. 2, at 54–56.

41. Danzon, *supra* note 26; Chin & Peterson, *supra* note 24, chap. 2; Peterson, *supra* note 25, chap. 2; Bovbjerg et al., *supra* note 6, chap. 4; Taragin et al., *supra* note 6, chap. 4.

42. *See* Vidmar, *Empirical Evidence, supra* note 35, chap. 2, at 222. However, in the rewritten version of the AMA Report, Johnson, Phillips, Orentlicher & Hatlie, *supra* note 3, chap. 1, cite the 1986 Department of Justice Report referenced *supra* in footnote 1, chap. 17. How the authors of the latter report

arrived at the 80 percent figure is unclear and will probably forever remain a mystery.

43. The primary source that is cited by Weiler and the AMA is Patricia A. Danzon, *Report on Awards for Noneconomic Loss in* Fla. Med. Malpractice Guidebook, at 132 (Henry G. Manne, ed., 1985). Danzon's study is critiqued in detail in Vidmar, *Empirical Evidence, supra* note 35, chap. 2 and other studies are discussed in Neil Vidmar, *Making Inferences, supra* note 34, chap. 2.

44. Bovbjerg et al., *supra* note 6, chap. 4.

45. *Empirical Evidence, supra* note 35, chap. 2; Vidmar, *Making Inferences, supra* note 34, chap. 2.

Chapter 18

1. This experiment and the analyses are described in more detail in Neil Vidmar, *Empirical Evidence, supra* note 35, chap. 2. This experiment was conducted with the collaboration of Laura Ann Helstern and Susan Smith.

2. *Id.* at 224–27.

3. With respect to varying the number and type of defendants, see *id.*, at 231. See also chapter 3. For research involving other contexts, see Valerie Hans & David Ermann, *Responses to Corporate versus Individual Wrongdoing*, 13 L. & Hum. Behav. 15 (1989); Valerie Hans, *Attitudes toward Corporate Responsibility: A Psycholegal Perspective*, 69 Neb. L. Rev. 158 (1990); Valerie Hans, *Lay Reactions to Corporate Defendants*, paper presented at the annual meeting of the Law & Society Association, Phoenix, Arizona (June 18, 1994); Robert MacCoun, *Differential Treatment of Corporate Defendants by Juries: Are "Deep Pockets" the Cause?* paper presented at the annual meeting of the Law & Society Association, Phoenix, Arizona (June 18, 1994).

4. There is support for the hypothesis that the cause of the injury and number of defendants interact with one another. However, further statistical analyses indicated that this interaction effect was due to the fact that the mean award was *lower* in the condition involving two defendants who were medically negligent ($67,709); the award in the two-defendant motor negligence condition ($83,655) was not statistically different from the other conditions.

5. A qualification to this conclusion will be discussed in chapter 19.

6. More details about this experiment are contained in Neil Vidmar, Jessica Lee, Elaina Cohen & Anne Stewart, *Damage Awards and Jurors' Responsibility Ascriptions in Medical versus Automobile Negligence Cases*, 12 Behav. Sci. & L. 149 (1994).

7. Chin & Peterson, *supra* note 24, chap. 2.

8. Jane Goodman, Edith Greene & Elizabeth Loftus, *Runaway Verdicts or Reasoned Determinations: Mock Juror Strategies in Awarding Damages*, 29 Jurimetrics J. 285–309 (1989).

9. This unpublished study is described in Vidmar, *Empirical Evidence, supra* note 35, chap. 2, at 259, n. 146.

10. See endnote 3, *supra* chap. 8.

Chapter 19

1. D. Dobbs, Handbook on the Law of Remedies (1973), at 135–38. *See also* Frank M. McClellan, *supra* note 6, chap. 3, at chap. 7.

2. For a review and references, see Bovbjerg, Sloan & Blumstein, *supra* note 17, chap. 17.

3. *Id.* at 911–18.

4. *Id.* See also, Peter H. Schuck, *supra* note 1, chap. 1.

5. Johnson, Phillips, Orentlicher & Hatlie, *supra* note 3, chap. 1, at 1383. The judge's decision, including presumably the damage award, would be subject to review by an administrative board.

6. This study, including additional details, was published in the Iowa L. Rev. *See* Neil Vidmar & Jeffrey J. Rice, *Assessments of Noneconomic Damage Awards in Medical Negligence: A Comparison of Jurors with Legal Professionals*, 78 Iowa L. Rev. 883–911 (1993).

7. *See* Valerie Hans & Neil Vidmar, *supra* note 25, chap. 1, at chap. 11.

8. *Id.*, Michael Saks, Jury Verdicts (1977); Hans Zeisel, . . . *And Then There Were None: The Diminution of the Federal Jury*, 38 U. Chi. L. Rev. 710–24 (1971).

9. Shari Diamond & Jonathan Casper, *supra* note 3, chap. 15.

10. This study was previously described in Neil Vidmar & David Landau, *What Animates Jury Awards for Pain and Suffering in Medical and Automobile Negligence Cases? An Empirical Study*, presented at the annual meeting of the Law & Society Association, Phoenix, Arizona (June 14–17, 1994).

11. Data from a few additional jurors—not included in the previous study because their response had been misplaced during data analysis—were included in the new analyses.

12. *See* Vidmar & Landau, *supra* note 10, chap. 19.

13. *See* Dobbs, *supra* note 1, chap. 19; McClellan, *supra* note 7, chap. 3.

14. Gerald R. Williams, Legal Negotiation and Settlement (1983).

15. Michael Brady & Peter Cubanske, *The Judicial Arbitration System: Its Promise and Its Shortcomings*, For the Defense, Aug. 1993, at 29–31.

16. For California, *see* Rice & Vidmar, *supra* note 6. My reference to Oregon is based on personal oral communication from John E. Hart at the fourth annual Risk Management Symposium, East Carolina University School of Medicine (Mar. 17, 1992).

Chapter 21

1. *See generally*, Gary Schwartz, *supra* note 12, chap. 17; Weiler, *supra* note 17, chap. 1, at 48; and chapters 1 and 2 of this book. Taragin et al., *supra* note 6, chap. 4. For their specific finding, see page 782.

2. *Id.* at 782.

3. Bovbjerg, Sloan & Blumstein, *supra* note 17, chap. 17.

4. *Id.* at 920.

5. Saks, *supra* note 1, chap. 1.

6. Bovbjerg et al., *supra* note 17, chap. 17, at 923.

7. *Id.* at 923.

8. Sloan, Githens, Clayton, Hickson, Gentile & Partlett, *supra* note 6, chap. 4. This study was discussed previously in chapter 14.

9. More details of the calculations are contained in chapter 7 of their book, *id.*

10. *Id.* at 136–40.

11. *Id.* at 141.

12. *Id.* at 141–44.

13. *Id.* at chap. 9.

14. *Id.* at 191–96.

15. *Id.* at 195. I calculated the latter figure from the data summarized in their table 9.3.

16. *Id.* at 193, table 9.1.

17. *Id.* at 220. In this light, the pain and suffering awards by the juries and legal professionals in the simulation experiments reported in chapter 18 are not out of line. In each of those experiments the claimants suffered injuries that can be categorized as less serious. The pain and suffering awards in each experiment were substantially larger than economic losses. This observation in no way reduces the importance of the findings that were unsupportive of the hypotheses that there is a "deep pockets effect" or that legal professionals can yield more reliable judgments of pain and suffering. It does caution against extrapolating from the studies to conclude that the jurors in these experiments would have given proportionately higher pain and suffering awards in cases involving much more serious injuries, although whether they would or would not is an empirical question.

18. Richard Mahoney & Stephen Littlejohn, *Innovation on Trial: Punitive Damages versus New Products*, 246 Sci. 1395 (1989); Sales & Coles, *Punitive Damages: A Relic that Has Outlived Its Origins*, 37 VAND. L. REV. 1117 (1984). *See also* Stephen Daniels & Joanne Martin, *Myth and Reality in Punitive Damages*, 75 MINN. L. REV. 1 (1990), for a literature review of claims and assertions.

19. Pacific Mutual Life Insurance Co. v. Haslip, 111 Sup. Ct. 1032 (1991); TXO Production v. Alliance Resources, 419 S.E. 2d 870 (1992).

20. *See* chapter 3, table 3.1.

21. Sloan et al., *supra* note 6, chap. 4, at 206.

22. Mark Peterson, Syam Sarma & Michael Shanley, PUNITIVE DAMAGES: EMPIRICAL FINDINGS (1987).

23. *Id.* at 22 and 50.

24. *Id.* at 45.

25. Daniels & Martin, *supra* note 18, chap. 21.

26. *Id.* at 45.

27. *Id.* at 42.

28. *Id.* at 55–56.

29. Thomas Koenig & Michael Rustad, *His and Her Tort Reform: Gender Injustice in Disguise*, paper presented at the annual meeting of the Law & Society Association, Phoenix, Arizona (July 13–17, 1994).

30. *Id.* at 94.
31. *Id.* at 100.
32. *Id.* at 108.

Chapter 22

1. Ivy Broeder, *Characteristics of Million Dollar Awards: Jury Verdicts and Final Disbursements,* 11 Just. Sys. J. 349 (1986).
2. Michael Shanley & Mark Peterson, Posttrial Adjustments to Jury Awards (1987).
3. Berkeley Rice, *The Malpractice Shootout in Washington,* 71 Med. Econ. 106 (1994); Randall Bovbjerg, *Lessons for Tort Reform from Indiana* 16 J. Health Pol., Pol'y. & L. 467 (1991).

Chapter 23

1. For a review, *see* Valerie Hans, *Attitudes toward the Civil Jury: A Crisis of Confidence? in supra* note 1, chap. 1, at 261.
2. Richard Posner, *The Uncertain Future of Legal Education,* address delivered to the annual meeting of the Association of American Law Schools (Jan. 15, 1991); Marc Galanter, *News from Nowhere: The Debased Debate on Civil Justice,* 71 Denver U. L. Rev.
3. *Id.* at 101.
4. *Id.* at 100.
5. Neil Vidmar, *Empirical Evidence, supra* note 35, chap. 2; Neil Vidmar, *Making Inferences, supra* note 34, chap. 2; Neil Vidmar, *Are Juries Competent to Decide Liability in Tort Cases involving Scientific/Medical Issues? Some Data from Medical Malpractice,* Emory L. J. (1994).
6. F. Patrick Hubbard, *The Physician's Point of View concerning Medical Malpractice: A Sociological Perspective on the Symbolic Importance of "Tort Reform,"* 23 Ga. L. Rev. 295 (1989). The quotation appears on pages 296 and 297.
7. DeVille, *supra* note 20, chap. 1.
8. *Id.* at 26, 25.
9. *Id.* at 25.
10. Hubbard, *supra* note 6, chap. 23; Schuck, *supra* note 1, chap. 1; Daniels, *supra* note 8, chap. 1; Kenneth Chesebro, *Galileo's Retort: Peter Huber's Junk Scholarship,* 42 Am. U. L. Rev. 1637 (1993); Marc Galanter, *The Regulatory Function of the Civil Jury,* in *supra* note 1, chap. 1.
11. *E.g.,* Richard Mahoney & Stephen Littlejohn, *Innovation on Trial: Punitive Damages versus New Products,* 246 Sci. 1395 (1989); Huber, Liability, *supra* note 10, chap. 1; Olson, *supra* note 2, chap. 8; and generally, Peter Huber & Robert Litan, eds., *supra* note 1, chap. 21.
12. See Hubbard, *supra* note 6, chap. 23; Schuck, *supra* note 10, chap. 23.
13. Daniels, *supra* note 8, chap. 1; Daniels & Martin, Civil Juries and the Politics of Reform (1995); Daniels & Martin, *supra* note 23, chap. 2; Daniels & Martin, *Myth and Reality in Punitive Damages,* 75 Minn. L. Rev. 1 (1990).

14. Daniels, *supra* note 8, chap. 1; Saks, *supra* note 1, chap. 1; Vidmar, *supra* note 34, chap. 2.

15. Daniels, *supra* note 8, chap. 1.

16. *Id.; see also* Mahoney & Littlejohn, *supra* note 11, chap. 23.

17. Vidmar, *Empirical Evidence, supra* note 35, chap. 2; Vidmar, *Making Inferences, supra* note 34, chap. 2; Vidmar, *Are Juries Competent? supra* note 5, chap. 23.

18. Randall Bovbjerg, *Medical Malpractice: Research and Reform*, 79 VA. L. REV. 2155, at 2185 (1993), has made a similar criticism.

19. Randall Bovbjerg, *supra* note 18, chap. 22.

20. Hubbard, *supra* note 6, chap. 23; Galanter, *supra* note 10, chap. 23; Schuck, *supra* note 1, chap. 1.

21. Stephen Sugarman, *Doing Away with Tort Law*, 73 CAL. L. REV. 555 (1985); Stephen Sugarman, *Taking Advantage of the Torts Crisis*, 48 OHIO ST. L. J. 328 (1987); Jennifer Arlen, *Compensation Systems and Efficient Deterrence*, 52 MD. L. REV. 1093 (1993).

22. Valerie Hans, *Lay Reactions to Corporate Defendants*, paper presented at the annual meeting of the Law & Society Association, Phoenix, Arizona (June 18, 1994); Valerie Hans & William Lofquist, *Attitudes toward Corporate Responsibility: A Psycholegal Perspective* 69 NEB. L. REV. 158 (1990); Robert MacCoun, *Differential Treatment of Corporate Defendants by Juries: Are "Deep Pockets" the Cause? supra* note 3, chap. 18.

23. Huber, *supra* note 10, chap. 1; Olson, *supra* note 2, chap. 8; Stephen Sugarman, *supra* note 29, chap. 7; Gary Schwartz, *Product Liability and Medical Malpractice in Comparative Context*, in *supra* note 1, chap. 21.

24. William Schwartzer, *Reforming Jury Trials*, 1990 U. CHI. LEGAL F. 119 (1990); Schuck, *supra* note 1, chap. 1.

25. *Id.*

26. Schedules and related procedures are discussed in more detail in Bovbjerg, Sloan & Blumstein, *supra* note 17, chap. 17.

27. David Baldus, John MacQueen & George Woodworth, 1 COMPARATIVE ADDITUR/REMITTITUR REVIEW OF AWARDS FOR NONPECUNIARY HARMS (Preliminary report, The University of Iowa, July 20, 1993).

28. Joseph Sanders, *From Science to Evidence: The Testimony on Causation in the Bendectin Case*, 46 STAN. L. REV. (1993); Joseph Sanders, *The Jury Deliberations in a Complex Case*, 16 JUST. SYS. J. 45 (1993).

29. Shari Diamond, Jonathan Casper & Lynne Ostergren, *Blindfolding the Jury* 52 LAW & CONTEMP. PROBS. 247 (1989).

30. *See, e.g.*, Robert MacCoun, *Inside the Black Box: What Empirical Research Tells Us about Decisionmaking by Civil Juries* in Robert Litan, ed., *supra* note 1, chap. 1.

31. Catherine Meschievitz, *Mediation and Medical Malpractice: Problems with Definition and Implementation*, 54 LAW & CONTEMP. PROBS. 195 (1991); Patricia Danzon, *The Frequency and Severity of Malpractice Claims: New Evidence*, 49 LAW & CONTEMP. PROBS. 57 (1986).

32. Neil Vidmar, Laura Donnelly, Thomas Metzloff & David Warren, AN

Empirical Examination of a Legislated Procedural Reform: Court-Based Management of Medical Malpractice Litigation (The Private Adjudication Center, Duke University School of Law, January 1992).

33. Joseph Sanders & Craig Joyce, *"Off to the Races": The 1980's Tort Crisis and the Law Reform Process*, 27 Hous. L. Rev. 207 (1990); *see also* Robert MacCoun, *Unintended Consequences of Court Arbitration: A Cautionary Tale from New Jersey*, 14 Just. Sys. J. 229 (1991); *see* generally Jeffery Pressman & Aaron Wildarsky, Implementation (1973).

34. Edith Greene, *On Juries and Damage Awards: The Process of Decisionmaking*, 52 Law & Contemp. Probs. 225 (1989); Saks, *supra* note 1, chap. 1, at 1268.

35. Vidmar & Rice, *Jury-Determined Settlements and Summary Jury Trials: Observations about Alternative Dispute Resolution in an Adversary Culture* 19 Fla. St. U. L. Rev. 89 (1991).

36. Hans & Vidmar, *supra* note 25, chap. 1; Peter Sperlich, *The Case for Preserving Trial by Jury in Complex Civil Litigation*, 65 Judicature 394 (1982); Harry Kalven & Hans Zeisel, The American Jury (1966).

37. Alexis de Tocqueville, Democracy in America (1835).

References

Alvarado, Donna. 1987. N.C. trails nation in malpractice claims. *Raleigh News and Observer,* August 15, 24c.

AMA/Specialty Society Medical Liability Project. 1988. *A Proposed Alternative to the Civil Justice System for Resolving Medical Liability Disputes: A Fault-based Administrative System.* Chicago, Ill.: American Medical Association.

Anderson, Cerisse. 1990. Malpractice award withstands challenge. *New York Law Journal,* December 27, 1.

Andrews, Lori B. 1994. *Medical Error and Patient Claiming in a Hospital Setting,* American Bar Foundation Working Paper 9316. Chicago: American Bar Foundation.

Arlen, Jenifer. 1993. Compensation systems and efficient deterrence. *Maryland Law Review* 52:1093.

Avery, Sarah. 1994. The avenging angel of plaintiffs. *Raleigh News and Observer,* June 17, 1c.

Baldus, David; MacQueen, John; and Woodworth, George. 1993. *Comparative Additur/Remittitur Review of Awards for Nonpecuniary Harms,* Vol. 1: Preliminary Report. Iowa City: University of Iowa.

Begley, Sharon. 1993. The meaning of junk. *Newsweek,* March 22, 62.

Bermant, Gordon; Cecil, Joseph; Lind, Alan; and Lumbard, Patricia. 1981. *Protracted Civil Trials: View from the Bench and Bar.* Washington, D.C.: Federal Judicial Center.

Black, Henry C. 1979. *Black's Law Dictionary.* 5th ed. St. Paul: West Publishing Co.

Blackstone, William. 1803. *Commentaries.* Philadelphia: W. Y. Birch and A. Small.

Bovbjerg, Randall. 1991. Lessons for tort reform from Indiana. *Journal of Health Politics, Policy, and Law* 16:467.

———. 1992. Medical malpractice: Folklore, facts and the future. *Annals of Internal Medicine* 117:788.

———. 1993. Medical malpractice: Research and reform. *Virginia Law Review* 79:2155.

Bovbjerg, Randall; Sloan, Frank; Dor, Avi; and Hsieh, Chee. 1991. Juries and justice: Are malpractice and other personal injuries created equal? *Law and Contemporary Problems* 54:5.

Bovbjerg, Randall; Sloan, Frank; and Blumstein, James. 1993. Valuing life and limb in tort: Scheduling "pain and suffering." *Northwestern Law Review* 83:908.

Brady, Michael, and Cubanske, Peter. 1993. The judicial arbitration system: Its promise and its shortcomings. *For the Defense,* August 29.

Brennan, Troyen; Localio, Russell; and Laird, Nan. 1989. Reliability and validity of judgments concerning adverse events suffered by hospitalized patients. *Medical Care* 27:1148.

Broeder, Dale. 1959. The University of Chicago Jury Project. *Nebraska Law Review* 38:744.

Broeder, Ivy. 1986. Characteristics of the million dollar awards: Jury verdicts and final disbursements. *Justice System Journal* 11:349.

Browder, Sue. 1993. Deadly doctors. *Woman's Day,* September 12, 100.

National Law Journal, 1991's largest verdicts. January 20, 510.

Caplan, Robert; Posner, Karen; and Cheney, Frederick. 1991. Effect of outcome on physician judgments of appropriateness of care. *Journal of the American Medical Association* 265:1957.

Casper, Jonathan; Benedict, Kennette; and Perry, Jo. 1989. Juror decision-making, attitudes, and the hindsight bias. *Law and Human Behavior* 13:291.

Casper, Jonathan D., and Diamond, Shari S. 1993. Estimating damages and predicting violence: The influence of experts in the courtroom. Paper presented at the annual meeting of the Law and Society Association, Chicago, Ill.

Chesebro, Kenneth. 1993. Galileo's retort: Peter Huber's junk scholarship. *American University Law Review* 42:1637.

Chin, Audrey, and Peterson, Mark. 1985. *Deep Pockets, Empty Pockets: Who Wins in Cook County Jury Trials.* Santa Monica: Rand Corporation.

Church, George. 1986. Sorry, your policy is cancelled. *Time,* March 24, 16.

Clark, Robert C. 1981. Why does health care regulation fail? *Maryland Law Review* 41:1.

Clermont, Kevin. 1988. *Civil Procedure.* 2d ed. St. Paul: West Publishing Co.

Clermont, Kevin M., and Eisenberg, Theodore. 1991. Trial by jury or judge: Transcending empiricism. *Cornell Law Review* 77:1124.

Cohen, Steve. 1990. Malpractice: Behind a $26-million award to a boy injured in surgery. *New York,* October 1, 41.

Coffee, John C., Jr. 1986. Understanding the plaintiff's attorney. *Columbia Law Review* 86:669.

Cooter, Robert; Marks, Stephen; and Mnookin, Robert. 1982. Bargaining in the shadow of law: A testable model of strategic behavior. *Journal of Legal Studies* 11:225.

Cox, Gail. 1992. Tort tales lash back. *National Law Journal,* August 3, 1

Daniels, Stephen. 1989. The question of jury competence and politics of civil justice reform: Symbols, rhetoric, and agenda-building. *Law and Contemporary Problems* 52:269.

———. 1990. Tracing the shadow of the law: Jury verdicts in medical malpractice cases. *Justice System Journal* 14:4.

Daniels, Stephen, and Martin, Joanne. 1986. Jury verdicts and the "crisis" in civil justice. *Justice System Journal* 11:321.

Daniels, Stephen, and Andrews, Lori. 1989. The shadow of the law: Jury decisions in obstetrics and gynecology cases, in *Medical Professional Liability and the Delivery of Obstetrical Care*, vol. 2, ed. Victoria Rostow and Roger Bulger. Washington, D.C.: National Academy Press.

Daniels, Stephen, and Martin, Joanne. 1990. Myth and reality in punitive damages. *Minnesota Law Review* 75:1.

———. 1995. *Civil Juries and the Politics of Reform*. Evanston, Ill.: Northwestern University Press.

Danzon, Patricia A. 1985a. *Medical Malpractice: Theory, Evidence and Public Policy*. Cambridge, Mass.: Harvard University Press.

———. 1985b. Report on awards for noneconomic loss, in *Florida Medical Malpractice Policy Guidebook*, ed. Henry G. Manne. Miami: Florida Medical Association.

———. 1990. The "crisis" in medical malpractice: A comparison of trends in the United States, Canada, the United Kingdom, and Australia. *Law, Medicine and Health Care* 18:48.

Dawson, Neal; Arkes, Hal; Siciliano, Carl; Blinkhorn, Richard; Lakshmanan, Mark; and Petrolli, Mary. 1989. Hindsight bias: An impediment to accurate probability estimation in clinicopathologic conferences. *Medical Decision Making* 8:259.

Dentzer, Susan, and Friedman, Dorian. 1990. America's scandalous health care. *U.S. News and World Report*, March 12, 14.

DeVille, Kenneth A. 1990. *Medical Malpractice in Nineteenth-Century America: Origins and Legacy*. New York: New York University Press.

Diamond, Shari; Casper, Jonathan; and Ostergren, Lynne. 1989. Blindfolding the jury. *Law and Contemporary Problems* 52:247.

Diamond, Shari, and Casper, Jonathan. 1992. Blindfolding the jury to verdict consequences: Damages, experts, and the civil jury. *Law and Society Review* 26:401.

Dobbs, Dan B. 1993. *Handbook on the Law of Remedies*. 2d ed. St. Paul: West Publishing Co.

Domenici, Pete, and Koop, C. Everett. 1991. Sue the doctor? There's a better way. *N.Y. Times*, June 6, A25.

Durkin, Tom. 1991. *Framing the Choice to Sue: Victim Cognitions and Claims*. American Bar Foundation Working Paper 9119. Chicago: American Bar Foundation.

Eisenberg, Theodore. 1990. Testing the selection effect: A new theoretical framework with empirical tests. *Journal of Legal Studies* 19:337.

Engle, David. 1984. The ovenbird's song: Insiders, outsiders, and personal injuries in an American community. *Law and Society Review* 18:551.

Evans, Rowland, and Novak, Robert. 1994. America's most powerful lobby. *Reader's Digest*, April, 131.

Farber, Henry, and White, Michelle. 1991a. Medical malpractice: An empirical examination of the litigation process. *Rand Journal of Economics* 22:199.

Farber, Henry, and White, Michelle. 1991b. A comparison of formal and informal dispute resolution in medical malpractice. *Journal of Legal Studies* 23:777.

Farrell, Christopher. 1986. The insurance crisis: Now everyone is in a risky business. *Business Week*, March 10, 88.

Fienberg, Stephen. 1989. *The Evolving Role of Statistical Evidence in the Courts.* New York: Springer-Verlag.

Galanter, Marc. 1974. Why the haves come out ahead: Speculations on the limits of legal change. *Law and Society Review* 9:95.

———. 1983. Reading the landscape of disputes: What we know and don't know (and think we know) about our allegedly contentious and litigious society. *UCLA Law Review* 31:4.

———. 1987. Jury shadows: Reflections on the civil jury and the "litigation explosion" in *The American Civil Jury*, ed. Chief Justice Earl Warren Conference on Advocacy in the United States. Washington, D.C.: The Rosco Pound–American Trial Lawyers Foundation.

———. 1993a. News from nowhere: The debased debate on civil justice. *Denver University of Law Review* 71:77.

———. 1993b. The regulatory function of the civil jury, in *Verdict: Assessing the Civil Jury System*, ed. Robert Litan. Washington, D.C.: Brookings Institution.

Gass, J. Ric. 1992. Defending against day in the life video. *For the Defense*, July, 8.

Genn, Hazel. 1987. *Hard Bargaining: Out of Court Settlement in Personal Injury Actions.* New York: Oxford University Press.

Gibbs, Nancy. 1989. Sick and tired: Uneasy patients may be surprised to learn their doctors are worried too. *Time*, July 31, 49.

———. 1990. Do you want to die? The crisis in emergency care is taking its toll on doctors, nurses, and patients. *Time*, May 28, 59.

Goodman, Jane; Greene, Edith; and Loftus, Elizabeth. 1989. Runaway verdicts or reasoned determinations: Mock juror strategies in awarding damages. *Jurimetrics Journal* 29:285.

Goodman, Jane, and Loftus, Elizabeth. 1991. *Lawyer Overconfidence in Dispute Resolution.* Technical Report G2-8804. N.p.: Fund for Research on Dispute Resolution.

Greene, Edith. 1989. On juries and damage awards: The process of decisionmaking. *Law and Contemporary Problems* 52:225.

Greene, Edith; Goodman, Jane; and Loftus, Elizabeth. 1991. Jurors' attitudes about civil litigation and the size of damage awards. *American University Law Review* 40:805.

Griffith, James. 1982. What will it take to solve the malpractice crisis. *Medical Economics*, September 27, 195.

Gross, Samuel. 1991. Expert evidence. *Wisconsin Law Review* 1991:1114.

———. 1992. Settling for a judge: A comment on Clermont and Eisenberg. *Cornell Law Review* 77:1178.

Gross, Samuel A., and Syverud, Kent D. 1991. Getting to no: A study of settlement negotiations and the selection of cases for trial. *Michigan Law Review* 90:319.

Guinther, John. 1988. *The Jury in America.* New York: Facts on File Publications.

Hammitt, James K.; Carroll, Stephen J.; and Relles, Daniel. 1985. Tort standards and jury decisions. *Journal of Legal Studies* 14:751.

Hans, Valerie. 1990. Attitudes toward corporate responsibility: A psycholegal perspective. *Nebraska Law Review* 69:158.

———. 1993. Attitude toward the civil jury: A crisis of confidence? in *Verdict: Assessing the Civil Jury System,* ed. Robert E. Litan. Washington, D.C.: Brookings Institution.

———. 1994. Lay reactions to corporate defendants. Paper presented at the annual meeting of the Law and Society Association, June 18, Phoenix, Ariz.

Hans, Valerie, and Ermann, David. 1989. Responses to corporate versus individual wrongdoing. *Law and Human Behavior* 13:15.

Hans, Valerie, and Ivkovich, Sanja. 1994. Jurors and experts. *Advocate: The Magazine for Delaware Trial Lawyers* 16:17.

Hans, Valerie, and Lofquist, William. 1990. Attitudes toward corporate responsibility: A psycholegal perspective. *Nebraska Law Review* 69:158.

———. 1992. Jurors' judgments of business liability in tort cases: Implications for the litigation explosion debate. *Law and Society Review* 26:85.

———. 1994. Perceptions of civil justice: The litigation crisis attitudes of civil jurors. *Behavioral Science and Law* 12:181.

Hans, Valerie, and Vidmar, Neil. 1986. *Judging the Jury.* New York: Plenum Press.

Harvard Medical Malpractice Practice Study Group. 1987. *Medical Care and Medical Injuries in the State of New York: A Pilot Study.* Cambridge, Mass.: President and Fellows of Harvard College.

Havighurst, Clark C. 1988. *Health Care Law and Policy.* Westbury, N.Y.: Foundation Press.

Hayden, Robert. 1990. Neocontract polemics and unconscionable scholarship. *Law and Society Review* 24:863.

Hilts, Phillip. 1991. Bush enters malpractice debate with plan to limit court awards. *N.Y. Times,* May 13, A1.

Hirsh, H. L., and White, E. R. 1978. The pathologic anatomy of malpractice claims. *Journal of Legal Medicine* 6:25.

Hubbard, F. Patrick. 1987. Patterns in civil jury verdicts in the state circuit courts of South Carolina: 1976–1985. *South Carolina Law Review* 38:699.

———. 1989. The physicians' point of view concerning medical malpractice: A sociological perspective on the symbolic importance of "tort reform." *Georgia Law Review* 23:295.

Huber, Peter. 1988. *Liability: The Legal Revolution and Its Consequences.* New York: Basic Books.

———. 1990. Junk science and the jury. *University of Chicago Legal Forum* 1990:273.

———. 1991. *Galileo's Revenge: Junk Science in the Courtroom.* New York: Basic Books.

Huber, Peter, and Litan, Robert, eds. 1991. *The Liability Maze.* Washington, D.C.: Brookings Institution.

Hylton, Keith. 1991. *Asymmetric information and the selection of disputes for litigation.* American Bar Foundation Working Paper 9115. Chicago: American Bar Foundation.

Imwinkelreid, E. J. 1983. A new era in the evaluation of scientific evidence. *William and Mary Law Review* 23:261.

Johnson, Kirk; Phillips, Carter; Orentlicher, David; and Hatlie, Martin. AMA report 1989: A fault-based administrative alternative for resolving medical malpractice claims. *Vanderbilt Law Review* 42:1365.

Julian, Thomas; Butler, Julius; Ogburn, Paul; Anderson, Mark; Preisler, Williams; and Capell, Melvin. 1985. Investigation of obstetric malpractice closed claims: Profile of event. *American Journal of Perinatology* 2:320.

Kalven, Harry. 1958. The jury, the law and the personal injury damage award. *Ohio State Law Journal* 19:158.

———. 1964. The dignity of the civil jury. *Virginia Law Review* 50:1055.

Kalven, Harry, and Zeisel, Hans. 1966. *The American Jury.* Boston: Little, Brown.

Kane, Mary Kay. 1991. *Civil Procedure in a Nutshell.* 3d ed. St. Paul: West Publishing Co.

Keeton, Page. 1979. Medical negligence: The standard of care. *Texas Tech Law Review* 10:351.

King, Resa. 1985. Stopping the bloodbath in medical malpractice. *Business Week,* April 22, 93.

Kinney, Elanor, and Wilder, Marilyn. 1989. Medical standard setting in the current malpractice environment: Problems and possibilities. *University of California at Davis Law Review* 22:421.

Koenig, Thomas, and Rustad, Michael. 1994. His and her tort reform: Gender injustice in disguise. Paper presented at the annual meeting of the Law and Society Association, June 15–19, Phoenix, Ariz.

Kritzer, Herbert M. 1991a. *Let's Make A Deal: Understanding the Negotiation Process in Ordinary Litigation.* Madison: University of Wisconsin Press.

———. 1991b. The propensity to sue in England and the United States: Blaming and claiming in tort cases. *Journal of Law and Society* 18:428.

Kritzer, Herbert; Bogart, William A.; and Vidmar, Neil. 1990. The aftermath of injury: Cultural factors in compensation seeking in Canada and the United States. *Law and Society Review* 25:499.

Landsman, Stephan. 1993. The civil jury in America: Scenes from an unappreciated history. *Hastings Law Review* 44:579.

Landsman, Stephan, and Rakos, Richard. 1994. A preliminary inquiry into the effect of potentially biasing information on judges and jurors in civil litigation. *Behavioral Sciences and the Law* 12:113.

Langley, Monica. 1986. Generous juries. *Wall Street Journal,* May 29, 1.

Lavery, J. Patrick. 1988. The physician's reaction to a malpractice suit. *Obstetrics and Gynecology* 71:138.

Lempert, Richard. 1993. Civil juries and complex cases: Taking stock after twelve years, in *Verdict: Assessing the Civil Jury System,* ed. Robert E. Litan. Washington, D.C.: Brookings Institution.

Litan, Robert E.; Swire, Peter; and Winston, Clifford. 1988. The U.S. liability system: Backgrounds and trends, in *Liability: Perspective and Policy,* ed. Robert E. Litan and Winston Clifford. Washington, D.C.: Brookings Institution.

Lloyd-Bostock, Sally. 1991. Propensity to sue in England and the United States of America: The role of the attribution process. *Journal of Law and Society* 18:428.

Localio, A. Russell. 1985. Variations on $962,258: The misuse of data on medical malpractice. *Law, Medicine and Health Care,* June, 126.

Loftus, Elizabeth, and Wagenaar, Willem. 1988. Lawyers' predictions of success. *Jurimetrics Journal* 28:437.

McClellan, Frank M. 1993. *Medical Malpractice: Law, Tactics and Evidence.* Philadelphia: Temple University Press.

MacCoun, Robert. 1991. Unintended consequences of court arbitration: A cautionary tale from New Jersey. *Justice System Journal* 14:229.

———. 1993. Inside the black box: What empirical research tells us about decisionmaking by civil juries, in *Verdict: Assessing the Civil Justice System,* ed. Robert Litan. Washington, D.C.: Brookings Institution.

———. 1994. Differential treatment of corporate defendants by juries: Are "deep pockets" the cause? Paper presented at the annual meeting of the Law and Society Association, June 18, Phoenix, Ariz.

Mahoney, Richard, and Littlejohn, Stephen. 1989. Innovation on trial: Punitive damages versus new products. *Science* 246:1395.

Malott, Robert. 1986. America's liability explosion: Can we afford the cost? *Vital Speeches of the Day* 52:180.

Manhattan Institute for Policy Research. 1992. *Liability: Injustice for All.* Videotape. New York: Manhattan Institute.

Martin, Edward C. 1990. *Personal Injury Damages: Law and Practice.* New York: Wiley Law Publications.

May, Marlynn, and Stengel, David. 1990. Who sues their doctors? How patients handle medical grievances. *Law and Society Review* 24:105.

Melis v. Kutin. 1990. 20105-80, 88 L03317, Supreme Court (Trial Division), October. *New York Law Journal* 1990:21.

Meschievitz, Catherine. 1991. Mediation and medical malpractice: Problems with definition and implementation. *Law and Contemporary Problems* 54:195.

Metzloff, Thomas B. 1991. Resolving malpractice disputes: Imaging the jury's shadow. *Law and Contemporary Problems* 54:43.

Mnookin, Robert, and Kornhauser, Lewis. 1979. Bargaining in the shadow of the law: The case of divorce. *Yale Law Journal* 88:950.

National Law Journal. 1991. Big awards that time made small. *National Law Journal,* January 21, S6.

Neale, Margaret, and Bazerman, Max. 1991. *Cognition and Reality in Negotiation.* New York: Free Press.

Nocon, James, and Coolman, David. 1987. Perinatal malpractice: Risks and prevention. *Journal of Reproductive Medicine* 32:83.

O'Connell, Jeffrey. 1986. Neo-no-fault remedies for medical injuries: Coordinated statutory and contractual alternatives. *Law and Contemporary Problems* 49:125.

Olson, Walter K. 1991. *The Litigation Explosion.* New York: Dutton.

Pacific Mutual Life Insurance Co. v. Haslip. 1991. 111 S. Ct. 1032.

Peterson, Mark A. 1987. *Civil Juries in the 1980s: Trends in Jury Trials and Verdicts in California and Cook County, Illinois.* Santa Monica: Rand Corporation.

Peterson, Mark; Sarma, Syam; and Shanley, Michael. 1987. *Punitive Damages: Empirical Findings.* Santa Monica: Rand Corporation.

Physician Payment Review Commission. 1991. *Annual report to Congress, 1991.* Washington, D.C.: GPO.

————. 1992. *Annual report to Congress, 1992.* Washington, D.C.: GPO.

Posner, Richard. 1991. The uncertain future of legal education. Address delivered at the annual meeting of the Association of American Law Schools, San Antonio, Tex.

President's Council on Competitiveness. 1991. *A report from the President's Council on Competitiveness: Agenda for civil justice reform in America.* Washington, D.C.: GPO.

Priest, George. 1985. Reexamining the selection hypothesis. *Journal of Legal Studies* 14:215.

————. 1987. The current insurance crisis and modern tort law. *Yale Law Journal* 96:1521.

Priest, George, and Klein, Benjamin. 1984. The selection of disputes for litigation. *Journal of Legal Studies* 13:1.

Pressman, Jeffery, and Wildavsky, Aaron. 1973. *Implementation.* Berkeley: University of California Press.

Pruitt, Dean G., and Rubin, Jeffrey Z. 1986. *Social Conflict: Escalation Stalemate and Settlement.* New York: Random House.

Rice, Berkeley. 1994. The malpractice shootout in Washington. *Medical Economics* 71:106.

Richards, Bill. 1988. Doctors seek crackdown on colleagues paid for testimony in malpractice suits. *Wall Street Journal,* November 7, B1.

Roberts, Gerald. 1987. Requirements for a malpractice suit. *Contemporary Obstetrics and Gynecology* 29:33.

Rosen, Paul. 1983. Nature of jury response to the expert witness. *Journal of Forensic Sciences* 28:528.

Rosenblatt, Robert, and Hurst, Andy. 1989. An analysis of closed obstetric malpractice claims. *Obstetrics and Gynecology* 74:710.

Rosenthal, Douglas. 1974. *Lawyer and Client: Who's In Charge?* New York: Russell Sage.

Saks, Michael. 1977. *Jury Verdicts.* Lexington, Mass.: D. C. Heath.

————. 1986. In search of the "lawsuit crisis." *Law, Medicine, and Health Care* 14:77.

————. 1992. Do we really know anything about the behavior of the tort litigation system—and why not? *University of Pennsylvania Law Review* 140:1147.

————. 1994. Medical malpractice: Facing real problems and finding real solutions. *William and Mary Law Review* 35:693.

Sales, James, and Coles, Kenneth. 1984. Punitive damages: A relic that has outlived its origins. *Vanderbilt Law Review* 37:1117.

Sanders, Joseph. 1993a. The jury deliberations in a complex case. *Justice System Journal* 16:5.

————. 1993b. From science to evidence: The testimony on causation in the Bendectin cases. *Stanford Law Review* 46:1.

Sanders, Joseph, and Joyce, Craig. 1990. "Off to the races": The 1980's tort crisis and the law reform process. *Houston Law Review* 27:207.

Sastoque v. Maimonides Medical Center et al. 1990. 566 N.Y. Supplement, 2d Series 108, 161 A.D. 2d 754.

Schuck, Peter H. 1993. Mapping the debate on jury reform, in *Verdict: Assessing the Civil Jury System*, ed. Robert Litan. Washington, D.C.: Brookings Institution.

Schultz, Marjorie. 1985. From informed consent to patient choice: A new protected interest. *Yale Law Journal* 95:219.

Schwartz, Gary. 1991. Product liability and medical malpractice in comparative context, in *The Liability Maze: The Impact of Liability Law on Safety and Innovation*, ed. Peter Huber and Robert Litan. Washington, D.C.: Brookings Institution.

Schwartzer, William. 1990. Reforming jury trials. *University of Chicago Legal Forum* 1990:119.

Seidelson, David. 1966. Medical malpractice cases and the reluctant expert. *Catholic University Law Review* 76:158.

Sentell, R. Perry, Jr. 1991. The Georgia jury and negligence: The view from the bench. *Georgia Law Review* 26:85.

————. 1993. The Georgia negligence jury: Judged by the judges. *Georgia State Bar Journal* 29:200.

Shanley, Michael G., and Peterson, Mark A. 1987. *Post Trial Adjustments to Jury Awards*. Santa Monica: Rand Corporation.

Shreve, Gene, and Raven-Hansen, Peter. 1989. *Understanding Civil Procedure*. New York: Matthew Bender.

Sloan, Frank, and Hsieh, Chee Rhuey. 1990. Variability in medical malpractice payments: Is the compensation fair? *Law and Society Review* 24:997.

Sloan, Frank; Githens, Penny; Clayton, Ellen; Hickson, Gerald; Gentile, Douglas; and Partlett, David. 1993. *Suing for Medical Malpractice*. Chicago: University of Chicago Press.

Sowka, M., ed. 1980. *Malpractice Claims: Final Compilation*. Milwaukee: National Association of Insurance Commissioners.

Spencer, Leslie. 1990. Troubling days for trial lawyers. *Forbes Magazine,* June 11, 37.

Sperlich, Peter. 1982. The case of preserving trial by jury in complex civil litigation. *Judicature* 65:394.

Staw, Barry. 1981. The escalation of commitment to a course of action. *Academy of Management Review* 6:577.

Strasser, Fred. 1987. Tort tales: Old stories never die. *National Law Journal*, Feb. 16, 39.

Sugarman, Stephen. 1985. Doing away with tort law. *California Law Review* 73:555.

———. 1987. Taking advantage of the torts crisis. *Ohio State Law Journal* 48:328.

———. 1990. The need to reform personal injury law leaving scientific disputes to scientists. *Science* 248:823.

Taragin, Mark; Willett, Laura; Wilzek, Adam; Trout, Richard; and Carson, Jeffrey. 1992. The influence of standard of care and severity of injury on the resolution of medical malpractice claims. *Annals of Internal Medicine* 117:780.

Teger, Alan. 1980. *Too Much Invested To Quit.* New York: Pergamon Press.

Tocqueville, Alexis de. 1953. *Democracy in America.* Trans. Henry Reeves. Ed. Henry Steele Commager. London: Oxford University Press.

Trubek, David; Sarat, Austin; Felstiner, William; Kritzer, Herbert; and Grossman, Joel. 1983. The costs of ordinary litigation. *UCLA Law Review* 31:72.

Tulsky, Frederic N. 1986. Did jury's award consider psychic's loss of "powers"? *National Law Journal*, April 14, 9.

Twerski, Aaron, and Cohen, Neil. 1988. Informed decision making and the law of torts: The myth of justiciable causation. *University of Illinois Law Review* 1988:607.

TXO Production v. Alliance Resources. 1993. 125 L.Ed.2d 366.

University of Chicago Legal Forum. 1990. The roles of the jury in civil dispute resolution. *University of Chicago Legal Forum* 1990 (whole issue).

U.S. Department of Justice. 1986. *Report of the Tort Policy Working Group on the causes, extent and policy implications of the current crisis in insurance availability and affordability.* Washington, D.C.: GPO.

U.S. General Accounting Office. 1986. *Report to congressional requesters, medical malpractice: Case study in North Carolina.* December. Washington, D.C.: GPO.

———. 1987. *Medical malpractice: Characteristics of claims closed in 1984, Report to congressional requesters.* April. Washington, D.C.: GPO.

Vargo, John F. 1993. The American rule on attorney fee allocation: The injured person's access to justice. *American University Law Review* 42:1567.

Vidmar, Neil. 1993. Empirical evidence on the "deep pockets" hypothesis: Jury awards for pain and suffering in medical malpractice cases. *Duke Law Journal* 43:217.

———. 1994a. Are juries competent to decide liability in tort cases involving scientific/medical issues? Some data from medical malpractice. *Emory Law Journal* 43:885.

———. 1994b. Making inferences about jury behavior from jury verdict statistics: Cautions about the Lorelei's lied. *Law and Human Behavior* 18:599.

Vidmar, Neil, ed. 1989. Is the jury competent? *Law and Contemporary Problems* 52, no. 4 (whole issue).

Vidmar, Neil; Donnelly, Laura; Metzloff, Thomas; and Warren, David. 1992.

An Empirical Examination of a Legislated Procedural Reform: Court-based Management of Medical Malpractice Litigation. January. Durham, N.C.: Private Adjudication Center, Duke University School of Law.

Vidmar, Neil, and Landau, David. 1994. What animates jury awards for pain and suffering in medical and automobile negligence cases? An empirical study. Paper presented at the annual meeting of the Law and Society Association, June 14–17, Phoenix, Ariz.

Vidmar, Neil; Lee, Jessica; Cohen, Elaina; and Stewart, Anne. 1994. Damage awards and jurors' responsibility ascriptions in medical versus automobile negligence cases. *Behavioral Sciences and the Law* 12:149.

Vidmar, Neil, and Rice, Jeffrey J. 1991. Jury-determined settlements and summary jury trials: Observations about alternative dispute resolution in an adversary culture. *Florida State University Law Review* 19:89.

———. 1993. Assessments of noneconomic damage awards in medical negligence: A comparison of jurors with legal professionals. *Iowa Law Review* 78:883.

Vidmar, Neil, and Schuller, Regina. 1989. Juries and expert evidence: Social framework testimony. *Law and Contemporary Problems* 52:133.

Viscusi, W. Kip. 1991. *Reforming Products Liability.* Cambridge, Mass.: Harvard University Press.

Weiler, Paul. 1991. *Medical Malpractice on Trial.* Cambridge, Mass.: Harvard University Press.

Weiler, Paul; Hiatt, Howard; Newhouse, Joseph; Brennan, Troyan; and Leap, Lucian. 1993. *A Measure of Malpractice: Medical Injury, Malpractice Litigation and Patient Compensation.* Cambridge, Mass.: Harvard University Press.

Weis, Samuel; Curtis, Peter; and McNutt, Robert. 1990. Expert testimony based on decision analysis. *Journal of General Internal Medicine* 5:406.

Wells, Gary. 1992. Naked statistical evidence on liability: Is subjective probability enough? *Journal of Personality and Social Psychology* 62:739.

Wiggins, Elizabeth, and Breckler, Stephen. 1990. Special verdicts as guides to jury decision making. *Law and Psychology Review* 14:1.

Williams, Gerald R. 1993. *Legal Negotiation and Settlement.* St. Paul: West Publishing Co.

Zeisel, Hans. 1971. . . . And then there were none: The diminution of the federal jury. *University of Chicago Law Review* 38:710.

Index